Charles
MANSON

MUSIC

MAYHEM

MURDER

Printed in the United Kingdom by Biddles Ltd, Surrey

Published by Sanctuary Publishing Limited, Sanctuary House, 45–53 Sinclair Road, London W14 0NS, United Kingdom

www.sanctuarypublishing.com

Copyright: Tommy Udo, 2002

Photographs: © CORBIS with Bettmann, Ted Streshinsky, Lynn Goldsmith, Hulton-Deutsch Collection, Davis Factor. Memorabilia courtesy of the author

Cover photograph: © CORBIS

ISBN: 1-86074-388-9

Charles
MANSON

Music Mayhem Murder

Tommy Udo

Sanctuary

Contents

Preface: LA Confidential

'The world began in Eden,
but it ended in Los Angeles'
– *Phil Ochs*

Sightseers and murder junkies are not encouraged at 10050 Cielo Drive. The original 'rambling ranch-style house' – home at one time or another to Cary Grant, Candice Bergen, Terry Melcher, and to Roman Polanski and his wife Sharon Tate – was torn down a few years ago and the numbering of the other houses altered to confuse would-be visitors. My driver, Saul (an almost rectangular man in his late 50s, a one-time West Hollywood Sheriff's Department deputy and, he claims, former bodyguard to Ronald Reagan) stands near the black Lincoln smoking a Dunhill. A double rarity in modern Los Angeles: smoking and smoking British cigarettes. It's tempting the powers that be in LA.

I gingerly snap photos of the view down Benedict Canyon. An awesome LA view; you can see the whole of the downtown area laid out like a 2D plan, stretching all the way to the ocean.

I think about what Susan Atkins said: 'It was so quiet you could almost hear the sound of ice rattling in cocktail shakers in the homes way down the canyon.'

I can hear the faint and distant chirping of insects. The air is still. I can hear Saul – standing about 20 feet away from me – exhaling smoke. Somewhere – is it up or down? – I hear a splash. Someone has just dived into their pool.

LA is weird. Not the people: despite what its detractors would have you believe, they aren't actually any weirder than the denizens of any major city. It's LA's *lack* of people that is eerie. You drive at peak hours of the day or night along Sunset Boulevard and you never see a pedestrian. You could almost believe that you were driving through an uninhabited city, that you were part of some huge exodus from some plague-devastated conurbation that was being abandoned. Everyone is in cars or behind the high, vine-covered chain-link fences and walls that surround the houses. Up on Cielo it's beautiful and peaceful. I feel oddly relaxed, calmed and soothed by the rays of the late afternoon sun, thinking it would be great to live here instead of flying back to a London in the grip of a November freeze.

Then I snap back down to earth and realise that I'm at the scene of a crime. One hot August night in 1969, a group of black-clad hippies turned up at this address and slaughtered all of the inhabitants. The most infamous murder trial of the post-war era followed. It just shouldn't feel this peaceful. I'm starting to wonder what I'm doing here, why I bothered to come up here in the first place, wondering what I've learned when suddenly another car speeds towards us and screeches to a halt. Two men leap out. They are both white, youngish or middle-aged – it's often hard to tell with the absurdly healthy Californians – dressed in anonymous plain clothes. Chinos. Jeans. Salmon-pink polo shirts. They are dressed for a day at a country club rather than for enforcing the law. They have police badges worn on lanyards around their necks. One has a shoulder holster containing a gun.

'Sir. Place the camera on the ground. That's right. Now place the bag on the ground. Now walk towards me. That's right. You sir, please step away from the vehicle.'

The orders aren't barked or shouted. There's no malice or anger. It's instructional, the way you would talk to a kid learning to swim or ride a bicycle. Of course, the ultimate sanction is that if we don't comply he will shoot us.

The cop asks me my name. I tell him and nervously start blubbing out every detail of why I'm here. I'm a journalist. It's a piece for a magazine in Britain. Well England actually. (Please God let him know where England is!)

He holds up his hand and asks where I'm staying. I tell him. A hotel on Sunset. He asks for ID. I produce a colour photocopy of my passport. He asks if I have anything else. A driver's licence? I tell him that I don't drive. He raises an eyebrow. I produce my union card and my employee card for IPC Publications (which was where I worked at the time). He seems satisfied. He goes off to talk to his partner who has been questioning my driver. I can't hear what is being said but every few seconds he turns to look at me with a gaze that would turn milk into yoghurt. I am, frankly, shitting it. Every 'bad cop' true story, novel and movie about the LAPD – James Ellroy, the Rodney King beating – races through my brain. They're going to kill me. They're going to fit me up with something and send me to one of those jails where they fuck new cons up the ass. How would I get bailed out? My mouth is completely dry and I think I'm going to vomit. The cop comes back.

'Who is Tommy?' he glares at me.

'Ah, that would be me, officer. It's a pseudonym that I write under.'

'So why did you give us this name?' he holds up the photocopy of my passport as though it's some surprise evidence that I have never seen before.

I launch into a stuttering explanation: 'It's a nom de plume. Lots of writers use them. George Orwell...er...Lenin. Ed McBain...'

The cop shakes his head, goes back to his car and makes a call on the radio, reading details off the passport. I notice for the first time that I am shaking uncontrollably. The driver and the other cop seem to be swapping jokes. Saul looks over at me, holds up both hands as if to say, 'Everything is OK.'

Then there is a long pause. I'm just standing there wondering what they could charge me with. Trespassing? We're not on private property. I think of the Ray Bradbury short story 'The Pedestrian' where in a near-future dystopia the last pedestrian tries to explain to a robot cop why he is out for a walk and where he is going. There's an apocryphal tale about a Londoner in LA who went for a walk, was picked up and questioned, and then told 'You wanna walk, go to the gym and use the treadmills.'

There's a burst of static and something comes back on the radio. The cop nods and walks back to me. He hands me the photocopy of the passport, tells me to pick up the camera and the bag. He takes the camera from me and opens it, exposing the film, then hands it back to me.

He then lectures me: in future I am to carry my passport or some better form of ID such as a California Driver's License. I nod compliantly. I don't want to argue that I don't drive and I don't live in California as these are probably statements that will result in my being run in. ('You don't DRIVE? Book him!') He turns to walk away.

'One more thing. Never come here again. Not this house. Not any others. And I think you know which others I'm talking about. These people want to be left alone. You want to go sightseeing, take the Universal tour. Do I make myself clear?'

I nod.

'Yes or no, sir. That was not a rhetorical question. Do I make myself clear?'

'Yes!'

'Don't feel too bad,' Saul tells me on the drive back. 'Those guys are just doing their job. There's a lot of money in those houses there. These people have political clout. The cop told me that they're called out here a lot. Some stoner kid wants to sell his soul to the Devil, some punks want to honour Manson, some freak just gets off on visiting murder scenes.'

In my paranoia, I wonder if he's talking about me.

There had, apparently, been a recent upsurge in strange, obsessed goth kids hanging out near the house. The LAPD feared some upsurge in Manson-related activities involving black-clad 13-year-olds creeping around the valley looking for victims to slaughter. But the truth was a little less terrifying. Trent Reznor of Nine Inch Nails had recently moved from the house where he recorded his second album, *The Downward Spiral*. Reznor claimed to have been unaware of the provenance of the house when he moved in, though anyone who knows anything about this most Byronic of rock stars will consider that highly unlikely. When the property was demolished, he took the door – the one on which the killers had scrawled the word 'pig' in the blood of their victims – to his new address, a funeral home in New Orleans.

'I'm not personally infatuated with serial killers. I find them mildly interesting at best. I have a curiosity about that, but by no means do I wish to glamorise them. From living in that house I've met every person in the world you can imagine who's obsessed with that whole thing and it's given me more of a perspective on it,' Trent told *Vox* magazine's Bob McCabe in 1995.

Like Trent, I have little or no interest in serial killers, mass murderers or true-life crime in general; but I am interested in Manson and have been since my teens. I'm not interested in the details of the murders, and while I do feel empathy for the victims, they are not primarily what interests me. It is the psychedelic nature of the Manson 'cult', the fact that he was able to order people to kill and all of the trappings – the apocalyptic ideology, the occult dimension, the rock 'n' roll – that fascinates me. I do not admire Manson and his followers; in fact, in many ways, the need to understand and explain is motivated by a need for the tools to recognise and combat similar cult leaders wherever they may arise. I am alarmed at the way that the 'new age' has crept into the mainstream, the way that everything from 'alternative' medicine – including such ludicrous things as aromatherapy, crystals and flower remedies – to Atlantis, alien abductions and astrology has a ready and willing audience. As the established churches decline, people replace them with any old crap that comes to hand. The new-age stuff, the conspiracy theories, the loopy world-views seem to be accepted easily because people want to believe that there is 'something' beyond the everyday world.

As it was for many of my generation, the Manson trial in 1970 – reported on the TV news and in lurid detail in the tabloid press – was, for me, like a horror movie in real life. It had everything: sex, Satanism and sadism.

I remember being fascinated by the image of Manson and the creepy shaven-headed girls with the swastikas carved into their foreheads sitting outside the court. Coincidentally, I also recall coming across the Process Church on a visit to Edinburgh. There were three of them, a man and two women, all dressed in black robes like monks – not in the purple capes with the Goat of Mendes on the back that they had sported earlier in LA – with the metal swastika/Iron Cross symbol made from four interlinked Ps around their necks. It is a long-standing regret that I lost the copy of *The Process* magazine that I bought from them. It was, in fact, the 'Death' issue. I was, however, 12 years old and the writing just seemed like so much gobbledygook.

Later, in my teens, I became an avid aficionado and collector of 1960s psychedelic music and writing. In the drab pre-punk mid-1970s, the spaced-out acid-crazed rock of The 13th Floor Elevators, Love, Sky Saxon And The Seeds, The Doors and The Jefferson Airplane seemed to offer a livelier alternative to the dismal mainstream bands that dominated music at that time. And among the dog-eared paperbacks that lined my shelves – the inevitable Penguin edition of *The Doors Of Perception/Heaven And Hell* by Aldous Huxley, *The Psychedelic Experience* by Dr Timothy Leary, *The Electric Kool Aid Acid Test* by Tom Wolfe, *The Teachings Of Don Juan* by Carlos Castaneda, *Demian, Steppenwolf* and *Siddhartha* by Herman Hesse – was a copy of *The Family: The Story Of Charles Manson's Dune Buggy Attack Battalion* by Ed Sanders. During my formative years, I read Sanders' book maybe seven or eight times, riveted by the story. I bought a copy of The Beatles' 1968 eponymous album, referred to as the 'White Album' (though that is not in fact its title), and searched for clues among the songs, particularly 'Helter Skelter' and 'Revolution 9'. The fact that Manson was in a band and had recorded with Terry Melcher, who had produced The Byrds (one of my favourite bands), and written songs for The Beach Boys (who were another) was also intriguing.

It's difficult to say exactly what the fascination was. I sometimes think that it was a bit like the knight in the Ingmar Bergman film *The Seventh Seal*. He comes to a village where the peasants are burning a young girl as a witch. The knight asks her if she has seen the Devil and knows how to summon him. The knight's squire asks him why he wants to meet the Devil. 'So that I could talk to him about God,' replies the knight. I wanted to believe that there was something cosmic, something magic, just beyond the excrementally dull everyday world of school and mundane small-town life. Even if it was diabolical and evil, it was evidence that there was more to existence than birth, toil and death.

It was a feeling on my part that, were it not for the murders, Manson could have been a great man. In retrospect, I now see that as naïve and ill informed – something along the lines of 'were it not for the attempted extermination of European Jewry, Hitler would be remembered as a great builder of motorways'.

Yet this is an idea that is growing today. As a music writer, I talk to a lot of bands – usually American metal and nu metal bands – and have been surprised at the way that Manson is gradually creeping into the mainstream. Many see him as an icon of evil, to scare people with, but some see him as a prophet of some kind.

There was also a feeling that, because the bands I liked were obscure and had been unfairly dealt with by record companies, press and agents at the time, Manson was another undiscovered musical genius like Arthur Lee, Tom Rapp or Iggy Pop (this was the mid-1970s and although it seems ludicrous now, classic albums like Love's *Forever Changes* and The Stooges' *Fun House* were actually deleted and very hard to come by). The descriptions of the bands that Manson and the Family, and associates like Bobby Beausoleil, were involved in sounded awesome. They had to be something mind-blowing and intense, the ultimate psychedelic experience, and I was desperate to hear what they sounded like. In my mind I imagined some fantastic cross between Deep Purple and The Incredible String Band.

When I was 17 I went to a record fair to look for rarities by The Standells, The Shadows Of Knight or Sagittarius or any other obscure hippy bands. In the cardboard boxes of one dealer I came across a copy of an album called *Lie* by Charles Manson and the Family. It was in a plain white cover, like most bootleg albums at the time, and had a white label with no track details or information as to who had put it out. It was £20 – a small fortune at that time – but I had to have it.

In retrospect I don't know what I expected: because there was something forbidden about the record, I felt like I was about to delve into the pages of *The Necronomicon* (a book that features in the horror fiction of HP Lovecraft and which used to drive anyone who read it insane) or to listen to the song of the sirens. What if, somehow, I let Manson into my head? What if it was the most awesome thing that I had ever heard? What if I woke up standing in a strange house, mutilated corpse on the floor, with a bloody knife in my hand? I felt the same way about putting on the record as I had about my first joint, my first tab of acid or my first line of speed: I was, of my own conscious volition, doing something that was wrong. I was not making a mistake; I was transgressing. I felt, in the language of the yellow press, a sick thrill.

The needle hit the groove and the record hissed badly, skipping on the first track because it was so badly warped. The music was just Manson and an acoustic guitar. It certainly was not the acid brainwashing that I expected. It was sort of...lame. Like James Taylor as a lounge act. Manson's voice was not what I had expected. I had expected – wanted? – him to sound angry and insane. I had expected to hear something that was closer to Black Sabbath than to Cat Stevens. It wasn't terrible, just not very good.

But to give the Devil his due, it's not the work of an untalented man; songs like 'Look At Your Game Girl' – covered by Guns N'Roses on *The Spaghetti Incident* to a clamour of disapproval and controversy – actually have a certain charm. You could, in all seriousness, imagine Sammy Davis Junior singing it. Sammy, or Barry Manilow.

Nowadays it is possible to walk into most independent cult record shops and find at least one piece of Manson product available on CD. You can buy *Lie* on CD through Amazon. Failing that, the songs are widely distributed on the Internet through file-sharing protocols like Napster, Audiogalaxy and Gnutella.

In the late 1970s, when punk seemed to be overturning the values of the 'love generation', Manson was a convenient stick with which to beat recalcitrant hippies. Smug teachers would shake their heads at our 'negativity'. I would usually reply with a rant about Manson, the killings at Altamont and the self-obsessed 'spiritual' supermarket that hippydom had degenerated into. Here's where your folksy love beads and communes ended up: in a brutal and essentially moronic slaughter.

When Siouxsie And The Banshees played their early shows, they covered The Beatles' 'Helter Skelter'. The Banshees were a band who liked to shock – at early gigs and when she danced onstage with The Sex Pistols, Siouxsie Sioux used to wear a Nazi armband – and their choice of 'Helter Skelter' was deliberately provocative. 'This song is dedicated to Roman Polanski,' she said, introducing it at one show in the late 1970s. Throbbing Gristle, another band that I became fanatically interested in as a teenager, also flirted with Manson: at an early gig at the Rat Club in the Pindar of Wakefield pub near King's Cross, they showed a 16mm film called *After Cease To Exist*. I didn't understand what it was about – it featured a castration sequence and the voice of a killer with the band providing an improvised soundtrack – but I knew that it was to do with the song 'Cease To Exist' on *Lie*. The Ramones namechecked him in 'Glad To See You Go' on their second album, *The Ramones Leave Home*, in 1977: 'Gonna take a chance on her/One bullet in the cylinder/And in a moment of passion/Get the glory like Charles Manson/Gonna smile, I'm gonna laugh/You're gonna get a blood bath/And in a moment of passion/Get the glory like Charles Manson'.

Manson was on his way, even then, to being a sort of underground punk icon.

It was a sick thrill, in the same way that Chrissie Hynde formed a band called The Moors Murderers after the perpetrators of a series of grisly child murders in the early 1960s, or even the way that The Sex Pistols recorded a single with exiled Great Train Robber Ronnie Biggs in Rio De Janeiro. It was something else to freak out straight society. It was, mercifully, less extreme than stabbing someone to death and daubing slogans on the wall in their blood.

1 The Fifth Beatle Of The Apocalypse

'I got the revolution blues; I see bloody fountains,
Ten million dune buggies comin' down the mountains.
Well, I hear that laurel canyon is full of famous stars,
But I hate them worse than lepers and I'll kill them in their cars'
– Neil Young, 'Revolution Blues'

The tiny, wizened man is led into the room. He wears a bright orange boiler suit, regulation issue by the California State Prison Authorities. He shuffles because of the manacles on his feet, though he'd still shuffle if you took them off. It's the jailhouse walk, a walk born of necessity, from wearing ill-fitting pants without a belt and shoes without laces; from clothes that don't fit properly because after they were issued you either got pumped up in the prison gym or lost weight through jailhouse food. He's asked his name and then asked to spell it.

'M-A-N-S-U-N!' he says with tired patience.

The parole hearing of Charles Millis Manson (California Department of Corrections Number B-33920, California State Prison, Corcoran, California) is the sort of charade that the California penal authorities go through every five years or so. They pretend to give serious consideration to giving Manson his freedom. Manson, on the other hand, knows that it's a game and uses the hearings as a forum for some rambling monologue or some clowning at the expense of the assembled press, TV cameras, lawyers, psychiatrists and social workers. Sometimes he remains mute. The verdict is always the same: parole denied on the grounds that Manson 'would pose an unreasonable risk and danger to society and a threat to public safety if released from prison'.

Manson then speaks: 'I accept this decision. That's cool. What I'd like for you to do in your own minds personally, everybody that has a personal mind of their own, could possibly consider that the longer that you let this conviction stand, and this little Helter Skelter scheme of the District Attorney to give his particular reality over into the play, that's going to be the reality that they're perpetuating. That's not the reality that I'm perpetuating. I'm not saying that I wasn't involved. I'm saying that I did not break man's law nor did I break God's law. Consider that in the judgments that you have for yourselves. Good day. Thank you.'

The little man shuffles out and smiles for the cameras, his eyes blazing with hate. It's unmistakably the same face with the same black eyes that gazed out from the cover of *Life* magazine's 19 December 1969 issue. It's still a look that chills you to the bone.

Currently being held in California's Corcoran State Prison, where he is serving his life sentence, Manson is currently under 'disciplinary custody' in the prison's Security Housing Unit (SHU). In his book *Lockdown America: Police And Prisons In The Age Of Crisis*, author and journalist Christian Parenti describes Corcoran as 'a land-locked slave-ship stuck on the middle passage to nowhere'. He describes prisoners 'warehoused' in SHUs, where they 'spend 23 hours a day in tiny cells, with no work, no educational programs, and often in total isolation'. The insanity this engenders among the inmates often infects the guards and the prison staff. The prison, like many others across America, is a simmering hate factory where offenders – the majority guilty of comparatively trivial crimes – are incarcerated alongside the violent outcasts, the murderers and the psychopaths. If you were not insane when you went in, the poisonous atmosphere would soon get to you.

In February 2000, after a comparatively short return to the general population, Manson allegedly threatened a prison worker and was returned to the SHU. He receives more mail than any other prisoner in the California State Prison system and probably more mail than any other prisoner in America. Manson has spent 31 of his 67 years incarcerated in juvenile detention and prison. Now that Nelson Mandela is free, he is perhaps the world's most famous prisoner.

He is a post-war figure as familiar as Che Guevara, Elvis Presley, John F Kennedy, Jim Morrison, James Dean, Marilyn Monroe, Mao Zedong or Madonna. As an icon of evil, Charles Manson is rivalled only by Hitler. He's not the mass murderer with the biggest body count, and the horrors of the Tate/LaBianca killings pale beside the grotesque cannibal holocausts of Idi Amin, Jeffrey Dahmer or Dennis Nilsen. The Manson Family's tally of nine (known) victims is paltry compared to even the lesser genocidal regimes of the past century. Kim Il Sung, dictator of North Korea, was responsible for the murder of at least 1.7 million people; a million or more Bengali and Hindu civilians were murdered in East Pakistan (now Bangladesh) in 1971 by the Pakistan military; at least 35,236,000 were murdered in Communist China – 7,731,000 during the Cultural Revolution and a further million during the period of 'liberalisation'. And in terms of a cult leader who sends out his fanatical followers to commit murders to further his Messianic purpose, he is dwarfed, both in terms of victims and panic engendered, by recent demons like Shoko Asahara of the Aum Supreme Truth sect (responsible for the nerve gas attacks on the Tokyo subway) or the new universal supervillain Osama bin Laden.

But somehow the little man with the piercing stare – the scar from the swastika crudely carved on his forehead, surrounded by an aura of blackness – is the bogeyman we have collectively chosen as king of all the real-life monsters.

'People worry about this man the way they worry about cancer and earthquakes,' said Vincent Bugliosi, the District Attorney who was assigned to the Tate/LaBianca murder case and whose book, *Helter Skelter: The True Story Of The Manson Murders*, is still the most authoritative text on the case.

Helter Skelter is an exhaustive, fact-heavy documentation of the investigation, the confession of Susan Atkins, the arrest, arraignment and associated trials of Charles 'Tex' Watson, Bobby Beausoleil, Paul Watkins and Bruce Davis. Disturbing and fascinating in equal measure, Bugliosi's is the 'authorised' version – that Manson, a mind-controlling psychopath, wanted, by sending his brainwashed goons off into the hills to slaughter the Hollywood elite, to spark off a race war between blacks and whites. Bugliosi makes a convincing case (obviously, since the jury found Manson guilty of murder), and while you may quibble and question his hypothesis, the facts are enough to convince you that nobody is the victim of a terrible miscarriage of justice. The 1974 book and the 1977 TV mini-series based on it did much to establish Manson as the icon of evil in the popular imagination.

Perhaps if the killings had taken place anywhere other than LA, backyard of Hollywood, story-teller and myth-maker to the world, they would not have the same resonance that they have today. Perhaps if they had taken place at another time, in the Eisenhower era or in the 1980s, we would view them differently.

There have been more brutal killings, weirder occult-related slayings. The Night Stalker killings, Fred and Rosemary West's 'House of Horror' in the UK, the unsolved Zodiac killings, the mass cult suicides of the Solar Temple Lodge and the Heaven's Gate sect and the bombing of the Oklahoma Alfred P Murrell building by 'Christian Identity' white supremacist fanatic Timothy McVeigh are all uglier, weirder and bloodier than the Manson murders. The assassinations of John Lennon, Gianni Versace, Tupac Shakur and Notorious BIG were murders of celebrities much more famous than Jay Sebring, Sharon Tate or Abigail Folger.

Yet Manson is still the 'king', the Elvis of mass murder. Manson is the rock 'n' roll killer, the fifth Beatle, the evil Beach Boy, the man who masterminded the execution of the 1960s with all its *laissez-faire* attitudes, with all its naïve and sometimes idiotic notions. Free love, free dope, free music. 'Come on people now/Smile at your brother/Everybody get together/Love one another right now,' as The Youngbloods sang. It's a cliché – Manson, the man who killed the 1960s – but, like all clichés, it contains a lot of truth.

The great psychedelic upsurge lasted roughly from 1965 until 1969, peaking in 1967 with the so-called Summer of Love. Fuelled on LSD and marijuana with equal parts idealism and bullshit, the hippies dreamed of a better world here and now, not in some imagined afterlife and not after some imagined social revolution. Thousands of teenage runaways, ageing beatniks, draft dodgers, peaceniks, leftists, activists, musicians, artists, crackpots and geniuses of every stripe came together in a vast social experiment, in the 'love ghetto' of San Francisco's Haight-Ashbury district and in experimental communes in the Hollywood Hills. There was a vast and vital upsurge of new music – acid-influenced rock 'n' roll that drew on jazz, folk, eastern music and developments in the electronic avant-garde – centred around bands like The Grateful Dead, The Jefferson Airplane and The Byrds. The hippies embraced everything from vegan diets and tie-dyed clothing to sexual liberation and a radical extension of the notion of civil rights. There was an upsurge of spiritual questing as youth looked for answers in the Sufi mystics, in Zen Buddhism, in the paperback novels of Herman Hesse and the psychedelic shamanism of Carlos Castaneda. There was an occult revival, with everything from a revived Wicca to Satanism being thrown into the hallucinogenic stew of ideas.

The downside of this sunny idealism was the casualties that soon littered the streets: kids who had 'blown their minds' on acid and the nastier variants, such as STP, that had started to circulate; 15-year-old middle-class girls who had never so much as thought about anything as mundane as earning a living prostituting themselves for food; drug dealers, pimps and cosmic headfuck merchants eager to exploit these naïve flower children for their own ends. 'Mind control' cults like Scientology, the Process, the Children of God, the Moonies, Divine Light and other assorted spiritual fascists proliferated, picking up the vulnerable children and weaning them off drugs and on to their own brand of Godly opium – from dribbling, cat-food-eating, drug-demented hippy to vacant, grinning religious zombie handing out flowers and tracts at the airport in just a few easy steps.

Manson, who was familiar with the 'mind control' techniques employed by Scientology from his time in prison, moved through this milieu, picking up the waifs and strays who drifted to California in search of the hippy dream. Like many aspiring artists and musicians at that time, he flitted around the edges of the scene, tailoring his image to suit the person he was talking to. He operated on different levels, enticing the runaways, the outcasts and the outsiders. He sang to them, softly, strumming an acoustic guitar, songs loaded with love and mysticism. He was what passed for a visionary. He hung out with Dennis Wilson, he knew the rest of The Beach Boys, he met Neil Young, Phil Kaufman, Terry Melcher (who was Doris Day's son and The Byrds' producer), who all respected him as a singer and songwriter.

His circle of disciples grew. Young, mostly female, they were like a cross between a travelling harem and the Apostles.

Manson had dreams of achieving fame through his music. He also had dreams of sparking off a revolution that would bring America crashing down in flames and sweep him to power, returning the world to a sort of joyous barbarism. He alternately believed that he was Jesus, the Antichrist and the Devil, that he was the angel written about in the Book of Revelation, the fifth angel with the key to the pit. He was Abraxas, the dark god that contains both good and evil, darkness and light. He would spark a race war between the white bourgeoisie and the oppressed blacks; the blacks would win, but they would be incapable of governing so they would turn to Charlie, ask him to be in charge.

All rock 'n' roll wannabes have such big egos, don't they?

2 Rock 'n' Roll Has A Heart Of Darkness

'The only black magic we were into was chocolates'
– *Ozzy Osbourne on Black Sabbath's Satanic connections*

There are those who have suggested that Manson is a scapegoat, that he was the target of the establishment who wanted to take a swipe at rock 'n' roll, free love, long hair, experimentation with drugs, the occult revival, the anti-war movement and the back-to-nature philosophy of the hippies.

It has been argued that prosecutor Vincent Bugliosi built his own career through prosecuting Manson and would have enjoyed a less star-studded legal (and literary) career had he, for example, prosecuted Charles 'Tex' Watson as the instigator of the killings, with Manson on a lesser charge of conspiracy to commit murder or accessory to murder. Certainly the coverage of the trial of Manson and his followers provided a convincing anti-hippy argument to anyone who had any doubts about the 'free love' philosophy. And while the sentences that were handed out – the death penalty – were later commuted to life in prison, one wonders if they would have been so severe had Manson been a Mafia gangster, had he chosen less high-profile targets or had he and his followers simply been crazies. Certainly Bobby Beausoleil, still incarcerated after over 30 years and unlikely to be paroled, has paid a high price for his association with the Family: there are very few other prisoners serving such a sentence for the killing of a drug dealer in the USA.

It was not any particular message that Manson preached or that his followers adhered to, it was the fact that they represented values, a way of life that was at odds with the mainstream of American society. Before Manson, people viewed the hippies as, at worst, an annoyance: most people on the outside saw the longhairs as comical, essentially harmless characters. They sympathised when they saw protesters beaten by cops and National Guardsmen, even if they didn't necessarily agree with what it was they were protesting about.

In the 1960s American society was polarised between the young longhairs and the crewcut 'squares' who were products of the Eisenhower era. The post-war consensus of what it was that constituted the American dream – a house in the suburbs, two cars in the garage and a TV in every room – was breaking down. 'Squaresville' – the white-bread world of the American middle class – was a product of Henry Ford and mass production. There was abundance, but it was standardised abundance. It was an America still bound by rules and conventions that governed everything from dating to religion.

But by the mid-1960s the values of the hippies started to creep into Squaresville: corporate executives started to grow their hair over their collars, to sport sideburns and moustaches and maybe – shock horror – to discard their neckties. Beneath the surface of appearances, new ideas started to influence the suburban white-collar middle classes. Ideas from the civil-rights movement and the anti-war movement started to find sympathetic ears in the heartland of the great 'silent majority' as well as on the radical fringes. The hippies were, after all, the children of this affluent suburban society.

The hippy critique of everyday life was all-encompassing: it was everything from food to clothes to political and religious philosophy. Soon they were questioning very fundamental tenets of the establishment.

It was, therefore, necessary for the threatened, 'traditional' American establishment to fight back. And it fought back through the rhetoric of politicians like Richard Nixon, who was able to paint the dissenters as enemies within. It fought back through brute force, using the police to attack demonstrators, as happened at the Chicago National Democratic Convention in 1968 and tragically at Ohio's Kent State University in 1969, when four students were killed. On the culture front, it fought back through television and movies, which either ignored or trivialised the radical upsurge that was taking place. But it also used 'dirty tricks' against its adversaries.

The weight of the US government was brought to bear on the rock 'n' roll counter-culture. The FBI maintained detailed files on John Lennon, bands like The MC5 and important youth culture figures like Bob Dylan. Phil Ochs, a contemporary of Dylan and a more overtly 'political' performer, had an FBI file so vast that when the Freedom of Information Act was passed it took six men to carry all the papers.

The FBI monitored and catalogued their actions, it set up drug busts, it spread rumours. When Lennon applied for a Green Card to remain in the USA, pressure was brought to bear on the Immigration and Naturalisation Service to refuse it on the strength of his conviction for possession of marijuana. Recently released papers reveal that Lennon was felt by the FBI to be a radical influence, a troublemaker.

There have been accusations of other, more deadly, dirty tricks by the paranoid fringe that blames the CIA/FBI/NSA for complicity in the deaths of Jimi Hendrix, Janis Joplin, Jim Morrison, Brian Jones, Elvis and John Lennon. In his book *The Covert War Against Rock*, Alex Constantine writes: 'The central revelation of this volume is the fact that the [CIA] and Organised Crime have, for over 30 years, engaged in a program to silence popular musicians whose influence subverts the cynical thought control tactics of American government and media.' Constantine's all-encompassing conspiracy theory involves everyone from the aforementioned 1960s icons to the assassinations of ex-Wailers star Peter Tosh, rappers Tupac Shakur and Notorious BIG, and the 'mysterious' death of INXS singer Michael Hutchence. It's a brilliant self-contained paranoid world-view where everything is connected and 'clues' are left in plain sight. No doubt if you were to check the number-plate of the Porsche that James Dean was driving the night he was killed, it would be an anagram of 'the CIA did it'.

Obviously the idea of secret service men in black being involved in the death of such an innocuous figure as Hutchence is ludicrous. But the FBI *did* run dirty-tricks campaigns against radical groups such as Students for a Democratic Society and the Black Panthers, and in 1972 the Watergate break-ins exposed a high-level campaign to subvert and undermine the legitimate opposition party in the USA.

Whether or not there has been any actual involvement in

monitoring or controlling events within rock 'n' roll, there are certainly powerful and noisy minority groups in the USA who believe that rock 'n' roll is 'Satanic'. For such people, the Manson trial – with all its revelations of Manson as wannabe rock star, Manson as revolutionary (albeit a revolutionary of the far right), Manson as Satan-Christ, Manson as mind manipulator – was a gift.

The rise of Christian fundamentalism in the 1970s and 1980s fed into a new ultra-conservative lobby determined to reverse the gains made in the 1960s for women's rights, the rights of black people and other ethnic minorities in US society and the rights of gay men and lesbians. The fundamentalists, under the leadership of the Reverend Jerry Falwell, organised under the umbrella 'the Moral Majority' to use their political and economic clout to try to turn back the clock; their major targets were abortion and family planning and what they perceived as 'immorality' in the classroom. They opposed sex education and in some states actually made it illegal to teach the theory of evolution in the classroom unless 'equal time' was given to so-called 'scientific creationism' – that is, that the events described in the Old Testament book of Genesis were literally true. The fundamentalists were able to wield their power to have TV shows taken off the air if they were offended by them; by threatening a boycott of the products advertised on the shows they were able to force editorial policy on programme makers. *Lou Grant*, *Dallas* and *Dynasty* were all targeted by the Moral Majority, and in 1989 it actually forced a pizza company to stop advertising during the comedy show *Saturday Night Live*. Rock 'n' roll, which had become more extreme and 'sinful' in the 1970s – as well as attaining even greater levels of popularity – also became a target for the Moral Majority's wrath.

In the 1960s the number of bands who were openly 'occultic' or 'Satanic' were few: Black Widow, forerunners of Black Sabbath, used to recreate a black mass or witches' sabbat – unaware, or unconcerned, that the two are not the same – as part of their stage show. The Beatles, The Rolling Stones, Judee Sill, Bram Stoker, Blue Öyster Cult and The Coven all flirted with occultism in their songs or album-cover art, but it was only in the 1980s and 1990s that bands like Slayer, Venom, Mercyful Fate, White Zombie, Angelwitch and even Iron Maiden began to adopt overt Satanic imagery, albeit more often than not drawn from mass-market horror paperbacks, comics and Hammer films than from a genuine desire to sell their souls to the Devil. For these bands, it was still all showbiz.

Public associations with Satanism, such as leather jackets emblazoned with pentagrams, Goats of Mendes, runes and demons, and tattoos of the same, have the power to 'freak out' only the most deluded and dim-witted of Christian (and Islamic) fundamentalists. British band Cradle Of Filth have been desperately trying to court controversy for years: their T-shirts emblazoned with the message 'JESUS IS A CUNT' have been seized by police after complaints have been made but have usually been returned the following day.

Perhaps the most celebrated Satanic-rock murder case of recent years took place in Norway, when the self-styled Count Grishnackh (aka 24-year-old Varg Vikernes), leader of 'black metal' band Burzum, murdered his rival Euronymous. Burzum, according to the American Nihilist Underground Society's website (www.anus.com), were 'created to "stimulate the fantasy of mortals". The music of Burzum is the vengeance of chaos against the propagation of administrative and technological models for human existence, ideas which demand allegiance to rules and "morality" or the wisdom of mercy and social compromise as seen by Judeo-Christian technocratic society. Thrusting his fist in the face of that evident death-worship, Grishnackh enfolds the rejected darkness in the lucidity of structure in the most forebodingly empty and threatening views of the world. Total nihilism reduces its belief in inherent nothing to nothingness and from that builds to absolutist ideologies which avoid the emptiness discovered; Burzum carries this passion in music and lyrics as well as artistic conception and presentation. This includes the darkly organic Pagan neo-Nazi post-Nietzschean philosophies which Varg spouts in fragments to a barely credible and barely listening press. He envisions his ideology and music as a continuation of Nazi Germany in the 1940s, as a pagan revolution against Jewish and Christian (Judeo-Christian, including Islam) influence, notably "morality," against which not only Nietzsche but other influential thinkers have railed (Burroughs, Schopenhauer, Wittgenstein, Pound, Shaw).'

That's one way to see it: you could also see it as a member of a tiny and obscure cult band taking his 'beliefs' – a mish-mash of Satanism, Nazism and Nordic paganism – a bit too seriously.

The Norwegian black metal underground has been linked to everything from burning down churches to a massive plot to assassinate centre-left politicians and free Varg from prison.

In his book *Lords Of Chaos: The Bloody Rise Of The Satanic Metal Underground*, Michael Moynihan writes: 'This is not the first time Rock and Roll has assumed a revolutionary mode, but it is the most fanatical and uncompromising such outbreak yet. It is also just the tip of the iceberg. Upon closer scrutiny, the plot to free Varg Vikernes becomes only the latest development in one of the most bizarre and outrageous sagas in musical history... The annals of Black Metal are fraught with violence – exploding in both self-administered suicidal shotgun blasts and cold-blooded knife-blade murders. It is a legacy comprised of innumerable strands of virulent rhetoric, from Satanism to fascism – some of it mere pomp, some stated in deadly earnest. Pulling back the genre's dark veil reveals a few certifiable loose cannons amidst numerous poseurs; the share of cartoon characters is counterbalanced by some genuine "demons" in human form. They all share a common desire to boldly step beyond the perimeters of acceptable society, be it in image or in deed, and plant their flags of defiance. All this is accomplished to the militant sound of Black Metal itself – a roaring cacophony of mind-bending dimensions.

'Rock music has always held seeds of the forbidden. As decades passed and the business swelled, the multinational corporations who came to control it could not allow such seeds to develop into uncontrollable stalks and vines. Simultaneous with Rock's descent into a commodity, sold through endless magazine advertisements and glitzy videos, a façade of pseudo-rebellion has been carefully cultivated, but Rock's "garden of earthly delights" is very well manicured indeed. Yet there are those who attempt to kick down the boundaries and allow it to rejuvenate its limbs in the fertile blood-soaked fields of real danger.'

The link between 'Satanic' rock 'n' roll' and Manson-style mayhem was drawn in the mid-1980s by Richard Ramirez, the so-called Night Stalker serial killer, who used to play AC/DC's 'Night Prowler' before going out to murder people in Los Angeles. (He was dubbed the Night Stalker because initial reports got the title of the song wrong.) He often mutilated bodies and once left a pentagram drawn with lipstick at the crime scene. He thought that the power of Satan would protect him from being caught and would prevent him from being harmed.

At his trial, his speech seemed to sum up the moral vacuum and nihilism of the times: 'It's nothing you'd understand, but I do have something to say. In fact, I have a lot to say, but now is not the time or place. I don't know why I'm wasting my time or breath. But what the hell? As for what is said of my life, there have been lies in the past and there will be lies in the future. I don't believe in the hypocritical, moralistic dogma of this so-called civilised society. I need not look beyond this room to see all the liars, haters, the killers, the crooks, the paranoid cowards – truly trematodes of the earth, each one in his own legal profession. You maggots make me sick— hypocrites one and all. And no one knows that better than those who kill for policy, clandestinely or openly, as do the governments of the world, which kill in the name of God and country or for whatever reason they deem appropriate. I don't need to hear all of society's rationalisations; I've heard them all before, and the fact remains that what is, is. You don't understand me. You are not expected to. You are not capable of it. I am beyond your experience. I am beyond good and evil. Legions of the night – night breed – repeat not the errors of the Night Prowler and show no mercy. I will be avenged. Lucifer dwells within us all. That's it.'

When he was sentenced to death, he shrugged: 'No big deal. Death always comes with the territory. See you in Disneyland.'

Bands like WASP – an over-the-top satirical band whose exploding codpieces owed more to Spiñal Tap than the *Malleus Maleficarum* – became targets of Christians who would picket their shows. There was also a proliferation of strange theories about rock. Chick Comics, a

Christian tract publishing house using comic books drawn by one Jack Chick, popularised the notion that rock 'n' roll was a Satanic conspiracy involving a secret cabal of witches who would literally press 'demons' into the grooves of records, which would then 'possess' the listener, driving them to immorality and suicide.

In an interview with Hezekiah Ben Aaron – then (he claimed) the third-highest ranking member of Anton LaVey's Church of Satan, now a devout Christian – circulated through fringe Christian magazines, he claimed that the Church of Satan had been involved in setting up bands like Black Sabbath, Blue Öyster Cult, The Who and others.

'I was working for the Church of Satan…the Church of Satan had other people who were middle-men for other companies. There were middle-men for Apple [The Beatles' label], Warner Brothers and other record companies. Someone would come to me and say, "I have a tape recording and I'd like for you to check it out. I'd like to see if you would be interested in sponsoring a rock group." I'd say, "All right, I'll check it out." A few days later I'd call back and set up another meeting. I'd hand you $100,000 and you wouldn't sign anything. What you wouldn't know is that a mirror on the back of the wall is a one-way mirror and we're tape recording and photographing or videotaping everything that goes on. The payback, if you fail to make the group work, is really bad. Sometimes it's up to 60 per cent on the dollar. We send you to a store, we provide you with uniforms and we provide you with amplifiers. It's all paid through the money we gave you. We set you up with a road tour. We set you up with engagements. We book you.' Aaron then explained that if the group did not make it he was given orders to collect the money or make 'other arrangements'. These other arrangements are the key to the dozens of reported rock-star 'suicides'.

Although this supposedly infernal arrangement doesn't sound very different from the gruesome contracts that most bands make with record labels – the closest thing to a real pact with the Devil that you'll find – it's actually widely believed by many Christian fundamentalists. What *is* 'true' is always of much less importance than what people believe to be true.

Members of the Church of Satan do not literally believe in an 'evil entity' – like many of the so-called Satanic metal bands, they are really in showbiz as much as in the religion business. However, members of a splinter group from the Church of Satan – the Temple of Set – actually do believe in and worship 'the horned one', though perhaps these subtle distinctions were too much for the born-agains to grasp.

In his book *Christian Rock Is The Devil's Music*, David L Brown writes: 'When Rock Music first came onto the scene, Bible-believing churches recognised it for what it was...the music of sex and rebellion. No Christian ministry praised Elvis' gyrating pelvis. Even Rock Stars called a spade a spade. For example, in 1969, *Life* magazine quoted Rock Star Jimi Hendrix: "Through music, you can hypnotise people...and when you get them at their weakest point, you can preach into the subconscious minds what we want to say." Rocker Hendrix knew what he was talking about. He continued, "Definitely I'm trying to change the world." Music has an awesome power to mould the thinking of the masses and particularly the youth and rock musicians know it. Crosby of Crosby, Stills And Nash made that plain enough when he bragged, "I figured that the only thing to do was steal their kids. I still think it's the only thing to do... I'm not talking about kidnapping...but about changing young people's value systems."'

Moral panics about rock 'n' roll are as old as the music itself: in the 1950s American TV was banned from showing Elvis below the waist because of concerns that his 'lewd pelvic gyrations' would so inflame the passions that western civilisation would be brought to its knees; no-neck southern preachers – including Jimmy Swaggart, the cousin of original hell-raising rocker Jerry Lee Lewis – used to organise boycotts of radio stations playing rock 'n' roll and 'race' music (what was later euphemistically rechristened R&B) to keep the Devil's music from corrupting their God-fearing flock. In the 1960s they burned records by The Beatles after John Lennon claimed they were 'bigger than Jesus' and evangelists would lead prayers outside Led Zeppelin gigs because the folks inside were unwittingly worshipping Satan.

Weird conspiracy theories continue to do the rounds on the far-right fringes: rock 'n' roll is controlled by Satanists; rock 'n' roll records contain hidden messages that brainwash listeners; The Beatles were used to hypnotise American youth and make them susceptible to communist propaganda; KISS stands for 'Knights In Satan's Service'!

Absurd as these beliefs may seem, it has actually resulted in the 'persecution' of artists in American courts. Holders of such beliefs have also managed to gain a foothold in mainstream American politics.

In the 1980s, the 'Washington Wives', a group of well-connected politicians' wives led by Tipper Gore, wife of failed presidential candidate and former Vice-President Al Gore, launched the Parents' Music Resource Center (PMRC) out of concern over lyrics to rock 'n' roll songs by WASP, Prince and others. By 1990, the PMRC was able to have record companies adopt a voluntary rating system ('stickering') of records that contained 'offensive' lyrics. Although the scheme backfired – the sticker became like a badge of free speech for some bands – it has resulted in prosecutions and fines by record retailers and has justified chain stores in closely vetting the content of the material they sell. While there is an understandable anxiety among American parents about the values propounded by rock 'n' roll, the PMRC also advocated the stickering of product that was deemed to be 'Satanic'.

This was a red rag to a bull in some cases. There is also a determination on the part of some bands to push back the boundaries as far as they will go: a band like Slipknot would have been unimaginable a decade ago, and despite attempts to put the genie back into the bottle, it is impossible to turn back the clock. There have been casualties along the way.

WASP was just one of the bands targeted by the PMRC; rappers were targeted, Madonna was attacked and even comparatively innocuous acts like Vanilla Ice were forced to 'clean up' their already squeaky-clean acts.

WASP, like Charles Manson's modern namesake Marilyn Manson, were entertainers first and foremost and, like Manson, they had an articulate frontman who could argue back. Although Blackie Lawless now seems convinced that the PMRC was more concerned with using him to promote the presidential ambitions of Al Gore, the campaign unleashed a potentially dangerous backlash against the band. They wanted to censor WASP the ultimate way.

'Eventually we had to call in the FBI,' Blackie told me. 'When I went onstage – and this has stayed with me to this day – they trained me to scan the audience, to look for things that weren't right. What's wrong with this picture?'

Bomb threats against WASP and a media hate campaign – usually wildly inaccurate – followed. But it did not stop there: the fundamentalists were not merely interested in censoring the 'cuss words' and provocative displays of lewdness and sexuality, they were after the 'hidden agenda'. Throughout the 1970s and early 1980s, such paranoid rantings about rock music and Satanism were confined to the badly printed tracts circulated by tinpot tabernacles. Then came the cases that would become like the Scopes trial (where a school teacher was put on trial in Tennessee for teaching that humans evolved from apes) of rock 'n' roll.

The court cases brought against Judas Priest and Ozzy Osbourne were landmarks for the Christian right. The case against Priest in 1990 was that they used 'backwards masking' in their records to spread 'Satanic messages' that drove two teenagers to a suicide pact.

On 23 December 1985, in Reno, Nevada, 18-year-old Raymond Belknap died of a self-inflicted shotgun blast to the head. His friend, James Vance, attempted to follow suit but survived. The two had been drinking alcohol, smoking marijuana and listening to Judas Priest's 1978 album *Stained Class*.

The Birmingham metal band were not overtly Satanic – their imagery was a sometimes comical blend of S&M and biker-chic – yet they were accused of having the words 'do it!' repeated over and over – reversed – on the track 'Better By You, Better Than Me' from *Stained Class*.

'I think the whole process was being bankrolled by one of these right-wing, fascist, Christian nut-case groups,' said Priest bass player Ian Hill. 'They were financing the whole thing and they were bringing it forward more than anybody else. I don't know, I might be wrong there, but that was the impression I got. It was stupid. It was stupid on a stick, what they were saying and accusing us of. At the time, it wasn't even technically possible – that album was 1978. It still isn't, really, for anything to have an effect on you if you can't hear it or you can't see it.'

The judge realised that perhaps there had been a mistake made in bringing the case to trial when the prosecution's 'expert' witness demonstrated how you can clearly make out demons in the cross-hatching of dollar bills and 'subliminal' images of the Pope having oral sex with the Virgin Mary in pictures of ice cubes in a glass in magazine advertisements for a brand of gin. The case was eventually thrown out and the band exonerated.

In the case of Ozzy Osbourne in 1985, a lawsuit claimed that the song 'Suicide Solution' (actually written about AC/DC's singer Bon Scott drinking himself to death) used 'hemi-sync' tones that made people unable to resist the message in the song and again drove a fan to kill himself. Both cases were thrown out after long and sometimes farcical trials, having more to do with the paranoid fantasies of right-wing Christian fundamentalists than any real violation of the law.

In the 'Slayer case', 15-year-old Elyse Pahler was raped and stabbed to death by Joseph Fiorella, Royce Casey and Jacob Delashmutt in 1996. After confessing, the three teenagers pleaded no contest and were given sentences of 25 years to life. Fiorella, Casey and Delashmutt were obsessive Slayer fans and heavy drug users. The murder, they reasoned, was a sacrifice to Satan to buy success for their band and Fiorella said that Slayer's music began to influence how he 'looked at things', though in a prison interview Jacob Delashmutt claimed that Slayer were less of a factor than Fiorella's obsession with Elyse Pahler. Nevertheless, the Pahler family went to court seeking unspecified damages and restrictions on the marketing of Slayer's music.

Had the judge found for the plaintiffs, the floodgates would have been opened to a raft of lawsuits against bands, whether or not they were purveyors of Satanic rock 'n' roll or the most innocuous pop acts, as parents sought to blame them for everything from school shootings to the fact that Junior is disobedient.

But the trial of Charles Manson – and later that of kidnapped heiress Patricia Hearst – established a precedent in American courts: that mind control was real. One individual actually could control the actions of others and make them commit acts that would normally be abhorrent to them. None of these cases were successful, but every year there are fresh calls to censor everything from TV to video games because they drive children to drug addiction, promiscuous sex and murder.

The scapegoating of rock 'n' roll still goes on, most notably that involving Marilyn Manson, a figure who provokes almost as much fear as the other Manson himself.

Within hours of the 1998 Columbine High School shootings, then Vice-President Al Gore was on TV denouncing video games and irresponsible Internet executives while the press unearthed connections with hitherto obscure 'gothic movement [sic]' bands like My Life With The Thrill Kill Kult and, particularly, Marilyn Manson.

Manson hit back at these accusations, quoting his namesake from his trial: 'You made your children what they are... These children that come at you with knives, they are your children. You taught them. I didn't teach them. I just tried to help them stand up... You can project it back at me, but I am only what lives inside each and every one of you. My father is your system... I am only what you made me. I am a reflection of you.'

In an essay posted on his website a few weeks after the killings, Marilyn Manson wrote: 'When it comes down to who's to blame for the high school murders in Littleton, Colorado, throw a rock and you'll hit someone who's guilty. We're the people who sit back and tolerate children owning guns, and we're the ones who tune in and watch the up-to-the-minute details of what they do with them. I think it's terrible when anyone dies, especially if it is someone you know and love. But what is more offensive is that, when these tragedies happen, most people don't really care any more than they would about the season finale of *Friends* or *The Real World*. I was dumbfounded as I watched the media snake right in, not missing a teardrop, interviewing the parents of dead children, televising the funerals. Then came the witch hunt.

'Man's greatest fear is chaos. It was unthinkable that these kids did not have a simple black-and-white reason for their actions. And so a scapegoat was needed. I remember hearing the initial reports from

Littleton that Harris and Klebold were wearing make-up and were dressed like Marilyn Manson, whom they obviously must worship, since they were dressed in black. Of course, speculation snowballed into making me the poster boy for everything that is bad in the world. These two idiots weren't wearing make-up and they weren't dressed like me or like goths. Since Middle America has not heard of the music they did listen to (KMFDM and Rammstein, among others), the media picked something they thought was similar.

'Responsible journalists have reported with less publicity that Harris and Klebold were not Marilyn Manson fans – that they even disliked my music. Even if they were fans, that gives them no excuse, nor does it mean that music is to blame. Did we look for James Huberty's inspiration when he gunned down people at McDonald's? What did Timothy McVeigh like to watch? What about David Koresh, Jim Jones? Do you think entertainment inspired Kip Kinkel, or should we blame the fact that his father bought him the guns he used in the Springfield, Oregon, murders? What inspires Bill Clinton to blow people up in Kosovo? Was it something that Monica Lewinsky said to him? Isn't killing just killing, regardless if it's in Vietnam or Jonesboro, Arkansas? Why do we justify one, just because it seems to be for the right reasons? Should there ever be a right reason? If a kid is old enough to drive a car or buy a gun, isn't he old enough to be held personally responsible for what he does with his car or gun? Or if he's a teenager, should someone else be blamed because he isn't as enlightened as an 18-year-old?

'America loves to find an icon to hang its guilt on. But, admittedly, I have assumed the role of Antichrist; I am the '90s voice of individuality, and people tend to associate anyone who looks and behaves differently with illegal or immoral activity. Deep down, most adults hate people who go against the grain. It's comical that people are naïve enough to have forgotten Elvis, Jim Morrison and Ozzy so quickly. All of them were subjected to the same age-old arguments, scrutiny and prejudice.'

In his autobiography *The Long Road Out Of Hell*, Marilyn Manson describes how years of being indoctrinated by Christian teachers with bizarre conspiracy theories and descriptions of the 'end times' caused him to eventually reject it.

According to Manson, his grade school teacher Miss Price told the class that President Ronald Reagan was the Antichrist (his name 'Ronald Wilson Reagan' had six letters in each name): 'The Antichrist was here on Earth and we must prepare for the coming of Christ and the rapture. My teachers explained all of this not as if it was an opinion open to interpretation but as if it were an undeniable fact ordained by the Bible.

'It was then that I began having nightmares – nightmares that continue to this day. I was thoroughly terrified by the idea of the end of the world and the Antichrist. So I became obsessed with it, watching movies like *The Exorcist* and *The Omen* and reading prophetic books like *Centuries* by Nostradamus, *1984* by George Orwell and the novelised version of the [strange campy 1972 Christian apocalyptic sci-fi] film *A Thief In The Night*, which described very graphically people getting their heads cut off because they hadn't received 666 tattoos on their foreheads. Combined with the weekly harangues at Christian school, it all made the Apocalypse seem so real, so tangible, so close that I was constantly haunted by dreams and worries about what would happen if I found out who the Antichrist was. Would I risk my life to save everyone else? What if I already had the mark of the beast somewhere on me where I couldn't see it? What if the Antichrist was me? I was filled with fear and confusion.'

As we shall see, such apocalyptic beliefs were to be pivotal to the career of Charles Manson. While his belief in an impending global 'race war' drove Charles Manson to send his followers out to kill the Hollywood rich, Marilyn Manson turned his indoctrination around and made it the subject of his high satire.

In a 1996 interview with *Alternative Press*, Manson spelled out his 'Nietzschean' line and his fear of growing fundamentalist influence in politics: 'I think Christianity itself is self-destructive because it's based on weakness, and I think as people are raised in this country you're meant to have faith in something you can't put your hands on. As you get older maybe you feel cheated, and you start to develop your own ideas of morality. So in a sense, for Christians, morality hasn't declined; it's just merely taken a different shape. The more you get government involved with religion, the worse off you are. They don't even see the irony in the Romans murdering Christ, if you want to buy into that story. It was because there was no separation of Church and State.'

The Christian right is still a potent force in the USA today and the censorship lobby has grown. Even before Columbine, artists such as Ozzy Osbourne, Judas Priest and Slayer were the targets of lawsuits brought and backed by Christian fundamentalists, blaming them for inspiring teenage murders, suicides and rapes through their music, lyrics and alleged hidden messages in the songs.

Manson baited them relentlessly. He told *Rolling Stone* in 2000: 'Christianity has given us an image of death and sexuality that we have based our culture around. A half-naked dead man hangs in most homes and around our necks, and we have just taken that for granted all our lives. Is it a symbol of hope or hopelessness?'

Part of his stage act consisted of Manson dressed up as a gigantic fascist Pope; he attacked Christianity in interviews and in articulate and well-thought-out rants on his website; his post-Columbine album, *Holy Wood (In The Shadow Of The Valley Of Death)*, was steeped in imagery about the Kennedy assassination and an absent God.

But central to all this was his identification with Charles Manson. While he was growing up, Marilyn Manson – then known as Brian Warner – bought Manson's album *Lie*. In his book he writes, '[This] was the beginning of my identification with Manson. He was a gifted philosopher, more powerful intellectually than those who condemned him. But at the same time, his intelligence made him seem eccentric and crazy, because extremes – whether good or bad – don't fit into society's definition of normalcy.'

By conflating the names of America's greatest sex symbol with the name of its greatest icon of occult terror, Marilyn Manson set out to subvert 'Christian' America.

'The balance between good and evil and the choices we make between them are probably the single most important aspects shaping our personalities and humanity... Marilyn Monroe had a dark side just as Charles Manson has a good, intelligent side,' he said.

His cover version of 'Sick City' – an acoustic rendering posted as an .MP3 file on his website in February 2000 as an 'impromptu Valentine's Day gift to fans' was probably the most widely circulated and played Charles Manson song to date, outstripping the Guns N'Roses cover of 'Look At Your Game Girl' on *The Spaghetti Incident*.

When Irish magazine *Hot Press* asked him why he had recorded the song, he said: 'We'd already warped another of his songs, "Mechanical Man", into a track on our first album, "My Monkey", and heard nothing. It was just my way of acknowledging his role in pop culture, as much as if I'd covered "Diamonds Are A Girl's Best Friend".'

Marilyn Manson is, perhaps, the greatest revenge that Charles Manson could have.

3 The New Atlantis

'This period in America resembles the Hellenistic era, when Rome
rose to rule the ancient Mediterranean. It was a sprawling,
cosmopolitan, polyglot world of sexual permissiveness and spiritual
anxieties. Mystical, New Age-like cults sprang up everywhere, and
major deities like Isis, Cybele and Juno were syncretistically merged.
The Heaven's Gate doctrine of a helpful spaceship whirring along in
the tail of Hale-Bopp is neither more nor less substantiated than
central Christian teachings about the resurrection of Jesus'
— *Camile Paglia, commenting on the Heaven's Gate
suicides in* Salon *magazine, 2 April 1997*

My visit to Cielo Drive and earlier to the Barker ranch and the remains
of the Spahn ranch were not in themselves especially useful to
understanding Manson, his followers, the victims, the circumstances
that would produce such a crime or even to the milieu in which they
moved. It's a quarter of a century later and everything is different.

But coming to LA itself and going to Death Valley instantly connect
me with insights into why so many people accepted Manson as a guru.

LA is a fantastic self-hating city: even the impoverished sections
like Watts seem much more affluent than my hometown in the west of
Scotland. It is a city of the 21st century, like a model that the rest of
the planet is working its way towards. There are more millionaires
here than anywhere else on Earth. The people seem blessed by absurdly
rude health, a gorgeous environment – from the lush fragrant hills to
the heart-achingly beautiful beaches – and a lifestyle that is the envy of
the rest of their nation and their world. Yet people who live here seem
to take great delight in running the city down. It's hard to find many

novels that celebrate the city: Raymond Chandler, Hollywood's own Dostoyevsky, described it as 'a city with all the personality of a paper cup'. Nathaniel West's *The Day Of The Locust* takes savage delight in describing an apocalyptic riot as the citizens tear everything to pieces, seemingly weighted down by their own meanness and greed. James Ellroy, perhaps the greatest of the post-war novelists the city has produced, has a love/hate relationship with the city and its history, where the hate more than outweighs the love. Although best known for his brilliant bestseller *The Black Dahlia* and *LA Confidential* – on which the successful 1997 film was based – he even based an early novel on the influence of Manson. In *Killer On The Road*, aka *Silent Terror*, killer/narrator Martin Michael Plunkett crosses paths with Charles Manson early in the book and goes on a killing spree across America in a rampage reminiscent of the real-life Jeffrey Dahmer. He vows, in the novel's closing sentence, to continue Manson's work 'in some dark form'.

Even films – the product that built the city, that gives it its importance – seem to delight in their contempt for it. *Chinatown*, directed by Roman Polanski – the first film he made after the murder of his wife – is about the rotten foundations of the City of Angels. Recent films like *Falling Down*, about a white-collar white male going on a gun rampage, and *8mm*, about the search for a 'snuff' movie in the city's porn-and-sleaze underground, depict LA as though Hell itself had erupted up through the San Andreas fault. To Christian fundamentalists, LA is Sodom, Gomorra and Babylon combined.

In a weird way, LA has no red-light district because most of the city is like one giant Soho or Reeperbahn. There seem to be as many adult bookstores, porno theatres and lap-dancing clubs as there are Starbucks, McDonald's and Burger Kings. You have to wonder about the capacity of the residents to consume porn. It also has the biggest and most public occult scene I have ever seen. You don't have to delve too deep to come into contact with Satanists, would-be witches, seers, psychics, gurus, reincarnated Cathars, UFO contact cults, Scientologists and all their disparate offshoots, and spiritual charlatans of every stripe. Driving along some of LA's seedier streets, for example, you notice that there are almost as many 24-hour psychic and tarot shop fronts as there are adult bookstores and XXX movie theatres. They are decorated in the same shabby style as the porno theatres, a 1970s/1980s skin-flick chic that must have looked dated the second they opened.

Most of the people that you come across in LA feel that they are in some way party to 'secret knowledge', an 'in' to the way the world really works, which evades all of us dumb slobs who soak up whatever they tell us on CNN. By 'most of the people', I mean that the most diverse people you come across – cops, hotel workers, music-biz folk, actors and would-be actors, cab drivers, 'just plain folks' as opposed to 'freaks' – seem to have the insider gossip on everything from the sexual preferences of movie stars and politicians to the fact that the government is being run by aliens.

Concurrent with an unquestioning acceptance of all things 'new age' there is a strain of fatalism: Los Angeles is doomed. Whether it's by earthquake – an inevitability – or other natural disaster, or whether it's by a nuclear meltdown or similar man-made ecological disaster, beneath the sunny West Coast optimism the average Angeleno actually believes that the Apocalypse, in one form or another, is just around the corner. You can see why: in the past century the city has been visited by fire, drought, earthquake, riot and mudslide. It's hardly the biblical plagues visited on Egypt, but Angelenos seem almost proud to recount their tales of woe and survival in the face of such adversity. Perhaps one set of beliefs strengthens the other: faced with the prospect of 'the big one', Angelenos seek refuge in strange cults that prey on their unreason.

California has been the promised land for every sort of idealist, spiritual seeker and pilgrim since the early years of the 19th century. Just as America itself was a haven for the religious dissidents from England, Scotland and the Netherlands in the 17th century and the apotheosis of the political idealists of the 18th, so the expansion continued westward. When groups and individuals felt they could not worship as they pleased or felt they did not belong in the prosperous and developing cities of the east, they packed up their worldly goods and headed west in wagons, heading out into new lands that were largely unknown, carving out new communities as they went.

The western seaboard is littered with the fascinating relics of failed social and religious communities, where pilgrims at one time hoped to establish a New Eden in the rich lands west of the Rockies.

In Visalia, the Kaweah Co-operative Commonwealth was established in 1885 in an attempt to create a socialist utopia based on the principles of Robert Owen, Karl Marx and the First International, which ended in disaster seven years later. Alturia, established in 1894, sought to found a New Jerusalem based on socialist ethics and Christian ideals; it too failed, amid allegations of financial mismanagement and the corruption of its leaders. North of Monterey, the Holy City – supposedly embodying the world's most perfect government – was established in 1906 by William E Riker, or Father Riker, who prophesied that on the day of Armageddon California would be destroyed by an earthquake and the only survivors would be Jews and Gentiles, 'the royal family of the Earth', with all the blacks, Asiatics and Indians being exterminated. The Theosophical Society, based on the occult writings of Madame Helena Blatavsky, established two colonies at Point Loma near San Diego and at Temple Home, north of Los Angeles.

This is the city that has always attracted more than its fair share of charlatans. The notorious Aimee Semple McPherson, pioneer radio evangelist and con-woman extraordinaire, built the impressively kitsch Angelus Temple on Glendale Boulevard before faking her own kidnapping. The State of California has produced or provided fertile ground for more religions, sects and cults than any other region of the world, including the spiritual Disneyland of the Indian subcontinent. Jim Jones and the People's Temple, the Heaven's Gate sect, the wonderfully bizarre Unarius all found havens in 'Cultifornia' before committing mass suicide/going to join with the space brothers. Maybe it is the sense of impending disaster that comes from living on a fault-line, though perhaps the real reason that they are attracted is the same one that pulls in everyone else who moves here: lots of money and great weather. If you're going to run a cult, you may as well do it where the sun shines all year round.

4 The Elvis Of Mass Murder

MICKEY: How 'bout Ted Bundy? Ever do one on him?
WAYNE: Yes. Yours got the larger Nielsen share.
MICKEY: Good...yuppie piece of shit.
WAYNE: What I'd like to do...
MICKEY: How 'bout Manson?
WAYNE: Yeah, it's pretty hard to beat the king.
– *Quentin Tarantino,*
from the script for Natural Born Killers

This book is about Charles Manson and rock 'n' roll. It's about how the music tied in with the man and how he has cast his shadow over the music, from cheap sickos who have adopted him as a T-shirt icon to freak out straight society, to a far nastier strain of far-right rockers who have adopted Manson as a revolutionary figurehead, taking him at his word as the messiah.

It's also about the dark side of rock 'n' roll and popular culture, particularly that which emanates from the city of Los Angeles in which Manson is both a player and a peripheral symbol.

Whenever a disaster strikes America – from the assassination of President John F Kennedy to the 11 September attacks – the great cliché that is trotted out by the majority of pundits and commentators is that 'America has lost its innocence'. But in many ways the Manson murders and the subsequent trial, when a creepy little ex-con and his army of all-American kids struck terror into the hearts of the nation, really was the end of innocence. Apart from the attack on Pearl Harbor, no enemy – not the Japanese, not the Nazis, not the Chinese communists, not the USSR – had ever succeeded in attacking American soil in modern times.

And despite the fact that black Americans struggling for civil rights had been the targets of domestic terrorist campaigns by the Ku Klux Klan and similar white supremacist terror groups, the 'mainstream' of American society – white, affluent, suburban – seemed almost immune to such horror. The ghettos of Watts, Harlem and Compton burned, yet in the suburbs it was still the Eisenhower era, albeit with longer hair and hipper clothes. The streets of Selma, Alabama, may as well have been in Vietnam; it was like another country.

Yet the Manson murders ended that complacency. The targets were young, hip and white. Not stuck-up East Coast WASP types, but the elite of the new, vibrant Hollywood set that was changing the nation. And the killers were boy- and girl-next-door types. They were former Sunday school teachers, college students, lords and ladies to be of the great white American middle class. They were the future educators, home-makers, trophy wives, bank presidents, corporate movers and shakers. Yet here they were, creeping around the Hollywood hills with knives, ready to carry out the most barbaric and bloody killings imaginable on the orders of their black-eyed little guru. This wasn't some messy domestic crime of passion nor some cold-blooded Mafia hit: this was murder that sent a message to America, to the world.

Just as only a few years earlier, the arrival of The Beatles seemed to herald a new and better world, a more optimistic one where there would be fewer bombs, fewer wars and a lot more love, Manson and his followers heralded the arrival of a more cynical and paranoid America. They were like the bloody curtain-raiser on the great republic after Watergate, the sleazy and troubled 1970s when the inner cities became virtual war zones and mayhem became a fact of life to which Americans resigned themselves. Manson is like a terrible footnote to The Beatles: inspired by the sounds, lyrics and titles of the songs on their seminal 1968 eponymous double 'White Album', Manson claimed that The Beatles were the four horsemen from the Book of Revelation.

The story of Beach Boys drummer Dennis Wilson is inextricably linked with the Manson story; a lesser talent than the troubled genius Brian Wilson, Dennis Wilson is, nevertheless, a rock 'n' roll figure whose reputation has blossomed in recent years as people rediscover his work on The Beach Boys' post-*Pet Sounds* and *Smile* albums, and his own brilliant 1977 solo album *Pacific Ocean Blue*. But the fact that he befriended, housed, clothed, nurtured and recorded Manson casts a dark shadow over his memory.

There is a lot of rumour and disinformation, and a number of downright lies surrounding Manson's connections to rock 'n' roll. For years people have been telling me that Manson was one of the applicants who auditioned for The Monkees' TV series. It's a great story, plausible too, given the number of other major rock celebs who auditioned and failed (Paul Williams, Stephen Stills, David Crosby) and what a fantastic group we would have had in a parallel universe with Charlie standing in for Davy Jones. Unfortunately, when the auditions were held, Manson was still in prison. Also, since the wording of the advertisement placed by Screen Gems in *Daily Variety* was seeking 'folk and rock musicians-singers' and 'four insane boys, aged 17–21 for acting roles in a new TV series', Manson, at 31, was already ten years too old. This does not stop others who attended the auditions, including legendary LA anglophile DJ Rodney Bingenheimer, swearing blind that they met Manson that day.

The other persistent urban myth is that the successful 1970s TV show *Charlie's Angels* – where an unseen boss called Charlie sends three beautiful girls to do his bidding – was inspired by the Manson Family. Highly unlikely.

Today Manson is namechecked as the inspiration behind a diverse group of artists and performers. Nine Inch Nails, The Lemonheads, Guns N'Roses, Pantera, System Of A Down, Psychic TV, GG Allin, Red Kross and Sonic Youth have all paid tribute to Manson one way or another, in interviews, in their own songs or in covers, and in other explicit links to the Tate/LaBianca killings. Composer John Moran wrote an opera, *The Manson Family*, based on the trial, using snippets and pastiches of Manson-related music. Marilyn Manson, one of the most influential figures in contemporary rock, makes an explicit link in his name between America's greatest sex symbol and its greatest symbol of evil. His song 'My Monkey' quotes lines from Manson's 'Mechanical Man'. He has also covered 'Sick City', a Charles Manson song. For some of these bands, Manson is just another piece of 1960s ephemera, a killer turned kitsch item. Others, though, feel that they wish to take up Manson's cause.

Just as there are historical revisionists who argue over the details of the Holocaust and even deny that it existed, so too there are Manson revisionists, ranging from those who deny that he is guilty of the crimes for which he has been imprisoned to those who assert that the Manson murders are actually part of a wider conspiracy involving the CIA's MK-ULTRA 'mind control' programme. The wilder fringes of conspiracy theory have portrayed Manson as being at the centre of a 'Manchurian candidate' operation to create programmed, brainwashed assassins. It's unclear whether they believe Manson was himself brainwashed or only his followers.

There's also another 'underground' explanation for the murders: that Manson was involved with a secret cabal of high-ranking Satanists, which later sparked off the 'Son of Sam' murders and the Jonestown massacre. In Maury Terry's book *The Ultimate Evil*, he makes this connection and also suggests that this Satanic conspiracy was the substance behind the outbreak of hysteria surrounding 'ritual child abuse' in the 1980s.

In *The Zodiac/Manson Connection*, by Howard A Davis, it is suggested that Manson Family members were responsible for the grisly Zodiac murders in San Francisco, which took place at roughly the same time. Bruce Davis, convicted for his involvement in the Tate/LaBianca killings, was singled out as the prime suspect. Prosecutor Bugliosi, in fact, suggests that there may have been as many as 35 Manson Family killings.

Others see Manson and his followers as prophets of the Green movement, as persecuted heretics, silenced from speaking the truth. Still others accept that he is guilty of the murders but admire him anyway; James Mason, self-styled leader of the Universal Order (formerly the National Socialist Liberation Front) is one of many on the extreme right who call Manson the 'greatest living philosopher of revolution'.

In his book *Taming The Beast: Charles Manson's Life Behind Bars*, Edward George, Manson's prison counsellor, recounts how Manson was approached by a neo-Nazi terrorist group called 'the Order' to be its leader. (Not to be confused with the Universal Order, the Order was a virulent white power/Aryan resistance movement ranging throughout Colorado and the Pacific north-west, led by white separatist/survivalist Robert Jay Matthews who murdered talk show host Alan Berg in 1984.) 'Searching for a resurrected Hitler they spoke of a grand coronation that glorified Manson's mystical qualities. The FBI busted some of their members and their previous guru was burned to death in a shoot-out leaving them leaderless. They came to Manson looking for a shepherd to recruit "true believers" like Timothy McVeigh, the man who bombed the Federal building in Oklahoma City, or Theodore Kaczynski, the infamous Unabomber.'

McVeigh and Kaczynski go some way to approaching Manson as American icons of evil, committing heinous acts motivated by quasi-religious notions of white supremacy or a twisted anti-technology, a fanatical anti-modernism. This militant irrationalism has led to a strange alliance of Nazis and ecologists.

ATWA (Air, Trees, Water, Animals) – a sort of pseudo-environmental sect fronted by Manson, and associates Sandra Good and Lynette 'Squeaky' Fromme – has a lot of common ground with the so-called 'Deep Green' and 'ecoterrorist' groups on the fringe, who see the mass murder of human beings as a good thing in that it is environmentally friendly. Good has claimed that the philosophy espoused by groups such as Earth First was actually taken from the Manson Family.

Even Manson's homespun apocalyptic ranting – Helter Skelter – has found its adherents in the modern world. In 1999, members of a Denver, Colorado, group called Concerned Christians were deported from Israel after intelligence reports indicated that they were going to be involved in some unspecified acts of mayhem and terrorism around the millennium celebrations. Their leader, Monte Kim Miller, a former anti-cult activist turned cult leader, believes he is the voice of God. His followers believe he is one of the two prophets of Revelation 11:3 ('And I will give power unto my Two Witnesses, and they shall prophesy a thousand two hundred and threescore days, clothed in sackcloth'); the other is Charles Manson. A taped message called 'I Am The Lawmaker' gives us some insight into the sect's beliefs. It focuses on the personal history of Manson and his supposed role as a divine 'lawmaker' or 'son of man'. The message seems to equate the life of Manson with that of Jesus. Manson is referred to as the 'Man Son', an allusion to Jesus as the son of man. 'The Charles Manson murders connect to the son of man judgments, that is the return of Jesus Christ,' the message says. The killings of Sharon Tate and four friends is said to have rendered a kind of divine judgement. By killing the foetus of Tate's unborn child, the Manson Family killed the 'Antichrist'. 'The killing of Sharon Tate's baby represents a killing of Rosemary's baby (the Roman Antichrists) by the Lord,' explains the tape.

Rosemary's Baby, directed in 1967 by Tate's husband Roman Polanski, is a seminal horror film about a plot by Satanists in modern-day New York to bring the Antichrist into the world. The Devil in the film's dream sequence was played by Church of Satan founder Anton LaVey. Susan Atkins, a Manson Family associate, was once a dancer in LaVey's cabaret revue. She would help to stab Sharon Tate to death. The film was set in the Dakota Building, where John Lennon lived with Yoko Ono until his assassination outside his own front door in 1981. And Charles Manson was a big John Lennon fan, as we shall see.

These connections are not mentioned here as evidence of some sort of conspiracy; they are intended to illustrate that circumstantial connections can be drawn that connect any number of unrelated or coincidental events or individuals. That there are deluded individuals and groups who have taken Manson's 'message' as their inspiration is not evidence of a far-reaching occult conspiracy, just evidence that nobody has really learned any lessons from the murders and the trial and the whole sordid story.

There are many more detailed books than this, which delve deeper into Manson's story, the stories of Sharon Tate, Abigail Folger, Rosemary and Leno LaBianca, Jay Sebring, Voyteck Kosinski, Stephen Parent, Gary Hinman and Donald 'Shorty' Shea, and of Mary Brunner, Bobby Beausoleil, Steve Grogan, Bruce Davis, Susan Atkins, Leslie Van Houten, Sandra Good, Lynette Fromme and Charles Watson. But before we talk about Manson's music, his ambitions and the artists who came after him, who have kept his flame burning within popular culture, it is important to look at the details of his life, the times he lived in and the Tate/LaBianca murders.

In a very small nutshell, Manson spent most of his life in jail, was released in 1967, tried to make it as a musician, assembled a following of young girls prepared to obey his every command, took a lot of acid and believed that he was both Jesus and the Beast, heard hidden messages in songs of The Beatles, sent some of his followers out to commit a series of grisly murders to divert suspicion from a friend and to help spark an apocalyptic race war, was arrested in 1969, tried, found guilty of murder and sentenced to death. The sentence was commuted to life in prison when the state of California abolished the death penalty and Manson remains incarcerated to this day.

5 That Ol' Black Magic

'Clang clang go the jail guitar doors'
— *The Clash, 'Jail Guitar Doors'*

The saddest thing about Manson – and yes you have to have at least a little sympathy for the Devil – is that he never really had a chance from day one of his unfortunate life. In a grandiose speech at his trial in 1970 he said, 'You can see me in the eyes of your ten-year-olds.' It's a theme Manson keeps returning to and reprising, that he is only a reflection of America, and in a sense he is right. To repeat the words noted in Chapter 2 (as quoted by Marilyn Manson after the 1998 Columbine High School shootings), Charles Manson proclaimed, 'You made your children what they are... These children that come at you with knives, they are your children. You taught them. I didn't teach them. I just tried to help them stand up... You can project it back at me, but I am only what lives inside each and every one of you. My father is your system... I am only what you made me. I am a reflection of you.' Manson may be evil, he may be mad, but he was made that way. There were a lot of people who helped shape Manson and 'the Manson Family' into a band of killers along the way.

When, at his trial, he was sentenced to death, he said, 'My father is the jailhouse. My father is your system. I have ate out of your garbage cans to stay out of jail. I have wore your second-hand clothes. I have given everything I have away. Everything! I have accepted things and given them away the next second. I have done my best to get along in your world and now you want to kill me, and I look at you and I look at how incompetent you all are and then I say to myself, "You want to kill me? Ha! I'm already dead! Have been all my life!" I've lived in your tomb that you built. I did seven years for a $37 cheque. I did 12 years because I didn't have any parents, and how many other sons do you think you have in there? You have many sons in there, many, many sons in there. Most of them are black and they are angry.'

'No Name' Maddox was born and christened in Cincinnati, Ohio, on 12 November 1934. (Manson was a name he adopted later after his mother was, briefly, married to a man named William Manson, though he was not Charles's father.) His mother was a teenage runaway turned prostitute who allegedly once traded him for a pitcher of beer. Raised by relatives and in orphanages, the young Manson was made to wear a dress to school by one uncle so he would 'learn to fight and be a man'. Violence was a normal part of the young Manson's upbringing, whether that violence was directed against him (he was often beaten by the relatives who raised him) or was just around him.

Another uncle and aunt were strict and religious. The young Manson was drilled in the Bible. When he attended church, he also discovered that he loved music and came to look forward to hearing the choir sing and to sing himself.

When his mother had custody of him, she often left him alone while she went on drinking binges. She moved around a lot, making his life uncertain and unsettled. Manson learned to fight and steal, and soon started out on the career of crime that would end up with him spending almost half of his life locked up before he was 35 years old.

He was sent to reform school for the first time at the age of nine and spent most of his teenage years in and out of state care, returning briefly to the custody of his mother. In 1949 he was sent to Boys Town. Boys Town, set up by Catholic priest Edward Joseph Flanagan in 1917, provided troubled youths with much-needed love, understanding and hope, taught vocational skills and tried to deal with the rage and frustrations of the social outcast youth with something other than a night stick and solitary confinement. Father Flanagan won accolades for his work and earned a reputation as an authority on discovering and developing the hidden talents of youths who had been discarded by society. Two movies, *Boys Town* (1938) and *Men Of Boys Town* (1941), were based on his work.

In 1945 Rene Spitz and William Goldfarb studied the effect of institutionalisation on children and the way it affected the development of personality. Goldfarb's comparative studies of children cared for in institutions such as orphanages and reform schools, and those removed to foster homes showed abnormal development in the institutionalised children in the areas of intelligence, motor coordination, behaviour and language. He used the phrase 'primitivisation of the total personality' to describe the effects of isolating children in regimented and unstimulating environments. His studies showed that these children manifested behaviour such as indiscriminate affection, extremely demanding or attention-seeking behaviour, 'social unrelatedness' with peers, autistic-like behaviour, hyperactivity, aggression (including acts of cruelty), temper tantrums, no cause-and-effect thinking and no concept of time, past or future. In effect, these institutions bred psychopaths unable to empathise with those around them. Worse, other studies showed that such environments could become 'addictive', so that those conditioned in this way would, from choice, seek out similar 'minimal' environments.

A psychiatric report written in 1951 concluded that Manson, because of his illegitimacy, small physical size and lack of parental love, was constantly striving for status with the other boys around him. He had to prove himself through contempt for the rules, through violence and through crime. 'This could add up to a fairly slick institutionalised youth,' the psychiatric report said, 'but one is left with the feeling that behind all this lies an extremely sensitive boy who has not yet given up in terms of securing some kind of love and affection from the world.'

All of the studies of Manson suggest that he adapted well to prison life and, in fact, preferred it to life on the outside. He also had problems adapting to environments where brutality and deprivation were not prevalent. An Indianapolis newspaper carried a photo of the young Manson, fresh faced, beaming, dressed in a suit and tie, with a story about how he had been taken out of a sinful home for a new life. Manson stayed only three days in Boys Town before absconding with another inmate, going on the run through Illinois on a stolen motorcycle, eventually robbing a supermarket. He was caught and sent to another reform school, escaping several times. In one attempt Manson and two others escaped again, this time in a stolen car, which they drove across the state line; it was now a matter for the federal authorities. Manson had graduated from reformatories to prisons.

He was paroled in 1954, married in 1955 to a woman who bore him a son and jailed that same year for stealing cars. Released again in 1958, Manson tried his hand as a pimp. He was given a ten-year suspended sentence in 1959 for trying to cash a stolen government cheque for $37.50. In that same year he conned a woman out of $700 in savings and drugged and raped her room-mate. He fled to Texas, was arrested and sent to prison to serve out his suspended sentence.

Prisons were Manson's school, his university, his social and professional network of contacts. The courses that were on offer were pimping, scams, con games, card sharping, lock picking, breaking and entering, car theft and fencing. If you wanted to get ahead, you studied hard so that next time you didn't get caught. It was in prison that Manson found himself, in the parlance of the 1960s.

Prison shapes ideas: given time to think, many men in jail undergo spiritual, political and intellectual awakenings while in the custody of the state. One thinks of the great Italian Marxist theorist Antonio Gramsci, or Malcolm X, or Fyodor Dostoyevsky, whose life and works were changed irrevocably by their incarceration.

American prisons at that time were divided between attempting to reform and rehabilitate the inmates and wanting to punish them. American prisons today are, more often than not, human warehouses. But in the middle of the 20th century there were genuine attempts to tackle the root causes of crime and to try to stop convicts from reoffending on their release, through education and using the encouragement of music and art therapy. These were brutal, violent places that were strictly segregated along racial lines (and prison gangs such as the Aryan Brotherhood, a violent white supremacist group allegedly responsible for numerous attacks and murders of inmates and correctional officers throughout the federal and state penal system, must also have fed some of Manson's racist ideology, which came to fruition later on), but it was also possible for an inmate to better himself while incarcerated.

While he was serving time in McNeil Island Federal Penitentiary in Washington State, the 27-year-old Manson took advantage of some of the educational programmes that the prison offered. He had never until that point been able to read or write proficiently, but he studied in his cell, struggling as he says to bring his education up to college entry level. He investigated Christianity; he also came into contact with other beliefs prevalent inside American jails. He followed some of the tenets of Islam, as practised by the Nation of Islam (or 'Black Muslims' as they were often referred to at that time). He came into contact with Native American beliefs and Buddhism, and possibly most importantly he discovered, through a cell-mate, the fledgling cult (or 'new religious movement') of Scientology.

Scientology, which has been called everything from a 'mind control cult' (an 'attempt to recreate the world of Orwell's *1984* as a religion', as one disgruntled refugee from the cult put it) to DIY psychiatry, was formulated by Lafayette Ronald (L Ron) Hubbard, a science-fiction writer who, along with the likes of Isaac Asimov, AE Van Vogt and Poul Anderson, was one of the mainstays of the pulp magazines of the 1940s and 1950s. Science fiction, however questionable its merits as literature at this time, is a genre concerned with ideas. At times the 'religion' that grew up around Hubbard's 1950 book *Dianetics: The Modern Science Of Mental Health* seems like a glorified self-improvement course and, at others, like something from the pages of one of Hubbard's science fiction stories. Scientologists believe that most human problems can be traced to lingering spirits of an extraterrestrial people massacred by their ruler, Xenu, over 75 million years ago. These spirits attach themselves in clusters to individuals in the contemporary world, causing spiritual harm and negatively influencing the lives of their hosts.

Scientology fought these negative forces through a process of 'auditing', which, according to their own definition, 'could be described as a very unique form of personal counselling which helps an individual look at his own existence and improves his ability to confront what he is and where he is. Scientology auditing can bring any person from a condition of spiritual blindness to the brilliant joy of spiritual existence.'

Scientology's celebrity adherents – John Travolta and Kirstie Alley, for example, but also soul legend Isaac Hayes, jazz pioneer Chick Corea and cult 1960s psychedelic folkies The Incredible String Band – have gone some way to normalising what they claim to be 'the world's fastest growing religion'.

Although Manson was never a Scientologist, he borrowed liberally from its ideas – what Scientologists call in their jargon *squirreling* – and must have been influenced by Hubbard's success in creating his own personal religion from scratch. Manson was manipulative, even when there was no need for him to be, and Scientology perhaps suggested to him the ultimate way to gain control over people.

Surviving in jail requires that you be able to assess a situation and deal with it, usually by violence. Manson did not have the advantages that a big or brawny man would have in jail and had to learn quickly to manipulate others. He became adept in the normal prison routine of assessing threats from other prisoners and looking at the options open to him. Scientology and its influence may be overestimated when discussing Manson: much of what he learned about manipulating others – telling them what they wanted to hear, thinking two or three moves ahead at all times – was just part of day-to-day survival in jail. Often it came down to just telling people what they wanted to hear.

In his speech to the judge at his trial in 1970, he said, 'I was released from the penitentiary and I learned one lesson in the penitentiary: you don't tell nobody nothing. You listen. When you are little you keep your mouth shut, and when someone says, "Sit down", you sit down unless you know you can whip him, and if you know you can whip you stand up and whip and you tell him to sit down. Well, I pretty much sat down. I have learned to sit down because I have been whipped plenty of times for not sitting down and I have learned not to tell people something they don't agree with. If a guy comes up to me and he says, "The Yankees are the best ball team", I am not going to argue with that man. If he wants the Yankees to be the best ball team, it's OK with me, so I look at him and I say, "Yeah, the Yankees are a good ball club." And somebody else says, "The Dodgers are good." I will agree with that; I will agree with anything they tell me. That is all I have done since I have been out of the penitentiary. I agreed with every one of you. I did the best I could to get along with you, and I have not directed one of you to do anything other than what you wanted to do.'

In a secret Scientology internal document seized by the FBI in 1977 that purported to show Scientology intelligence operations against other groups and individuals, there is a report of an interview with one Raul Morales: 'Raul arrived in prison on McNeil Island, Washington, in 1962 and became a cell-mate of Lafayette Raimer, allegedly a trained Scientology auditor (about Level I in Raul's estimation) and was introduced to Scientology at that time. Raimer was auditing in prison at that time and in one ten-man cell had managed to gather a group of about seven, all in Scientology. Charles Manson entered later and studied…along with his cell-mates and received approximately 150 hours of auditing from Raimer. Raimer kept records of his auditing. Manson got super-energetic and flipped out when he'd been audited and would, for a time, talk about nothing but Scientology to the extent that people avoided his company. After a while, however, Manson was screaming to get away from his auditor (in Raul's opinion, he'd been severely over-run or something). He eventually managed to get put in solitary confinement to get away from his auditor. Eventually prison officials got suspicious of the group's strange activities and broke up the group. Raul just found out yesterday that another friend, Marvin White, later sent Manson books (after the Scientology group was broken up) on hypnotism and black magic.'

Other 'science fiction' cults – such as the Martian 'love cult' described in Robert A Heinlein's classic *Stranger In A Strange Land* – remained on the printed page and in the imagination of their creator, but were also an influence on Manson, as we shall see. Other pseudo-scientific and quasi-mystical ideas that were prevalent in the popular pulp magazines at that time included the idea of the 'hollow Earth' – a long-held belief that the Earth has a vast underground civilisation residing at its centre or in vast caverns was undergoing a brief revival, thanks to the efforts of extraordinary pulp editor Ray Palmer – and were also to feed into Manson's personal mythology when he sought the entrance to a vast subterranean cavern in Death Valley where he and his followers would hide out during the Apocalypse he believed was at hand.

Also, one can't help but look at the comics and pulp magazines of the 1950s and 1960s with their small ads listing books that promised to give the reader the key to unlimited power through hypnotism, answers to 'all the secrets of the ages' courtesy of the Rosicrucians and countless self-improvement manuals based, more or less, on Andrew Carnegie's *How To Win Friends And Influence People*, and wonder how much of it went towards shaping Manson the master criminal cult leader.

Finally, The Beatles were something of an obsession with Manson. Their arrival in New York in 1964 to scenes of teenage hysteria was like an invasion from another planet. With their absurd hair, their incomprehensible accents and a sense of humour that often went right over the heads of the irony-free button-down minds of early 1960s straight America, The Beatles were the wedge that helped to open the generation gap, a fault-line that divided children born into post-war affluence from their parents, whose experiences had been the depression of the 1930s and the uncertainty of the Second World War. The Beatles had a quasi-mystical power over their flock of (predominantly teenage girl) fans, which actually had many similarities to the gospel revivals taking place at the same time, particularly the stadium crusade of the Reverend Billy Graham. Rock 'n' roll had always borrowed from the hot gospellers and holy rollers, the fiery and intense Pentacostalist and Baptist preachers of the Bible belt. It is said that the young Elvis Presley based some of his moves on the travelling tent revivalist preachers who would, literally, shake, rattle and roll as the holy spirit moved them. For Manson, the possibility of being able to reach people in the same way through his music must have been attractive. John Lennon famously declared that The Beatles were 'bigger than Jesus'. Manson felt – as did many of his contemporaries – that, with the right breaks, he could be bigger than The Beatles.

Manson also came across Alvin Karpis, top of the FBI's Most Wanted list in the 1930s and arrested by bureau chief J Edgar Hoover himself on a kidnapping charge. Karpis robbed banks, had shoot-outs with the police, kidnapped the wealthy for ransoms and held up trains like an Old West outlaw. He joined forces with Freddie Barker and his brothers to form the Karpis–Barker gang, known in crime mythology as the Ma Barker Gang. At one time, Karpis was wanted for murder in 14 different states. The police nicknamed him 'Old Creepy' or 'Creepy Karpis'. Karpis escaped the electric chair but went on to serve more time in Alcatraz than any other convict. He spent a quarter of a century in that jail – his cell-mates were Doc Barker, Machine-Gun Kelly and Al Capone – before being moved to McNeil. Although in prison nobody is anybody, despite what they 'achieved' on the outside, Karpis was a star. But on top of this notoriety, Karpis was also a musician. He played blues guitar, something that awakened a yearning in Manson to learn about music. He sought out Karpis and learned guitar from him.

In his autobiography, *On The Rock – 25 Years In Alcatraz: The Prison Story Of Alvin Karpis*, he recalls that '[a] kid…request[ed] music lessons. He wants to learn guitar and become a music star. "Little Charlie" is so lazy and shiftless, I doubt if he'll put in the time required to learn.

'The youngster has been in institutions all his life – first orphanages, then reformatories and finally a federal prison. His mother, a prostitute, was never around to look after him. I decide it's time someone did something for him and to my surprise, he learns quickly. He has a pleasant voice and a pleasing personality although he's unusually meek and mild for a convict. He never has a harsh word to say and is never involved in even an argument.

'He and some other kids in McNeil belong to the Church of Scientology, a religious cult which Charlie attempts to persuade me to join. "If you believe strong enough that you can do something, you can do it!" he explains, but I decline his invitation.

'When Charlie is getting good on guitar and vocals and also "getting short", he asks me to send him to some contacts in Reno or Las Vegas to get a job. Other prisoners, all good friends of mine, are Frankie Carbo, Mikey Cohen and Dave Beck, who have connections with nightclubs in Las Vegas. I think seriously about using my influence to get him started in the entertainment business.

'My decision in the end is to leave him on his own. If he has the talent, he'll make it to the top. The history of crime in the United States might have been considerably altered if "Little Charlie" had been given the opportunity to find fame and fortune in the music industry.'

6 Free At Last

'If you're going to San Francisco,
Be sure to wear a flower in your hair'
— *Scott MacKenzie, 'San Francisco'*

Although the demos he recorded in the 1960s show little evidence of his roots, later albums recorded in prison – like *Charles Manson Live At San Quentin* – are actually classic prison blues songs.

There's some suggestion that Manson actually enjoyed prison and felt comfortable there. Long-term prisoners – those, like Manson, who were raised in institutions from childhood – felt comfortable with the routines of prison life. They had status there, they knew the rules and they actually experienced a kind of freedom. The outside world was, to them, an unknown: details, from how to dress correctly to how to relate to women, were puzzling. In prison, for example, violence was the ultimate end of most arguments. In prison, your capacity for violence was an advantage, conferring respect and status. On the outside, however, this wasn't necessarily the case. When he was transferred to Terminal Island and then released in 1967, Manson even argued with his parole board to allow him to remain there.

Vincent Bugliosi claims in *Helter Skelter* that Manson left vowing to corrupt the youth of America. But his own testimony and that of Karpis – quoted in John Gilmore's *The Garbage People* – tells a different story: 'I shook Charlie's hand and when he'd gone off I shook my head. Manson was definitely ill prepared for life. He left McNeil and I saw nothing but a string of penitentiaries before him. Bad, bad news all the way down.'

In his 1986 book *Manson In His Own Words*, Manson's cell-mate

Nuel Emmons' is quoted as saying, 'I had spent the last seven years of my life looking forward to the day I would get out. I had dreams and plans, but as I was being processed for release I knew the dreams would never be realised and the plans were nothing more than wishful thinking... I had my music, but I was afraid that if I depended on it too strongly, I would fail at that too. No, I did not want to go out into a world of uncertainties. For the moment I was secure and that's how I wanted to stay.'

Manson In His Own Words, by 'Charles Manson as told to Nuel Emmons', is the *Satanic Verses* of Mansonia. This 1986 book was supposedly dictated by Manson to his cell-mate, though according to Manson it is 'Manson in Emmons's words, not mine'. The book is problematic because you suspect that, while some of this is based on actual conversations with Manson (it gives Manson's side of the story), according to Manson and other associates it describes situations that definitely did not take place. While one would normally take the assertions of Manson and his friends with a pinch of salt, there seems to be little reason for them to lie in this case. The book reads like a creative reinterpretation of other available books, though anyone with even a passing knowledge of Manson can tell that it is not his voice speaking. However, what is not in doubt is that he left prison with $35 and a suitcase full of old clothes, scared and unprepared to face the world.

Manson emerged into a world that was markedly different to the one he had left in 1961. The staid certainties of the Eisenhower era had dissolved following the assassination of John F Kennedy, the growing unpopularity of America's involvement in the Vietnam War and a rising challenge to the dominant culture of white, male, middle-aged protestant America. It was, ironically, the long post-war boom that produced a generation critical of the way that the system worked, who bit the hand that fed them. People openly questioned everything that only a few years before had seemed certain and immutable. Marriage, the family, God, church, nation, government – all were subject to scrutiny and rejection. Suddenly there were women questioning the 'legal slavery' of marriage, gay men questioning whether they really deserved to be abused and harassed by police and black people questioning the system that kept them as second-class citizens, still slaves in the land of the free. Although the changes that were taking place in America had deep-seated political, economic and demographic causes at their root, it was the stylistic changes that were the most radical and profound.

A bohemian lifestyle pioneered by the so-called beatniks in the 1940s and 1950s had taken root around North Beach in California and in Greenwich Village in New York. Confined at first to a small group of dissidents, pot-smokers, politicos, writers, poets, mystics and hangers-on obsessed by modern jazz, Zen Buddhism, art and ideas of free love, it had begun to mutate and become a mass-market overground phenomenon by the early 1960s.

The term *hippy* was coined as an insult, allegedly by a police officer at a press conference in 1966, though it most likely derived from the term *hipster* coined in the 1930s to describe the white denizens of Chinese opium dens (apparently because they stood with their hands on their hips) or from the 1940s term *hep cat*, which *Webster's Dictionary* defines as 'a person who is unusually aware of and interested in new and unconventional patterns especially in music; characterised by a keen informed awareness of or interest in the newest developments'. Insult or not, it is the name by which long-haired youths came to be known in the 1960s. While others preferred 'love generation', 'freaks' or 'free men', hippies they were.

Rock 'n' roll had supplanted jazz, cinema and TV as the major recreational activity of youth. The sound became softer, folkier, laden with new electronic effects supplied by gadgets such as the fuzzbox and the wah-wah pedal. Guitars began to sound like sitars. A new school of rock virtuosi – the 'guitar heroes' – such as Eric Clapton of The Yardbirds (and his successor Jimmy Page) and Jimi Hendrix emerged, pushing back the boundaries of musicianship ever further. Bob Dylan inspired bands to write lyrics that went beyond the simplistic teenage love songs, laments and double entendres about sex that had been the mainstay of rock 'n' roll throughout the 1950s. Songwriting became poetic. The Beatles and the so-called British Invasion, from 1964 onwards, had a radical impact on American bands, from their sound –

which became open to the same influences as The Beatles, The Rolling Stones *et al* – to the way they dressed and wore their hair.

Men began to grow their hair long, from collar length in the mid-1960s to full-flowing Jesus locks by 1967. It was a style that was feminine, while the dominant culture – epitomised by the severe crewcut of the advertising executive, the Marine and the astronaut – was aggressively old-school, red-meat-eating masculine. For all their radical, naïve and progressive ideas, the biggest challenge the hippies seemed to offer to straight America was their irritating refusal to visit the barber. Clothes changed too: eastern styles such as kaftans, Afghan coats, cheesecloth khurtans, sandals, peasant skirts, military surplus, denim, leather and suede became the norm. A walk along Sunset Boulevard in Los Angeles, Carnaby Street in London or Haight Street in San Francisco in 1967 would have been like a visit to the circus as people dressed in a riot of clashing colours, sporting body paint, long hair, no hair, dyed hair, old band uniforms (like The Beatles on the cover of *Sergeant Pepper's Lonely Hearts Club Band*) or fancy-dress costume. Women either wore vivid variations on the mod make-up of the time or rejected it entirely as plastic, preferring a natural look.

Drugs too were a vector in the changing cultural scene. Marijuana, plentiful since the turn of the century, when it was made illegal in black neighbourhoods like Watts and among the Hispanic immigrants to California, had been 'discovered' by white hipsters in the 1930s and 1940s, and particularly by the 'beats' in the 1950s. By 1967 it was commonplace, though still very much illegal. LSD (lysergic acid diethylamide 25) was first synthesised in Switzerland in the 1940s and was legal in the state of California until 1966. Thanks to the proselytising of, on one hand, Dr Timothy Leary and, on the other, Ken Kesey and his band of Merry Pranksters, LSD, or acid, was the chemical that every person who considered themselves to be hip in the 1960s wanted to try.

We now know that the CIA, through its MK-ULTRA programme, had experimented with LSD in its search for an effective truth drug or something that could be used to brainwash its enemies. It has even been suggested that LSD was used to undermine the growing political radicalism and opposition to the war, by literally blowing the minds of the throng of potential activists and agitators, diverting them from involvement in mass political action into meaningless hedonism, searching for spiritual answers and the navel-gazing cul-de-sac of personal growth and me-generation politics. The most extreme conspiracy theorists have even suggested a link between Manson and the CIA. In his modern paranoid classic *The Shadow Over Santa Susana: Black Magic, Mind Control And The 'Manson Family' Mythos*, author Adam Gorightly links Manson to MK-ULTRA, Sirhan Sirhan (allegedly brainwashed assassin of Robert Kennedy), 'Son of Sam' David Berkowitz, Mark David Chapman (murderer of John Lennon) and John Hinckley Jr (Jody Foster obsessive who tried to assassinate President Ronald Reagan). Gorightly, seemingly having read every primary source, book and article on Manson ever written, demonstrates that Manson, rather than being the illiterate hillbilly he portrayed himself as, was a magickal adept, a brilliant if malicious and manipulative man. Gorightly too wades through conspiracy theories, allegations of mind control and arcane lore to draw a picture of Manson that is more complex and that draws alternative conclusions to those of Bugliosi, Sanders *et al*. Others have suggested that, in fact, the whole Summer of Love psychedelic schtick was just fall-out from the CIA and the military's activities.

All these conspiracies fall apart when you look at them too closely; either that or they give birth to even bigger and more complicated conspiracy theories that keep on multiplying until you see entire streets full of government spooks, alien agents and Illuminati stooges. The fact is that the CIA found LSD to be comparatively useless as a truth drug, as a tool of mind control or as something that could be used to undermine foreign statesmen, agents and others that they wanted to compromise. And the truth behind what the CIA was really doing with MK-ULTRA may never be known because the Agency destroyed all records and papers pertaining to it.

What is not disputed was that there were some quite serious figures who saw LSD as a powerful weapon. Major General William Creasy, chief officer of the Army Chemical Corps, thought that LSD would be the weapon of the future. He suggested that dropping LSD in Moscow's water supply would be more humane than fire-bombing the city or using nuclear weapons. 'I do not contend that driving people crazy even for a few hours is a pleasant prospect. But warfare is never pleasant... Would you rather be temporarily deranged...by a chemical agent, or burned alive?' he asked readers of *This Week* magazine in May 1959.

But for all that the LSD experience could be negative, there were millions more who really did find it to be the door to perception, an evolutionary touch-pad that opened the mind. LSD has been successful in treating some forms of schizophrenia; studies have also shown LSD to be useful in treating alcoholism and other addictions. In the 1960s terminal cancer patients given LSD found that they were able to overcome the debilitating anxiety and depression from which they suffered.

Its role as a doorway to quasi-religious visionary experiences has been well documented, but there are also instances where mathematicians, theoretical physicists and chemists have gained insights through using the substance. Dr Harold A Abramson, an early LSD researcher, gave subjects doses of LSD to test their abilities to perform simple and complex mathematical problems. In *The Use Of Psychedelic Agents To Facilitate Creative Problem Solving*, published by the Institute for Psychedelic Research of San Francisco State College, he cites two instances in which marked improvements in performance occurred, somewhat to his surprise: 'One of our engineers, who was a subject, could get 100 per cent under LSD in certain of the tests we used, which he never did without LSD... There was another subject, a young woman, who was a technician working at Columbia, who was determined to get all her mathematics examples correct, and practised at home. Although she was very disturbed [over other matters]...under 100mcg of LSD, she got 100 per cent on her mathematics test.'

LSD changed people; users often reported that they gained insight into themselves and developed a much stronger empathy with others. Mainstream American research into LSD, however, ceased in 1966, when it became illegal.

The illegal trade in LSD and other psychedelic chemicals began with Timothy Leary's experiments at Harvard and later at Millbrook, in New York state, in the early 1960s, and also with Ken Kesey's Merry Pranksters and their 'acid tests' – multimedia 'happenings' involving film, music (their house band was The Grateful Dead) and Kool Aid spiked with LSD – on the West Coast. But they were still able to buy supplies of pharmaceutical LSD manufactured in the Sandoz Laboratories in Switzerland. There was also significant usage of LSD among the great and the good before it became associated with hippies. Roman Catholic priests enthused about its potential as an aid to spiritual growth. Christopher Mayhew, later a Labour MP, appeared on the BBC's prestigious current affairs programme *Panorama*, filmed experiencing an LSD trip. But it was not until 1966 that it became a street drug, manufactured in illegal laboratories and sold through a network of criminal suppliers.

Before being sent to prison in 1961, Manson was certainly familiar with marijuana. In his book, there's also a suggestion that, while in Mexico, Nuel Emmons tried smoking the sacred mushrooms that the Yaqui Indians used in their shamanistic rituals as a gateway to the other world. There are no details about his experiences with the mushrooms, only an anecdote about pulling a Magnum out when confronted by four Yaqui toughs, winning their respect and getting a bag full of the sacred mushrooms. Whether this is true or perhaps inspired by the bestselling *The Teachings Of Don Juan: A Yaqui Way Of Knowledge* by Carlos Castaneda – who has also been accused of being a fake, lying about his involvement with the Yaqui mystics – remains unclear.

The psychedelic experience began to affect everything. Artwork, which evolved from surfer iconography or hot rod designs, became intricate and vividly coloured; the posters of Rick Griffin or Mouse and Kelly mashed together comic-book art, movie stills, art-deco stylings and Day Glo colourings into a vivid and distinct psychedelic style. In fashion, in film, in light shows and in writing, LSD was a huge influence on culture, and it was the popular music of the time that wove all these elements together.

There was a great game of one-upmanship going on between all the major bands at this time as they tried to push forward the frontiers of their music, to move away from simple formulaic R&B and to create something that they felt was art truly worthy of them. The Beatles had released *Revolver* in 1966, an album that included the ground-breaking track 'Tomorrow Never Knows', which used looped sounds, reversed tapes and sampled orchestral notes to create a collage-like effect, backing Lennon's words, which were inspired by Leary's interpretation of the Egyptian *Book Of The Dead*. It was a song about the loss of ego, about becoming part of a greater cosmic whole. The Beach Boys responded with *Pet Sounds*, still regarded by many critics as the greatest pop album of the 20th century (and even as the greatest ever piece of recorded music). The Beatles went one up on *Pet Sounds* with *Sergeant Pepper's Lonely Hearts Club Band*, in many ways the ultimate psychedelic album, since it managed to shove everything from the clichéd faraway voice on 'Lucy In The Sky With Diamonds', the oblique lyrics of 'A Day In The Life' and the orchestra, the sound loops and the whimsical use of instruments like the harpsichord, onto two sides of vinyl. Brian Wilson of The Beach Boys famously began work on *Smile*, an album that would go one better than *Sergeant Pepper's Lonely Hearts Club Band* but that would, symbolically, lead to madness and burn-out.

Although The Beatles featured the great English magician Aleister Crowley on the cover of *Sergeant Pepper's Lonely Hearts Club Band*, it was not until The Rolling Stones released *Their Satanic Majesties Request*, one of the first rock 'n' roll albums with overt black magic overtones, that there was a real tangible link between the new psychedelic culture and the occult underground. Anita Pallenberg, girlfriend of Brian Jones and later of Keith Richards, was the occult conduit in the band, introducing Mick Jagger, Marianne Faithfull and Keith Richards to Kenneth Anger, about whom more will follow.

Other bands, like The Grateful Dead, incorporated elements of jazz, American jug-band folk, country and western, blues and soul into their music; their marathon jam sessions around songs like 'Dark Star' were recreating in rock music the kind of intense, rapid creativity that John Coltrane brought to jazz. On the East Coast, The Velvet Underground brought a more European avant-garde sensibility to their sound, involving *musique concrète*, the early minimalist music of Terry

Riley and Steve Reich and the possibilities of overloading people with light, noise and movement. In Britain, bands like Pink Floyd and The Soft Machine were breaking down the barriers between what was pop and what was 'serious music' or what was 'art'.

There was also, as we shall see in more detail later on, a great spiritual quest going on with The Beach Boys, The Beatles, Mia Farrow and others all making the journey to India to meet the Maharishi (though Ringo Starr was to return complaining, 'It was just like Butlins,' while John Lennon eventually tired of the Maharishi and, when the guru asked him why he was leaving, replied, 'You're so bloody cosmic, you tell me'). Significantly it was Beach Boys drummer Dennis Wilson who discovered the Maharishi and transcendental meditation first, although it was Mike Love who remained the only member of the band who stayed faithful, rather like George in The Beatles. Suddenly there were gurus everywhere; even the normally cynical Pete Townshend of The Who discovered the enlightened Meher Baba, though from the fact that you never saw a picture of Pete smiling, you might deduce that he never really found inner happiness or that, if he did, he wasn't letting on.

Everything seemed to come together in around 1967 on America's West Coast. It was where the best bands were, where the best drugs were to be found, where the best sense of community, of bohemian life, was to be found in the cold-water flats and psychedelic coffee shops around the Haight-Ashbury, with the Family Dog-organised dance concerts taking place at the Longshoreman's Hall or the Fillmore. San Francisco became the city of the moment, like *fin de siècle* Paris, Berlin in the 1920s or New York in the 1950s. It's often said that, in America, if you don't fit in, you move west. San Francisco is as far west as you can go, and if you don't fit in there, your next stop is a jump from the Golden Gate Bridge.

Folk singer Scott MacKenzie's cash-in hit 'San Francisco' – still tiresomely trotted out over footage of hippies dancing at the 'love-ins' in Golden Gate Park whenever the 1960s are discussed by the mainstream media – was like a clarion call to a nation full of discontented kids, urging them to head on out west. A century earlier it had been gold that drew the pioneers; in the 1960s it was the promise of a new way of life. The propagandists for the Summer of Love – ranging from poet Allen Ginsberg to the Haight Street merchants who were actually doing rather well financially from the anti-materialistic hippies – painted a picture of a city that was Utopia on the Pacific. But while man cannot live by bread alone, he does need the occasional sandwich to get by.

The Diggers, a radical group that combined Dadaist street theatre with political agitation, set up a free food programme in Panhandle Park, serving hot meals to the hippies whenever it could, begging and sometimes using moral blackmail to get donations from local markets and businesses. It wasn't so much a hip Salvation Army as a group trying to put into practice the principles of its namesakes, the millenarian puritan sect of 17th-century England that squatted and farmed the common land, giving away the surplus to the poor. Both groups of Diggers wanted to create a better world here and now, not after the revolution or the second coming of Christ.

In his brilliant and neglected 'fictionalised' autobiography *Ringolevio*, Emmett Grogan describes a rather different San Francisco to the rose-tinted psychedelic paradise. Grogan and the Diggers claimed that the hippy merchants were hyping up the Summer of Love in order to make a profit and it was attracting too many would-be hippies to the Haight-Ashbury who were simply unable to look after themselves. Kids arrived with nothing and were going hungry because they couldn't make a living, having bought the hype that San Francisco was a free-for-all where everything was provided by a community of like-minded 'love children'. The Diggers thought that keeping the neighbourhood out of the limelight was important because they foresaw that any publicity would bring trouble, such as the cops. They also objected to the merchants calling their burgers 'love burgers' and selling 'love beads' because they didn't think that love should be associated with materialism.

Manson, 32 years old, arrived in San Francisco with his guitar, a vague notion of becoming some sort of wandering minstrel and very little else. He was not unlike the thousands of other dippy kids who arrived hoping to make their living as poets or musicians, or with some similar notion but no real idea of how to go about it. But, thanks to the efforts of groups like the Diggers (despite their objection to the hippy hype) and the San Francisco Free Clinic, it *was* possible for the runaways, vagrants and penniless hippies to get free food and medical care.

Abigail Folger, heiress to the Folger Coffee Company millions and one of the victims killed at 10050 Cielo Drive in 1969, was one of the many rich liberal San Franciscans who worked closely with the Free Clinic, helping to raise funds (she was involved in a 1967 benefit concert at the Carousel Ballroom in 1967, which featured Big Brother And The Holding Company and The Quicksilver Messenger Service). Her mother, Inez Folger, helped the clinic to obtain grants and corporate donations, as well as working as a volunteer drug counsellor.

It was also possible in the balmy Mediterranean climate of San Francisco to sleep outdoors in the park, which is what Manson did in the first few months of 1967.

Manson had his first experience of LSD at this time courtesy of a would-be folk singer called Nancy Hart, who had access to 'Owsley acid' (literally LSD manufactured by legendary underground chemist Owsley Stanley III, who made the acid for Ken Kesey's acid tests and was also a close associate of The Grateful Dead), which she gave to him, saying, 'You're already there. You don't need it.' Manson then went to a Grateful Dead concert, joining in the communal ecstatic dancing and wondering if he had died and gone to heaven.

The importance of LSD and, in later decades, MDMA/MDA, or ecstasy, in creating a communal experience, almost a 'group mind', has never really been properly researched. There are numerous anthropological works detailing the peyote rituals of the Yaqui Indians, the Kava cult of the South Seas Islands and other assorted psychedelic group experiences of South American tribes. Yet the almost religious character of the mass dance experience, where many of the participants are using mind-altering substances has only been noted by a few non-professional observers and participants. But all of these emphasise the feeling of belonging, the feeling that you are in tune with the literally thousands of people in the same hall. This feeling may in fact be a hallucination, a delusion of security and happiness, but it is important, nonetheless; it is what drives the global rave scene, a phenomenon that shows no sign of abating.

The early Grateful Dead shows at the Avalon, the Fillmore, the Longshoreman's Hall and in Panhandle Park were notable for the fact that most of the crowd participated in frenzied dancing (hard to imagine when one thinks of lethargic stoners lying in big piles barely able to move at Dead concerts over the past two decades). They were the community band and their music was the glue that held all the Haight hippies together.

Manson, a perennial outsider, never able to become a part of the straight world outside of prison, found for the first time that he belonged. He was homeless, but everyone was homeless; it was, in fact, hip to be homeless. You slept where you could – in crash pads, the park, the street. For many of the runaways who ended up in San Francisco, the hippy experience was just a brief adventure in poverty. For Manson and many others, though, it was not a choice.

Whatever the effect of LSD on Manson's own internal world, it was of less importance than his discovery that it could be used to manipulate others. While conspiracy theorists have linked Manson and MK-ULTRA because both tried to use psychedelics as a mind-control drug, there need actually be no direct causal link. Timothy Leary was already talking about LSD as a means of 'reprogramming' the human mind and editing out 'bad patterns', something that conventional psychoanalysists and Scientologists also sought to do.

Manson was older than the other kids around him and they saw him as being wiser, hipper; he tailored his jailhouse rants into an anti-parent anti-establishment rap that the runaways were eager to hear. He had status with them – not, at first, as a leader, but certainly as a sort of tribal elder.

Mary Brunner, a 23-year-old librarian at the University of California, Berkeley, became Charles Manson's first disciple, the first of his harem and the mother of his third child. The son was named Valentine Michael Manson, after Valentine Michael Smith, the messianic hero of Robert A Heinlein's *Stranger In A Strange Land*. She also fed into his evolving mythology through her interest in environmental issues. Manson's raps now included tirades against the pollution of consumer society and the need to save animals, trees, water and air from pollution. He also threw in rants about 'racial pollution', how the black man was growing in strength and 'polluting' the races.

Then Manson brought home Lynette 'Squeaky' Fromme, another discontented, emaciated escapee from middle America, whom he allegedly seduced by announcing, 'I am the God of Fuck!'

In an excerpt from her (unpublished) book, posted on her website, Fromme recalls her first meeting with Manson: 'My father had kicked me out of his house at the height of an argument over an opinion difference. He had become so enraged. He told me never to come back, and that was all the severance it took. I had noplace to go. I stuck out my thumb on a freeway entrance, going through all my tears to Venice, where I remembered beatniks lived. Afraid, with all my books, my dictionary, my eye make-up clutched to me, I sat on a bench staring at the ocean.

'Suddenly, an elfish, dirty little creature in a little cap hopped over the low wall, grinning, saying, "What's the problem?" He was either old or very young – I couldn't tell. He had a two-day beard and reminded me of a fancy hobo, rather elegant, but my fear was up. "How did you know?" I started to say, and he smiled really bright and I had the strangest feeling that he knew my thoughts.

'"Up in the Haight I'm called the gardener," he said. "I tend to all the flower children." My mind was struck with the thought…that a gardener plants seeds, and I became more afraid and clenched my legs together. "It's alright," he told me, and I could feel in his voice that it was. He had the most delicate, quick motion, like magic, as if he glided along by air, and a smile that went from warm daddy to twinkly devil. I couldn't tell what he was.

'I was enchanted and afraid all at once, and I put my head down and wished he would go away, and when I looked up, really he was gone! And I turned my head, wanting to talk to him now with urgency. And as soon as I turned back around, there he was again, sitting on the wall, grinning at me. I had only conceived of such things in fairy tales.

'"So your father kicked you out," he said with certainty, and once again my mind went with the wind and I laughed and relaxed... We talked and I felt very good with him and freer, much freer. "The way out of a room is not through the door," he said, laughing. "Just don't want out and you're free." Then he unfolded a tale of the 20 years he's spent behind bars, of the struggle and the giving up and the loving of himself.'

Mary Brunner was reluctant to allow another woman to move in, with Manson rapping at her that 'nobody belongs to anybody else', but she accepted the situation. This informal polygamy was not unusual at the time and Manson was not exactly breaking new ground; people were experimenting with new ways to live and in the pre-women's liberation hippy milieu, a *ménage à trois* was just another lifestyle choice.

In David Crosby's 'Triad', a song that he wrote in 1967 and that ultimately resulted in his departure from The Byrds over their refusal to include it on their album *The Notorious Byrd Brothers*, he sings, 'You want to know how it will be/Me and her, or you and me/You both stand there, your long hair flowing/Eyes alive, your minds still growing/Saying to me, "What can we do now that we both love you?"/I love you too/I don't really see/Why can't we go on as three?' (When the song was covered by Jefferson Airplane on *Crown Of Creation*, sung by Grace Slick, it took on a whole new and much more subversive slant.)

The hippies are often confused with the anti-war protesters – groups such as the Free Speech Movement at Berkeley, the Students for a Democratic Society (SDS) – and other radical groups such as the Black Panther Party. In fact, while there were some crossovers between Haight-Ashbury and Berkeley, and while the war in Vietnam was unpopular, the hippies around Haight-Ashbury were largely apolitical. Their dissatisfactions, like the raps Manson delivered, were vague: 'the system', 'the man' and 'the establishment'. While the politically motivated students were, on the whole, on the left – and would move further to the left in 1968 and 1969, giving birth on the one hand to terrorist factions such as the Weathermen and rigid, almost Stalinist socialist parties like the Progressive Labour Party on the other – the hippies were also the germ of a libertarian right-wing movement. They were about individualism, self, the personal; despite being painted as 'pinkos' and 'comsymps' (communist sympathisers) by the hard-hat

Republican Party types, the hippies were less likely to be reading Karl Marx than 'free enterprise philosopher' Ayn Rand. Their interests were more likely to be spiritual than political – they felt themselves to be an elite, superior to the deluded masses who worked for a living at jobs they hated to buy consumer goods they did not need.

As we have already seen, Manson was a fan of Robert A Heinlein's *Stranger In A Strange Land* and told people he met that they should read it (although he claimed never to have read it himself). In many ways, Heinlein, with his hatred of centralised authority, along with his bloodthirsty militarism, as epitomised by novels like *Starship Troopers*, was an unlikely hippy hero. Although a socialist in his youth – he supported Upton Sinclair's 1934 EPIC (End Poverty In California) campaign for governor and unsuccessfully ran as a Democratic candidate for the state legislature – Heinlein became a committed anticommunist in his later years. Published in 1961, *Stranger In A Strange Land* was originally conceived as a parody or updating of Kipling's *The Jungle Book* with Valentine Michael Smith as a sort of descendant of Mowgli. The premise is that, in the future, the only survivor of an unsuccessful attempt to colonise Mars is a boy, Valentine Michael Smith, who is raised by the mysterious Martian natives when his own parents mysteriously die. Brought back to an oppressive bureaucratic Earth, it is discovered that the boy has strange powers and beliefs, having been raised by the incomprehensible aliens. He escapes the clutches of the State and forms a 'cult' of (mostly female) devotees, living communally, engaging in the ritual of 'water sharing' and engaging in 'free love' and group sex.

The Manson Family adopted the water rituals described in the book, passing water in a glass from person to person, using language from the book like *grok* (which means to intuitively understand something), and Manson even nicknamed his parole officer Jubal after a character in the book, a libertarian writer who acts as the Martian boy's protector on Earth. Michael is eventually killed by a mob, but his disciples, called *water brothers*, continue his work.

In fairness to Heinlein, it was not just Manson who picked up on the book; along with *The Lord Of The Rings*, *Stranger In A Strange*

Land was the counter-cultural Bible and words like *grok* passed into the day-to-day argot of the hippies.

The theme of a small elite acting against the prevailing, seemingly all-powerful mass society and triumphing is a theme common to much of Heinlein's work, which was bound to have some resonance with the hippies. In *Revolt In 2100*, America is ruled by a religious theocracy and the hero joins a shadowy cabal of free thinkers to overthrow the established order. *Starship Troopers*, for all its militarism and glorification of weaponry, was really about rugged individualism pitted against the inhuman collectivism of the intelligent insect enemy in the novel, clearly and crudely standing as a metaphor for the Soviet Union and Red China. His 1966 book *The Moon Is A Harsh Mistress*, about a war of independence fought by a lunar penal colony against the oppressive government of Earth, is one of the key works of modern libertarianism with the revolutionaries' motto 'TANSTAAFL' ('There Ain't No Such Thing As A Free Lunch') being adopted by right-wing anarchists today. His most disturbing work, however, is *Farnham's Freehold*, which has a white family propelled into a post-nuclear future ruled by blacks and where white people are kept as slaves. Depending on who you ask, this book is either a racist tract, a reaction to the ongoing civil-rights movement or a satire on racism, showing slavery with the boot on the other foot.

Heinlein, after learning about the connection to the Manson Family, was indignant and decided not to speak out about the subject. No statement was ever issued. In fairness again to Heinlein, he had always been a committed anti-authoritarian, as vigilant against the forces of fascism as he was against the 'anthill' levelling of communism. Heinlein had written prophetic stories warning of a clash between the Axis powers and the democracies before Pearl Harbor. Manson, on the other hand, regarded Hitler as a 'tuned-in guy who wanted to level the karma of the Jews', and for all his raps about freedom and being free, he became a little fascist at the centre of his own little crowd of acolytes.

At the height of the summer of 1967, Manson, Fromme and Brunner moved into a communal house in the centre of Haight-Ashbury at 636 Cole Street. Manson had begun to attract other followers as he wandered around the dazed hippies on the streets, talking to them and listening to what they had to say. He had started to acquire what he had always lacked: a family. He became a well-known figure on the streets of Haight-Ashbury. A few blocks away from the Manson base, on Cole Street, a man called Brother Ely, aka Victor Wild, sold leather goods and ran the San Francisco chapter of the Process Church of the Final Judgement (or the Process for short).

Wrongly seen as a black-magic cult or a Satanist group, the Process theology had four deities: Jehovah, Jesus, Lucifer and Satan. Members were urged to pick one that they could identify with and devote themselves to that deity. Satan was not seen as the opposite or enemy of God, as in traditional Christian theology. Sporting long hair and beards, black clothes and purple capes with the Goat of Mendes embroidered on the back, often accompanied by savage-looking German Shepherd dogs on leashes, the Processeans became familiar figures on the streets of many European and American cities in the 1960s. Like the Diggers, they ran free-food programmes as well as meditation classes and telepathy-developing circles in coffee houses.

LA was home to real Satanist groups like the Church of Satan. Anton LaVey, who founded the California-based Church of Satan in the 1960s, did not actually believe in the personal existence of the Devil. Satanism was not Devil worship but 'the worship of life' and, as such, 'concerned with the fullest gratification of the ego on this plane of existence'. With his shaved head and forked beard, LaVey resembled Ming the Merciless from the old *Flash Gordon* series. A former carnival hand, LaVey was at heart a showman: he claimed up to 25,000 adherents to the Church of Satan, including Sammy Davis Junior and Jayne Mansfield. There were other groups like the Temple of Set – a breakaway sect formed by a former associate of LaVey – who actually did believe in and worship the 'evil' entity, Lucifer, Loki, Satan or whatever name he/it goes by. The Process tried to form an alliance with the Church of Satan, but LaVey dismissed them as 'kooks'. Manson Family members were also described as 'kooks and creeps out of their minds on drugs' by LaVey, who had little time for hippies, be they knife-wielding or otherwise.

On his website, Robert Nicholas Taylor of the 'apocalyptic folk' band Changes, who made their live debut at a Process meeting house in Chicago and whose album *Fire Of Life* was finally released only in 1999, describes his attraction to the Process thus: 'Certainly, much of my attraction to the Process lay in my Grail Quest out of the morose atmosphere that soulless technology and bureaucracy had imposed on our lives. Ecology had not yet become the catch slogan of yuppie materialists, yahoo politicians and quarterly stockholder reports. We felt constricted under the thumb of a debased age in which advertised slogans supplanted poetry, contractual agreements replaced love and televangelism masqueraded as spirituality. Unlike that alien and decadent garb of the Guru cults from the East, the Process had a distinctly western, neo-Gothic exterior: neatly trimmed, shoulder-length hair and equally neat beards, all set-off by tailored magician's capes with matching black uniforms. Apocalypse was in the air, an impending feeling of doom. The multi-coloured dreams of psychedelia had begun to fade and for those of us who had crossed its rainbow bridge there would be no turning back. The world as we had known it would never quite seem the same again. The prevailing order of things – these and a panoply of similar assumptions formerly taken for granted with simple minded acceptance – now came into question, were scrutinised, dissected and exposed for the frauds we felt them to be. But what were these mainstays of our civilisation to be replaced with?'

Manson was certainly aware of the Process and apparently bought clothes from Victor Wild. He also wrote an article that appeared in the 1971 'Death' issue of *The Process* magazine called 'Pseudo-Profundity In Death', a stream-of-consciousness rant that reads, 'Death goes to where life comes from. Total awareness, closing the circle, bring the soul to now. Ceasing to be, to become a world within yourself... Death is peace from this world's madness and paradise in my own self. Death as I lay in my grave of constant vibrations, endless now.' It should be noted that other contributors to the magazine included Marianne Faithfull and Salvador Dalí.

The Process Church was formed in 1962 in Mayfair, London, by Robert Moore (who later assumed the name Robert DeGrimston) and

Mary Anne MacLean, both mid-level members in the London Scientology movement, which at that time was still a fledgling pseudo-psychoanalytical group and not a church. They called their group Compulsions Analysis, using a technique or 'process' similar to that of Scientology. They felt, however, that Hubbard had based his system on unproven, speculative and pseudo-scientific theories and wanted to bring a more objective approach to their techniques.

DeGrimston's interests widened, bringing in Jungian ideas about archetypes and higher powers, delving into a fusion of religion and analysis. The group moved to Xtul, in the Yucatan Peninsula of Mexico, where the idea of the Process as a sort of neo-gnostic religion gelled. Various offshoots of the church sprang up in Europe and America, and in 1967 the church launched its mission in the Haight-Ashbury district.

There are many parallels between the beliefs and activities of Manson and the Process – they believed in imminent Apocalypse as described in the Book of Revelation, which forecast that only 144,000 people would survive; both referred to their groups as 'the Family'; both tried to recruit members of outlaw motorcycle gangs such as the Hell's Angels, the Outlaws and the Bandidos as their troops; both borrowed heavily from Scientology; both held animals and nature in high regard; leaders of both sects believed themselves to be the reincarnation of Jesus Christ – but there is no evidence that Manson was ever a member as suggested by both Ed Sanders in *The Family* and Maury Terry in his book *The Ultimate Evil.*

The Family was written by beat poet, counter-culture spokesman and one-time member of The Fugs Ed Sanders, who set out to write a book whose premise was that Manson was innocent. Sanders wanted to exonerate the hippies from blame in the murders and spent months trawling around California interviewing Manson associates, members of the occult underground, police and prosecutors. He patently hates LA and describes it as wading through sleaze. He sticks close to the Bugliosi line, though the first editions of the book included the allegations that Manson was actually a member of the Process. The Process successfully sued and subsequent editions of the book have been edited to omit references to this. It's a better read than Bugliosi's denser work, although it occasionally lapses into annoying early 1970s hippyspeak and 'freak' jargon.

The Ultimate Evil is a bizarre and barely believable slab of pulp that links the Process, Manson, Son of Sam and the wave of alleged Satanic abuse that swept America in the 1980s. It is worth reading as an insight into the paranoid fringe but should be filed alongside tomes on alien abduction, the descendants of Christ being the French royal family and the thoughts of David Icke. The book, nevertheless, still has its adherents; people often propound Maury's 'theory' without being aware of its source.

During his arrest and trial, two members of the Process visited Manson in jail. The church was concerned that a link could be established between them and Manson, and some early reports did in fact claim that Manson was part of the Process. It is possible (although there is no evidence) that Manson had met DeGrimston during a visit that Moore/DeGrimston made to a house that was an occasional Manson Family hangout, known as the Spiral Staircase, in Topanga Canyon in 1967. Prosecutor Assistant DA Bugliosi asked Manson if he knew DeGrimston. He said that he did not, but that he did know Robert Moore. When asked where they had met, Manson replied, 'You're looking at him. Moore and I are one and the same.'

For all of the parallels, the Process was just another of the myriad occult 'kooks' that flourished briefly in the 1960s, although, as shall be discussed later, despite fizzling out in the 1970s, its influence lingers on in rock's fringes. It was an elitist group, though despite the quasi-swastika symbol it adopted (four Ps arranged in a cross, forming a swastika/Iron Cross design) not an overtly racist one. And, compared with Manson, the Process was comparatively benign.

There has been some suggestion (although no hard evidence) that Manson also came into contact with the Solar Lodge of the Ordo Templi Orientis (Order of the Temple of the Orient or Oriental Templars, or OTO), a group active in California that claimed descent from the OTO founded by German occultists and associated with the great English occultist Aleister Crowley. Often erroneously called a Satanist, Crowley, who styled himself the 'Great Beast', was the most public figure in the occult revival in the early years of the 20th century. A gifted poet and author and a very talented self-publicist, Crowley's maxim 'Do what thou wilt shall be the whole of the law' has been one of the most influential, and misunderstood, to subsequent counter-cultural rebels. With his heroic capacity for drugs, a flamboyant bisexuality and a theatrical flair for inventing rituals, Crowley was like a rock 'n' roll star born half a century too soon.

The OTO founded in California in 1966 or 1967 actually had no direct link to the original lodge, but it practised the same rituals and attracted a growing following. In Alex Constantine's *Ordis Templis Intelligentis*, the author writes, 'The OTO's Solar Lodge in San Bernardino was founded by Maury McCauley, a mortician, on his own property. The group subscribed to a grim, apocalyptic view of the world precipitated by race wars, and the prophecy made a lasting impression on Charles Manson, who passed through the lodge. In the LA underworld, the OTO spin-off was known for indulgence in sado-masochism, drug dealing, blood drinking, child molestation and murder. The Riverside OTO, like the Manson Family, used drugs, sex, psycho-drama and fear to tear down the mind of the initiate and rebuild it according to the desires of the cult's inner circle.'

The OTO also lived in a commune in the desert and, in August 1969, while the Manson Family was in the midst of its killing spree, the Solar Lodge was at the centre of a scandal when a six-year-old boy was discovered chained up in a packing crate. He had apparently been kept there for 56 days. Candace Reos, a former member of the Solar Lodge, told police that, when she became pregnant, the cult's leader, Jean Brayton, was outraged and ordered her to concentrate on hating the unborn child.

As well as occult/Satanic groups, there were other so-called 'Jesus cults' active in California. The Children of God organisation, which was at the centre of an alleged child-abuse scandal in the 1970s, was founded around the Huntingdon Beach area by a charismatic preacher called David Berg, who later adopted the name Moses or Moses David. Originally known as the Light Club, the Ontario Consultants on Religious Tolerance website reported, 'Many flower children were encouraged by rock music and free peanut-butter sandwiches to spend some time in the coffee house. Some were "saved" and abandoned their hippy life of alcohol, other drugs and free love. Some evangelised other hippies, a few on a full time basis. Berg received a revelation from God in 1969 that a disastrous earthquake was about to hit California and cause part of the state to slide into the ocean. He led the group out of Huntington Beach to wander throughout the American Southwest for eight months. During that time, they changed their name to the Children of God.'

As well as the obvious parallels with Manson − recruiting waifs and strays, the prophecy of impending disaster, a period of wandering − the Children of God now go by the name the Family (aka the Family of Love).

7 Good Lovin' Gone Bad

'Think I'll pack it in and buy a pick-up,
Drive it down to LA'
       – *Neil Young, 'Out On The Weekend'*

As the Summer of Love peaked, life in Haight-Ashbury began to sour. Tourists arrived in buses to gawp and take snapshots of the freaks. As stocks of relatively pure LSD were exhausted, underground chemists flooded the streets with all manner of chemicals masquerading as acid. Strychnine, amphetamine and atropine in various combinations, sometimes with and sometimes without actual LSD, began to cause terrifying bad trips that often left profound psychological scars. Other substances, like STP – a synthetic variant of mescaline whose initials stood for 'serenity, tranquillity and peace', though its effects were anything but – caused some legendary 'three-day freakouts' and in some cases resulted in hospitalisation and suicide. Phencyclidine, commonly referred to as PCP or angel dust, also started to appear on the streets; this is a substance that induces intense paranoia, psychosis and extreme violence and which was to become one of the inner-city substances of choice in the late 1970s. Biker gangs moved in on the drug trade, meting out violence to the hippies. Rapes and rip-offs started to occur. The police began to crack down on the longhairs, harassing them often for little or no reason. The Diggers staged a 'Funeral of Hippie (Beloved Son of Mass Media)' involving a coffin procession through Haight-Ashbury, where people were encouraged to throw in their love beads, granny glasses, headbands and other symbols of the commercialised Summer of Love. As more and more runaways poured in, pimps, hustlers and drug dealers moved in to exploit them. The Grateful Dead, community band and symbols of the San Francisco scene, removed themselves to a house north of the city. Other original hippies began to leave, forming communes, going to the countryside or, in some cases, dropping back in after they had tuned in, turned on and dropped out. They called themselves free men and freaks rather than hippies.

Ironically, worried by all the petty crime and the rip-off climate around him, Manson moved his Family out of Haight-Ashbury to Santa Barbara in southern California. There was also far too much competition from the plethora of holy hucksters, Jesus freaks, divine lighters and spiritual shamen who crowded the sidewalks and coffee shops. Manson wasn't the only reincarnation of Jesus on the block.

The Family grew, taking in Patricia Krenwinkel, an 18-year-old middle-class insurance clerk from Inglewood; Bruce Davis, one of Manson's few male disciples; Susan Atkins, a pivotal figure; and Ruth Ann Morehouse. Also at around this time, Manson discovered a school bus for sale. He bought it and he and his followers ripped out the seats at the back and installed a refrigerator, cooker, beds and living quarters. Then they hit the road with Manson at the wheel, consciously or not imitating the original psychedelic family, Ken Kesey's Merry Pranksters, who criss-crossed America in their school bus, painted in daubs of Day-Glo and rainbow colours, making films and dropping acid, with Neal Cassady – the actual hero of Jack Kerouac's *On The Road* – at the wheel giving a stream-of-consciousness rap regardless of whether or not anyone was actually listening. But Manson's bus was painted black, windows and all.

Patricia Krenwinkel had once considered becoming a nun. She suffered from low self-esteem because she was unusually hairy, so when Manson made love to her, telling her how beautiful she was, she rapidly fell in love with him. She quit her job and moved into the house, sharing a bed with Charlie, Lynette and Mary.

Bruce Davis had come west from Tennessee and had met Manson in Seattle. Manson had gone up to visit some old prison associate and to look up his mother who had settled there. Davis had been heavily involved in drugs and had also been involved in Scientology. He and

Manson made a connection and he then moved into the house, adding another component to the Family.

Ruth Ann Morehouse was the daughter of Methodist preacher Dean Morehouse. A liberal cleric, Morehouse was upset that his 16-year-old daughter had run off to join Manson and swore out a complaint with the local police to have him arrested. Manson turned up at Morehouse's front door and not only managed to convince him to call off the police but also took acid with him, actually winning him over as a convert.

Susan Atkins had already spent time in jail and was on probation, working as a topless dancer, when she met Charles Manson. Atkins, then 19, was also an occasional topless dancer at Anton LaVey's Church of Satan black masses, her act involving her emerging naked from a coffin.

In her 1978 book *Child Of Satan, Child Of God*, about her involvement in the murders and eventual conversion to Christianity, she remembers, 'I looked at my two-inch-long false fingernails, painted brilliant red. And my face was something special, as I looked up into the mirror. It was eerie – milky white, broken by bright red lips that matched the colour of the fingernails and by seemingly sunken blue-black eyes expertly twisted upward at the outside corners... Jet-black hair framed it all. I was the perfect, sexy vampire, ready for my casket lying at the center of the stage.

'Using care because of my fingernails, I reached into my big, black handbag and fished out a pill. Rehearsals had gone well – we were ready for the weirdest show on the strip, but I knew I'd never be able to get into that casket for real without being stoned. I popped the acid tab into my mouth, carefully avoiding any lipstick stains...

'The show was a smash hit along the strip. [The owner of the North Beach topless club] had scored big. But the witches' sabbath, and my total sell-out to LSD, marijuana and hashish, and to sex with virtually any attractive man, landed me in the hospital in four months. I was half-dead from gonorrhoea and had a complete physical breakdown.'

Atkins was a runaway with a history of family problems. On the night that she met Manson, he sang to her and took her to bed. He gave her acid and told her to imagine that he was her father when he fucked her, something that, according to Atkins, produced the most intense experience she had ever known. In her book, she recalls meeting Manson for the first time: 'Standing for a moment inside the door of the big brown house, I heard the pounding of my heart. I was stoned.

'Faintly I heard music. "Someone's singing," I thought… Somebody was singing upstairs. I climbed the stairs slowly, my bare feet silent on the carpeting… Passing through the massive, oak double doors, I was startled. My eyes landed instantly on a little man sitting on the wide couch… I could see he was singing, his eyes seemingly closed. Without moving his head, he opened his eyes and stared directly into my face.

'A slight smile flickered on and off the skinny little man's clean-shaven face. His voice was middle range and expressive. He played guitar magnificently.

'There was a space on the floor to the man's right. I tip-toed to it and eased myself cross-legged to the floor… He looked at me and smiled. I studied him unsmiling… "He's like an angel." I don't think I spoke the thought aloud, but I was so loaded I couldn't be sure.

'I was aware that the man with the guitar had stopped singing. Voices and low laughter rose up and down almost lyrically. The little man's spell still prevailed.

'He was talking quietly and smiling. But he never looked at me… I stared at the man's guitar. It seemed a thing of magic and wonder. "I'd like to play it," I thought. "I bet I can play it."

'In a split second he turned his head slowly to look into my eyes. "Why don't you play it?" He started to move the instrument toward me. My mind swirled. Had I said that aloud? No. I had only thought it. How did he know it? "No, thanks," I said softly. "I can't play."

'He smiled and looked, unblinking, into my eyes… It was as though our minds were speaking.

'In a second or two, he looked away and joined in conversation in the middle of the room.

'"Who is this man?" I was shaken. "He's really strange."

'I got up and walked to the record player, flipping through the pile of records on the floor... I danced formlessly around the player as the record concluded. I stopped and dropped on another Doors record. It was alive and furious.

'I threw myself into the music and danced, lost within. "I'll dance for him." He began to dance behind me... I felt his hands on my hips, and he began to move my body. "What's he doing?" He was leading my body in movements I had never tried... He whispered into my left ear, "That's right. That's good. Yes. In reality – in your God-self – there's no repetition. No two moves, no two actions, are the same. Everything is new. Let it be new."

'We swung to face one another... Suddenly, something happened that has no explanation. I experienced a moment unlike any other. This stranger and I, dancing, passed through one another. It was as though my body moved closer and closer to him and actually passed through him... We danced savagely.

'He smiled. "You are beautiful," he said. "You are perfect. I've never seen anyone dance like you. It's wonderful. You must always be free."

'For a few moments, I could only smile. I watched his face. "Thank you," I finally said. I paused. "My name is Susan Atkins," I said. "Who are you?"

'The eye contact was broken and he lowered his head, brushing his hair with one hand. "Who? Me? Oh, I'm Charlie. Charlie Manson."'

Atkins became the most evangelical of Manson's followers and was renamed Sadie Mae Glutz, something that would have added resonance when The Beatles released their classic eponymous double album the following year. The Beatles song 'Sexy Sadie' on the 'White Album' was actually written about the Maharishi and their disappointment with him (he allegedly tried to get Mia Farrow to have sex with him), although Paul McCartney has also suggested that they were turned away from the elderly Indian guru by the machinations of jealous former associate Alex Mardis, aka Magic Alex.

People around the nascent Family describe Charlie's control over everything. When they tripped or when they had group sex, Manson was always directing everyone and telling them exactly what to do. At this point, his control over them was 'fatherly and benign'; he made them feel good about themselves, made them feel loved and wanted.

Atkins, who was a troubled soul, felt that there was more of Jesus than Satan in Manson at this time: 'He personally never called himself Jesus, but he represented a Jesus Christ-like person to me. He said Jesus Christ was but a man like any other man and with awareness of the world and the universe, and he gave up his life willingly so that we could live in order to become the same. Not Jesus Christ, but the same consciousness that Christ endowed us with.'

Perhaps the other most significant meeting at this time was that between Manson and a young musician called Bobby Beausoleil. The story of Manson is inextricably bound up with that of Bobby Beausoleil. Although Beausoleil was never a 'member' of the Family, the fact that he was a friend and associate of Manson, Susan Atkins and others at the Spahn ranch and was actually living there when the Tate/LaBianca murders took place was enough to damn him in the eyes of the media and the law. Beausoleil had to undergo a retrial after the Manson murders and, like Manson and his associates, he spent two years on death row before California abolished the death penalty. Beausoleil is still in prison for killing Gary Hinman – a murder that he does not deny he committed and that he has expressed regret for – but could not have had any part in the other slayings because he was incarcerated at the time.

Beausoleil was Manson's biggest conduit to the music scene before Dennis Wilson and Beausoleil was also friendly with The Beach Boys' drummer independently of Manson. Beausoleil continues to make music from his prison cell in the Oregon State Penitentiary in the Pacific Northwest, releasing albums of complex instrumental jazz rock fusion through his own White Dog label as well as working as an audio-visual technician in the prison and being involved in a music-therapy outreach programme aimed at young offenders.

Beausoleil was born and grew up in Santa Barbara. As a child, he was surrounded by music and fell in love with early rock 'n' roll and rockabilly. He taught himself to play guitar on an instrument that was actually set up as a Hawaiian guitar, and it was this spirit of improvisation that was to infuse the music he would later play. His childhood and adolescence was troubled and he spent time in a reform school after being made a ward of the court when he ran away.

The first book to be published in the wake of the arrest and trial was *The Garbage People* by John Gilmore, a young crime writer who had written about the so-called Pied Piper of Tucson killer Charles 'Smitty' Schmid. Manson was aware of Schmid and Gilmore's book and granted him access while he was still held in Independence on property damage charges. Ron Kenner, an *LA Times* reporter, saw Manson as a symptom of American society, not as some demon outsider. *The Garbage People*, published in 1971, was actually unavailable until the mid-1990s, when it was republished. A recent Amok edition, retitled *Manson: The Unholy Trail Of Charlie And The Family*, corrects some inaccuracies from the original text and adds an extensive section on Bobby Beausoleil and his relationship with Kenneth Anger. Again, it is a better read than Bugliosi's *Helter Skelter*, though the section that includes crime scene and coroners' photos of the victims is strictly for sick puppies.

In the updated edition of *The Garbage People*, Beausoleil is quoted as saying that he left home and hit the road when he was 12. Vicky Devin, a Hollywood girlfriend, recalls that he was abused as a small child by an aunt and uncle: 'Bobby went through that mill. It was bad, typical of the worst sexual and other abuse brought down on a little kid. But he couldn't tell anyone – he didn't tell anyone and it went on and he kept trying to get away from it. He wanted to run… Underneath the cool attitude, he was filled with some kind of ugliness. The abuse had twisted him something awful.'

He was released into the custody of his grandmother, who lived in El Monte, 'just east of LA, where the new Nazis were hanging out'. In the mid-1960s, he drifted to Hollywood, where he met a woman who made clothes for Sonny and Cher (including the huge furry vests that they wear in that hoary old TV footage of them singing 'I Got You Babe') and started to experiment with marijuana and the pharmaceutical LSD. He also came into contact with the emerging LA music scene. He had friends who knew Dino Valenti and The Quicksilver Messenger Service, a band less celebrated than the better-known Grateful Dead and Jefferson Airplane, though one whose influence still permeates music today.

Beausoleil went to see The Byrds playing in LA but was more taken by the support group, known as The Grass Roots. The Grass Roots featured a young black musician called Arthur Lee, a charismatic frontman at that time heavily influenced by Mick Jagger. He was the first musician to sport the LA style – fringed buckskin jacket, beads, cheesecloth, long hair – and was unique in that he was a black man fronting a white rock band. Beausoleil describes himself as their number-one fan at that time and sat in at a few gigs playing guitar, improvising, becoming friends with Lee. When the band got a gig playing a Santa Barbara gay bar called the Brave New World, Beausoleil travelled down with them and played with them. The crowd – all male, dancing with each other – loved Beausoleil, who was a pretty boy known by the nickname Cupid at this time. Lee saw the potential of having Beausoleil in the band full time, but he never joined because another contender, the late Bryan MacLean, auditioned for the group and became Lee's writing partner.

Beausoleil remained friends with Lee but resented MacLean, partly because he had taken his place in the group but also because he damaged a guitar that Beausoleil had lent him. At this time, a manufactured pop group called The Grass Roots had just enjoyed a hit single with a cover of Bob Dylan's 'Ballad Of A Thin Man' and Arthur Lee's Grass Roots were forced to change their name.

There are a number of stories about how the name Love was adopted, but according to Beausoleil, Arthur Lee told him that it was in honour of him, Cupid, that they chose it.

Love signed to Elektra and recorded two albums of sub-Byrds LA rock before releasing their timeless masterpiece *Forever Changes* in 1967. Interestingly, another artist that Elektra was interested in at this time was also a fan of Love. 'People told me Manson used to come to my shows,' Arthur said in a 1993 interview, 'but I never knew that.'

Beausoleil had made other connections, most notably with Frank

Zappa, who knew the 17-year-old from the street scene in LA and actually recorded him. If you listen to Frank Zappa And The Mothers Of Invention's debut album, *Freak Out*, recorded in LA in late 1965, Beausoleil's is one of the voices you can hear on the disturbing 'Who Are The Brain Police?' and 'Help, I'm A Rock'. *Freak Out* is one of the most adventurous releases ever, bringing together improvised music, 'free jazz', unusual instrumentation, a neo-Dadaist aesthetic – Zappa once performed on the Steve Allen TV show 'playing' a bicycle as both a wind and percussion instrument – with the disreputable 'low culture' of rock 'n' roll. Although Zappa was militantly anti-drug, 'Help, I'm A Rock' sounds like the work of somebody undergoing a bad acid trip, built around a shout of 'Help, I'm A Rock', a rambling monologue from Zappa and a studio full of percussion instruments played by a bunch of self-styled freaks. Zappa's sprawling experimental collective (people drifted in and out of the Mothers Of Invention line-up almost on a whim) was to prove influential on Beausoleil's future musical direction.

He was listening to the modal jazz of John Coltrane, who was making his most ground-breaking work at this time, most notably 'A Love Supreme' and 'Ascension' as well as eastern music, particularly Indian classical (or raga) musician Ravi Shankar, whose influence on everyone from Coltrane to The Beatles and The Byrds (Roger McGuinn's guitar style, particularly on 'Eight Miles High', was dubbed 'raga-rock'), was starting to be felt.

Beausoleil then moved to San Francisco, where he joined a comparatively ordinary working rock 'n' roll band called The Outfit, who rehearsed in a space that would later become the Straight Theater.

'I brought as much innovation to it as I could. It was good for me as I got an opportunity for more performing experience. I took to the stage like a fish to water, naturally. I loved performing for people; I was comfortable and it wasn't anything I had to force at all. I became a lead-guitar player, more melodically oriented as opposed to just strumming chords, during the period when I played with The Outfit,' he said in his 1998 interview with Michael Moynihan.

Beausoleil claims that he upstaged the rest of the band with his stage movements and dancing; record company talent scouts, including one from Sun Records, allegedly came to see the band and wanted to sign Beausoleil on his own without the rest of them. True or not, he was starting to become known on the underground as a stunning performer and as a character around Haight-Ashbury. He wore a top hat and was accompanied at all times by his white dog, Snofox. Even before he met occultist and film-maker Kenneth Anger, he was cultivating a personal style that was part stage magician, part black magician.

Eager to experiment with new instruments, he bought a student sitar and a Greek bouzouki and taught himself to play; later, he added a dulcimer. These were not traditional rock instruments, and while there were groups like The Incredible String Band in Britain who were starting to play with similar unusual stringed, bowed and plucked stringed instruments, the LA scene in 1965 was still surprisingly conservative. Dissatisfied with The Outfit, Beausoleil started recruiting for a new project, the first 'electric symphony orchestra', to be known as the Chamber Orkustra or just Orkustra. The first member to join was a young classically trained violinist called David LaFlamme, who at that time was playing in a gay bar performing 'Turkey In The Straw' on violin while dressed in tight velvet clothes. He had also played in the original line-up of Dan Hicks And His Hot Licks, one of the bands that would be a mainstay of the West Coast scene for almost a decade. The Orkustra added other musicians, including – at one time – a concert harp, and at any moment there would be 12 to 15 people in the rehearsal space that they rented, all trying to play together. There are no known surviving recordings of Orkustra, though they did make a demo for Atlantic and Kenneth Anger paid for some studio time. When Orkustra split, however, many of the musicians ended up coalescing around David LaFlamme in his new outfit, It's A Beautiful Day. It's A Beautiful Day showcased LaFlamme's violin as well as his rich, sonorous voice. They were in many ways the archetypal San Francisco band, almost lounge/easy listening, playing languid, melodic songs with ethereal female backing vocals, quasi-mystical lyrics and extended onstage jams. 'Bombay Calling', a live favourite recorded for their debut, was an Orkustra song performed, according to Beausoleil, almost exactly as Orkustra had performed it.

By 1966, just before the Summer of Love kicked off in earnest, Orkustra was regularly playing second or third on the bill at the Avalon, the Fillmore and the Carousel, along with other bands from San Francisco's fecund music scene, such as Buffalo Springfield (featuring Neil Young), Big Brother And The Holding Company (with Janis Joplin), The Sir Douglas Quintet and The Charlatans (no relation to the baggy British band of the same name active today); indeed, when Orkustra disbanded in 1967, drummer Terry Wilson joined The Charlatans.

Orkustra member Henry Rasof recalls in an interview in *Fuzz Acid & Flowers* by Vernon Joynson, an extensive who's who of the US psychedelic scene, 'I joined the group in the summer of 1966 after seeing an ad in the Psychedelic Shop on Haight St. There were a lot of people in the band at that time. By Christmas, when we played our first gig at St John's the Evangelist Episcopal Church, there were, as I recall, six people and instruments – guitar, drums, violin, acoustic bass, flute and oboe. I played the oboe, amplified with a harmonica pick-up. I have a tape of that concert, which I got long ago from David LaFlamme. The flute player then dropped out, and there were five of us. The group disbanded the next year. Emmet Grogan, founder of the Diggers, never played in the group whilst I was in it.'

But the legendary Diggers founder did allegedly sing with Orkustra, even though they were ostensibly an improvised instrumental ensemble, and Orkustra became renowned as the Diggers' house band. They performed at one of the first free concerts the Diggers staged in Panhandle Park, sharing a stage consisting of two flatbed trucks with The Grateful Dead, and played a number of Diggers benefits. Beausoleil took part in the Funeral of Hippie and was a regular visitor to the Free Frame of Reference, the closest that the Diggers had to a headquarters.

Despite this connection with the leftist/anarchist Digger faction, there's some evidence that the band – or at least Beausoleil – had another philosophy. 'I had the idea of making an album for the Pacific label, *The Golden Sword*,' he says in *The Garbage People*. 'I had this image in my mind of a sword – like it's pictured on the cover of a book called *Imperium*, by a guy the FBI was hounding and busted into infinity.'

Imperium, The Philosophy Of History And Politics, by Francis

Yockey, written under the pen name Ulick Varange, is an obscure though important text in the annals of post-war fascism. In a turgid and confused 700-page-plus tome, which purported to be the new *Mein Kampf*, Yockey – an American who spied for the Nazis during the Second World War – set out his anti-Semitic and anti-American philosophy. More importantly, he was among the first to put forward the idea that the gassing of 6 million Jews never happened. Ironically, Yockey ended up working for communist Czech intelligence because, according to Martin Lee in his study of neo-Nazism, *The Beast Reawakens*, 'Yockey looked at the United States as more of a threat to Nazism than the Soviet Union. In his mind, at least the Russians were white, while the United States was a mongrel culture.' Yockey committed suicide – though the circumstances are 'suspicious' – in a San Francisco jail cell in 1960.

Whether Beausoleil accepted the premise of this godfather of Holocaust denial is tantalisingly unclear. Beausoleil said, 'It was a big book and I read it a lot – studied it and tried to make as much of it as I could – but my course was different... I would finally come to believe that I was a man of action. I had to go through things no matter what they were or how dangerous they may have seemed to someone on the outside.'

The album was never recorded.

In 1967 Orkustra performed at the Glide Memorial Festival, a three-day event organised by the Sexual Freedom League, one of the many 'happenings' taking place in San Francisco at that time.

Beausoleil told Michael Moynihan, 'What this turned out to be was perhaps the most remarkable event that I experienced in San Francisco, the "Human Be-in" notwithstanding. It was never publicised and there were no posters put out for it. The Diggers and whoever else it was rented the Glide Memorial Church for three days, a long three-day weekend. They essentially just turned it into a free-for-all. They lined up all these people to come in and do different things to get the activity going but they wanted it to be a people's event. The [Diggers] mime troupe was there. Essentially they wanted people to groove on each other, and not just to be passively entertained. The talent and artists who they brought in were there for the purpose of encouraging people to launch interaction... It was crazy, and incredible things happened during those three days – people made love in front of the altar... It was wild. The intention of the organisers was to get people interacting, making love with each other and celebrating freedom. And it was successful in doing that. The police left it alone. It was amazing. I think that was the reason why it was not publicised; there were just a few radio announcements and then it was word of mouth.'

The gig was chaotic, with lights exploding, background noise tapes breaking, the band playing behind a screen while belly dancers cavorted in front. In attendance was underground film-maker Kenneth Anger, who spotted Beausoleil and fell in love with him. Afterwards, when they met, Anger, who was casting his latest film *Lucifer Rising*, told Beausoleil, 'You are Lucifer.'

'To me, Devil worship was a lot of shit,' said Beausoleil. 'The friends Kenneth Anger had were weak. They were fakes to me.' Nevertheless, he agreed to participate in the film, to write and perform the soundtrack, and he moved in with Anger who lived at the Russian Embassy, a Victorian mansion which had actually been the Russian Embassy in the USA during the Czarist period, with a 360-degree view of the city.

Anger was a celebrated film-maker: *Scorpio Rising*, released in 1964, caught the Pop Art mood of the times. It was controversial – there were flashes of nudity – and was actually seized as pornographic.

The Magick Powerhouse Of Oz was a more professional outfit put together to work on the soundtrack. Beausoleil hired some free jazz players, though he was not as close to any of the musicians in that band as he was to LaFlamme or the others, and claimed in an interview not to actually remember their names.

On 21 September 1967 they played their last gig, at a show staged by Anger called *Equinox Of The Gods*, where he unveiled what he had so far of *Lucifer Rising*.

In an interview with *Off The Wall* magazine, psychedelic poster artist Reginald Eugene Williams recalls the gig: 'Headlining was the ill-fated Bobby Beausoleil's Magick Powerhouse Of Oz, the SF Mime Troupe, Charlatans, Congress of Wonders and Straight Dancers and

Lights by North American Ibis. Bobby "Snofox" Beausoleil had been portraying Lucifer in Kenneth Anger's work in progress *Lucifer Rising*, which was projected as part of the "show".

'Kenneth returned to the theatre office the next day and accused us of stealing the now-missing film. We said that we had not, and as I rose to show him the way out he accused me of towering over him and threatening him. We cleansed ourselves of the situation by performing a ceremony at the public trashbasket to rid ourselves of two bad elements on Haight Street and felt we were protected from both situations at once.

'Kenneth soon decided that Bobby had the missing film. Bobby split for LA...looking for stardom.'

The other version of the story, according to Anger, is that they fell out after he allegedly loaned Beausoleil $10,000 to buy gear for the new band and allowed him to store his amps at the house. One of his dogs ripped open a box that Beausoleil had left there. It contained a bale of marijuana. Enraged, and aware that such a quantity of dope could bring down a hefty prison sentence, Anger threw the bales out of the house. Beausoleil allegedly made off with the reels of *Lucifer Rising* and, Anger claimed, buried them in Death Valley. Kenneth Anger had sworn out a warrant for his arrest and declared that he was 'dead' as a film-maker.

Beausoleil, on the other hand, has since claimed that what happened was that Anger had never actually completed the film and that the story that it was stolen and 'buried in Death Valley' was a suitably dramatic riposte to investors and fans waiting to see the finished product. Sort of like 'the dog ate it'.

Beausoleil fled to the Spahn ranch to hide out with Manson. Now we have to backtrack a few months to their first meeting.

In an interview with writer Michael Moynihan posted on his personal website, Beausoleil recalls, 'The first time I met the Manson people was at the Spiral Staircase house down in Malibu, just at the base of Topanga Canyon. I went there visiting a friend that I had known previously from the Hollywood scene, a guy named Paris. He was one of the Hollywood regulars, actually more from the "beat generation" I think. He was quite a bit older. I was visiting him and there was what

CHARLES MANSON: MUSIC, MAYHEM, MURDER

seemed to be a party going on next door – people smoking pot and playing music. So I just wandered over there and it was Charlie Manson singing and playing guitar, and there were some other guys and some girls. I sat down, I listened for a while and I picked up this thing called a melodica. It's designed on the same concept as a harmonica, except it has keys. There was one sitting on the table next to me, and I picked it up and started improvising some counterpoint melodies, which kind of blew everyone's mind – maybe they were all loaded on acid. I played along for a little while and checked out what was going on, then I left... When I ran into them that time in Malibu, it was just a real brief thing; it wasn't that significant to me. I heard later on that it was fairly significant to them – apparently it seemed pretty strange to them that someone could come in cold and harmonise with Charlie's music without any previous familiarity.'

Like Manson, the young Beausoleil had been raised in orphanages and reform schools and had a talent and passion for music. Although the occult aspects were significant, it was initially the fact that Beausoleil was a working musician – unsuccessful though undoubtedly talented – that attracted the two. Beausoleil was never a follower or a disciple of Manson, and in many ways he could actually have been a rival to Manson.

'The first day Bobby showed up at the Spiral Staircase, I thought I saw too much vanity and conceit in his make-up to ever like him, but when I heard him play his guitar, I had a lot of respect for his ability,' Manson is quoted as saying in Nuel Emmons' book. 'The two of us could jam and improvise in perfect harmony, always anticipating the other's moves.'

The Manson Family arrived at the Spiral Staircase in their black school bus in the autumn of 1967. The Spiral Staircase – so named by one of the Manson girls because, surprisingly, it had a spiral staircase – was a house owned by a woman allegedly with connections to Anton LaVey's Church of Satan. It is therefore probable that they knew of it through Susan Atkins. She met Manson in San Francisco and gave him a standing invitation to visit. It was a 'party' house and Manson stayed there for a few months, meeting various cultists and, according to Ed

Sanders, witnessed animal sacrifices and blood drinking as part of Black Masses and other rituals practised there.

They also met a lot of wealthy and influential people who wore business suits by day and crept out to the house at night to indulge in everything from orgies to drugs, something with which Manson was always happy to help them.

They made themselves known to their non-Satanic neighbours, too. In his *Easy Riders, Raging Bulls: How The Sex'n'Drugs'n'Rock'n'Roll Generation Saved Hollywood*, a freewheeling account of the movie scene in the 1960s and 1970s, Peter Biskind recounts a story about wealthy Malibu socialite Donna Greenberg in her words: 'One beautiful sunny Sunday morning I was having breakfast on the patio with my four-year-old, my nanny, my husband and our oldest son, who was 13 or 14. We had just had a paint-in, painting our seawall with peace signs, graffiti, that sort of thing. Suddenly the most frightening group of hippies walked onto our patio, stood around and stared at us, wandered through our house. I was petrified, but I didn't know what to say and it was also the '60s, being nice to people who wore lots of beads and jewels and bandanas. There was a piano covered with all the pictures one collects of children and family and loved ones and everyone I knew, in little silver frames. They gathered around the piano and looked at the pictures. Then they walked out, leaving us shaken. They got down to the end of the beach, but they couldn't get out, and a police car came and I found myself walking down there and telling the police to let them go, they were my guests. Don't ask me what the impulse was. It was the Manson Family.'

Stories like this – of encounters with the Manson Family in the wealthy millionaires' colony of Malibu – are commonplace, though in fact at the time people were not quite so scared and 'freaked out' as they were when they recounted the tales years later. Manson, in fact, was able to move in the very wealthy LA circles and make an astonishing number of contacts in the film, music and entertainment industries. If he was able to win over the father of one of his followers – a Methodist minister, no less – then the Hollywood circles discovering kinky sex, exotic drugs and rock 'n' roll were easy game.

He had secured, through a prison contact, studio time at Universal Studios to record several demos of his songs after impressing a middle-ranking player at the label with an impromptu audition with an acoustic guitar. There was also a vague proposal to make a movie based on the second coming of Christ, although this project came to nothing. His initial recording session was impressive enough to secure the promise of more time, though not an immediate contract with the label. As it happened, the second session did not take place.

The Manson group relocated to the home of Gary Hinman, who Manson met through Bobby Beausoleil. The group then hit the road, travelling through the Mojave Desert, through small towns seldom visited (and often unmarked on the map) away from the main highway. Manson thought of the desert as a place where he could put down some permanent roots, though most of the girls found it too desolate and remote. The group would arrive at the home of friends and on occasions squatted in unoccupied properties, staying for a few weeks before moving on. By the time Mary Brunner gave birth to Manson's son in 1968, the Family's ranks had swollen to between 15 and 20. The bus was becoming cramped and the girls were becoming fractious.

In the summer of 1968, the group visited the Spahn movie ranch, which had been used as a backdrop in films like *Duel In The Sun*. Manson arranged with the owner George Spahn – then in his 80s, nearly blind, and crippled with arthritis – to take over the day-to-day running of the place, looking after the horses that were hired by visitors and taking care of George's cooking and cleaning needs. In return, the Family moved into the ramshackle huts and cabins dotted around the decaying set.

The relationship with George Spahn involved mutual dependence – he came to rely on having one of the girls around for housework, companionship and as much sex as man in his 80s requires while they needed a hideout – but also terror. There is a story that, when they first arrived at the ranch, Manson paid the old man $5,000, but that he got most of the money back through intimidation and threats. One night, Manson entered Spahn's room, held lit matches and swung punches just a few millimetres from his face to test if he was really blind. Then Spahn heard the door close. Terrified, he sat in the darkness. After an hour, he reached out his hand and felt Manson's head. 'That's right, George, I'm still here,' Manson said.

They would move on and return to the Spahn ranch several times, staying a few weeks and moving on, and in the wake of the murders in 1969 it provided them with a hideout, being only half an hour away from LA but remote enough for the activities of a band of nude hippies to go comparatively unnoticed.

8 Dumb Angel

'I'm gonna kill surf city with a loaded gun
Got to blow surf city like a nuclear bomb
I'm gonna fight surf city, got to get it down
I'm gonna kill, kill, get it down
I got to get, get, surf city
– *The Jesus And Mary Chain, 'Kill Surf City'*

Dennis Wilson was the 'hidden' talent in The Beach Boys. He was the only one of the band who actually surfed and, at a time when the whole music scene – the whole world – was undergoing radical change, it was Dennis who connected The Beach Boys to these changes. He was the seeker; he was the one who knew the counter-culture. It was Dennis who helped to take control of the band when Brian was unable to give them direction and it was his growing influence that redeemed many of their post-*Pet Sounds* albums. It was this desire to prove himself as an individual and as a musician that in part drew him to Manson. Dennis was looking for something and Manson just happened to come along at the right time.

In the sleeve notes to The Beach Boys album *All Summer Long*, Dennis is quoted as saying, 'They say I live a fast life. Maybe I just like a fast life. I wouldn't give it up for anything in the world. It won't last forever, either. But the memories will.'

Dennis, the youngest of the Wilson brothers, was only included in the band at his mother's insistence. While Brian and Carl Wilson made their heartbreaking harmonic teenage hymns into modern-day Gregorian chants, Dennis was used as seldom as possible. His was not the angelic voice of the spheres. As a drummer, they regarded him – like

Ringo Starr – as something of a joke, bringing in session men to play his parts on record and limiting him to a flourish-free 4/4 backbeat live.

But Dennis was handsome and athletic where the rest of the band were geeky, podgy and toothy; he personified the character that the band sang about in their dramas of wood-sided cars driving down to the beach, getting around all the girls and surfing all day long. Dennis *was* The Beach Boys.

Dennis was the one the girls screamed for: the band saw him as Ringo – a musical liability, a clown – but the little girls saw him as Paul, George and John rolled into one. When Dennis ventured from behind the kit to deliver a rare harmony part with his brothers and cousin, the screams of a hall full of pre-pubescent teenage girls would drown out everything else.

Dennis took full advantage of the opportunities that his charisma and popularity afforded him. He was the best dressed of all of The Beach Boys, revelled in the attention of groupies and indulged in the plethora of exotic substances that came his way. Dennis was the first to smoke pot, the first to try acid. He loved motorcycles and fast cars and made a point of crashing them as often as he could. He epitomised the new school of rock 'n' roll high living.

But there was also a spiritual side, an intellectual side that drew him first to the Maharishi, then to the frothy surface of the counter-culture and eventually to Manson. It was this side that also drove him to make the cult flick *Two Lane Blacktop* (a post-*Easy Rider* road movie in which he co-starred with James Taylor) and the seminal solo record *Pacific Ocean Blue*, arguably the last great musical statement from any of The Beach Boys.

By 1967, Dennis was dissatisfied with life and with the artistic direction that the band had taken. The great project known as *Smile* (aka *Dumb Angel*, Brian's pet name for Dennis) had fallen apart, although fragments – songs like 'Heroes And Villains', 'Cabinessence', 'Surf's Up' and 'Wind Chimes' – were to crop up on Beach Boys releases for the next decade. The Beach Boys hit 'Good Vibrations' – arguably the greatest pop single ever – promised that *Smile* would be the most progressive, cerebral album ever made, eclipsing The Beatles and all the other 1967 releases by The Byrds, The Who, The Rolling Stones and the new psychedelic groups like Pink Floyd, Love and Jefferson Airplane.

Smile was planned for release in January 1967. Half a million record sleeves were printed up, including a 12-page booklet that was to be included in the package. But something happened on the way to the record plant. *Smile* just never appeared. Brian had stopped performing live with the band and was replaced by Bruce Johnston. In early 1967, The Beach Boys returned from the UK to find Brian mixing these incomprehensible tracks with the flow-of-consciousness lyrics of Van Dyke Parks. At that time, The Beach Boys were in the process of suing Capitol Records and were supposed to headline the Monterey Pop Festival. The Beach Boys and their management were also hard at work trying to start up The Beach Boys' own label, Brother Records, at this point. Even if Brother would eventually release the album, it was uncertain whether Capitol would distribute it, pending the outcome of the lawsuit. The other Beach Boys did not want to depart from the commercial formula that had made The Beach Boys the defining band of the early part of the decade. They also had to go out and perform the material live, and as the songs became increasingly complicated – relying on multiple overdubs, orchestras and unusual instrumentation, such as the theremin on 'Good Vibrations' – the band had serious difficulties recreating the sound in concert. Also, Mike Love simply did not 'get it'. They did not want to release *Smile*. As the delays and fights dragged on, The Beatles released *Sergeant Pepper's Lonely Hearts Club Band*; it was the equivalent of the Americans winning the space race, with The Beatles as the Americans and Brian in the role of the USSR. Brian withdrew more and more from reality.

In his book *Dumb Angel: The Life And Music Of Dennis Wilson*, author Adam Webb describes Brian Wilson's attempt to make *Smile* as being like the work of a scientist granted total freedom in the studio, engaged in a covert cold-war arms race with The Beatles. It was also Dennis who supported the progressive direction that Brian was taking: 'After the relative commercial failure of *Pet Sounds* in the US, it was Dennis who stood up for Brian's new direction when the rest of the group were worried that, to paraphrase Bruce Johnston, "we were gonna have the biggest hit in the world or the career was over". Interviewed by the *NME* in early 1967, it was he who made the grandiose claim that *Smile* was so good that it made its predecessor "stink".'

This may be partly because, at last, Dennis had more of a role to play in the band. Although his claim to have played keyboards on 'Good Vibrations' was not borne out by anyone else who was there, Dennis did appear as a vocalist, singing a mournful version of 'You Are My Sunshine' (recontexted as 'You Were My Sunshine') on a track called 'The Old Master'. He also recorded a piano instrumental called 'I Don't Know'. Both tracks have subsequently been lost.

Dennis loved 'Cabinessence', unarguably the paramount psychedelic track from the *Smile* sessions: divided into three sections, starting with folksy banjo picking and the strange refrain 'doing doing doing', 'Home On The Range' on acid, moving into the fugue-like middle section, involving what sounds like a multi-tracked choir before coming to the strange 'Have you seen the Grand Coulee Dam?' section, with its layered harmonies, almost like a medieval church Mass. It's an acid trip contained in a pop song, going from the slightly skewed feeling that normality has something wrong, through the rapid-fire hallucinogenic vistas at the peak to the mellower and more contemplative comedown. It's still an enigmatic song, a direction for music that no one really followed, though it was to be Dennis's guiding light in times to come.

In the summer of 1968, Patricia Krenwinkel and Ella Bailey, a new addition to the Family, were hitchhiking through LA. They were picked up by a man they immediately recognised as Beach Boys drummer Dennis Wilson. Wilson, then in the wake of a messy divorce, was in the habit of picking up female hitchers and taking them back to his Sunset Boulevard home for sex and drugs. The two talked almost exclusively about 'Charlie'; Wilson allowed them to stay at his house while he went off to a recording session. Returning in the middle of the night, he was alarmed that there was a black school bus in his driveway and a party going on in his house. As he entered his own home, he found various hippies helping themselves to food and drink from his refrigerator. In the living room of his house, he found a group of nude or semi-naked women with Manson at the centre. 'Are you going to hurt me?' he asked.

'Do I look like I'm going to hurt you, brother?' Manson replied, kneeling down and kissing Wilson's feet.

The Family moved right on into Wilson's three-acre estate on Sunset. Although Wilson later claimed that Manson was not a talented musician or songwriter ('Charlie never had a musical bone in his body,' he told Vincent Bugliosi), the two spent hours discussing songwriting, playing the guitar and singing close-harmony duets.

Dennis was desperately seeking ways to prove himself to the others in the band, to Brian and to himself. With *Smile* abandoned in May 1967, later that year The Beach Boys rush-released the inferior *Smiley Smile*, which included some of the finished tracks from the *Smile* sessions – most notably 'Heroes And Villains' and the gorgeous 'Wonderful' – but otherwise it was a disappointing record. In the context of the times – albums like The Doors' eponymous debut, *Forever Changes* by Love and the spectacular if overlooked *Electric Music For Mind And Body* by Country Joe And The Fish – *Smiley Smile* was a step backwards. The group was now under the control of Mike Love and Al Jardine, and while Brian was still a member and sang lead vocals in the studio, his influence had been marginalised. Looking at photos of the band from that time, they look like they are from another era. When they visited London in 1967, Dennis headed for Carnaby Street and newly opened boutiques like Granny Takes A Trip, Mr Fish and the Portobello Road market to kit himself out in the late-mod style of love beads, suede jackets and flared hipsters. The rest of the band went to Savile Row and bought tweed jackets and deerstalkers.

The follow-up, *Wild Honey*, released in 1968, was also poorly received; its optimistic summery white soul – almost evocative of the 1950s – grated with the more abrasive and revolutionary atmosphere in California.

By the time of his meeting with Manson, Dennis had grown as an artist – and grown in his ambitions – but found himself in a difficult position within the group, having aligned himself with his brother. He had written his first serious songs – 'Little Bird' and 'Be Still', which were to be included on the band's 1968 album, *Friends* – but found it hard to connect with the rest of the band. He looked for outside help and found it in his collaborations with poet Stephen Kallich and his friend Gregg Jakobson.

Wilson was instrumental in feeding Manson's ambitions as a musician, talking to people in the music industry about him and even at one point talking about signing him to The Beach Boys' own label, Brother Records.

'Fear is nothing but awareness,' Dennis Wilson said in a 1969 interview with *Rave* magazine. 'I was frightened as a child because I did not understand fear – the dark, being lost, what was under the bed! It came from within me. Sometimes The Wizard frightens me. The Wizard is Charles Manson, who is another friend of mine who says he is God and the Devil! He sings, plays and writes poetry, and may be another artist for Brother Records.'

'A lot of pretty well-known musicians around LA knew Manson, though they'd probably deny it now,' Neil Young recalled in Barney Hoskin's *Waiting For The Sun*, a history of the LA rock scene. 'The girls were around, too. They'd be right there on the couch with me, singing a song.'

At a party at Wilson's house, Manson met with producer Terry Melcher. Melcher was Doris Day's son and had once been in a band with Beach Boy Bruce Johnston (The Rip Chords) and had worked with The Byrds on the ground-breaking album *Turn Turn Turn* (and later in the decade returned at the helm of *The Ballad of Easy Rider* and *Byrdmaniax*), as well as signing to Colombia near-legendary LA band The Rising Sons, led by Taj Mahal and Ry Cooder. Melcher and girlfriend actress Candice Bergen lived at 10050 Cielo Drive, an address that Manson and associate Tex Watson visited several times.

Manson recorded several demos at Beach Boy leader Brian Wilson's Bel Air home in the studio installed in his house. Brian, suffering from mental illness, never saw Manson and the girls who accompanied him – or at least, Brian claimed not to have seen them.

Manson also recorded demos with Dennis's friend and Terry Melcher associate Gregg Jakobson at a studio in Van Nuys.

For all of the high-profile contacts that the Family had made, Manson was frustrated by the fact that nobody who mattered – apart from Dennis Wilson – seemed particularly enthused by his music. John Phillips of The Mamas And The Papas heard the tapes but wasn't particularly interested. In his autobiography *Papa John*, Phillips recalls his introduction to the Family when Dennis Wilson phoned him up and said, 'This guy Charlie's here with all these great-looking chicks. He plays guitar and he's a real wild guy. He has all these chicks hanging out like servants. You can come over and just screw any of them you want. It's a great party.' Rudi Altobelli, Melcher's landlord, was a big-shot agent but was also uninterested in his music or his philosophy.

The relationship between Manson and Wilson soured; the Family stole everything that wasn't nailed down, took Wilson's clothes to wear or to give away to strangers and wrecked his Ferrari, and Manson had the Family girls – all of whom were riddled with assorted venereal diseases – treated by Wilson's personal physician, running up 'the largest gonorrhoea bill in history'. Wilson left the house on Sunset Boulevard and moved into an apartment, leaving his business manager to evict the Manson Family, who then returned to the Spahn ranch.

The Beach Boys bought one of Manson's songs, 'Cease To Exist', which appeared on their album *20/20* as well as on the B-side of their single 'Bluebirds Over The Mountain' (although the song was credited to Dennis Wilson, who retitled it 'Never Learn Not To Love', and the chorus was changed from 'Cease to exist' to 'Cease to resist'). Manson was angry, claiming that, if The Beach Boys had recorded the song the way he wrote it, it would have sold a million copies. 'Dennis Wilson's Brotherhood took my songs and changed the words,' Manson said. 'His own devils grabbed his legs and pulled him under water.'

Charlie was not to prove too popular with the rest of the group. In an interview with *Goldmine* magazine's Ken Sharp in July 2000, Beach Boys member Al Jardine recalled, 'It was just irritating 'cause they were always around and it was "Charlie this, Charlie that." And then he had this little thing that he and Charlie worked out. It was just a melody, a melody in "Never Learn Not To Love". Not the melody, but there was a mantra behind that. Then Dennis wanted to put it in everything. I thought, "Oh boy, this is getting to be too much."'

Manson allegedly presented Dennis with a bullet and threatened the life of his children – the breaking point in their relationship. Manson later claimed, 'I had a pocket full of bullets. I gave one to Dennis. I gave them out to a lot of people. It didn't mean nothin'.'

9 Meanwhile, Back At The Ranch...

'Once I had a little game. I liked to crawl back into my brain.
I think you know the game I mean. I mean the game called go insane.
Now you should try this little game,
Just close your eyes, forget your name
Forget the world, forget the people,
And we'll erect a different steeple.
This little game is fun to do. Just close your eyes, no way to lose.
And I'm right there, I'm going too.
Release control, we're breaking through'
The Doors, 'The Celebration Of The Lizard'

Back at the Spahn ranch, Manson and his followers started on the journey that would lead to Cielo Drive.

The Family grew with the addition of Paul 'Little Paul' Watkins, Steve 'Clem' Grogan, Charles 'Tex' Watson, Linda Kasabian and Sandra Good, all hanging out together at the ranch, their routine involving day-to-day chores and, at night, eating a meal, listening to Charlie talking for a couple of hours, playing music and then having sex, either all together or in smaller individual groups. Charlie still dictated everything: how they would fuck and, occasionally, who would fuck whom. At least once a week they would take acid, which Manson used to build a strong group bond. He forbade anyone in the group to take acid alone. Despite their reputation as drug-deranged berzerker killers, their consumption was comparatively limited. There was marijuana and acid, and occasionally other psychedelics like peyote and mescaline, but not heroin or cocaine. Charlie could see the havoc that the influx of heroin was having on the hippies in Haight-Ashbury and as an ex-convict he saw addicts and former addicts in jail. As well as his altruistic revulsion against these narcotics, though, he also knew that he would lose control of anyone who became addicted to heroin. Their first loyalty would be to skag, not to Charlie.

Charles 'Tex' Watson, in an interview posted on his *Abounding Love Ministries* website (Watkins, like Susan Atkins, is now a born-again Christian and runs a prison ministry), recalls his first meeting with Manson after being picked up by Dennis Wilson while hitchhiking: 'I walked into Dennis's log-cabin-style mansion and I was very impressed. Dennis introduced me to an old white-bearded man named Dean [Morehouse, father of Ruth Ann Morehouse], who smiled and said, "You've got to meet Charlie!" It seemed like everybody I met who knew Charlie worshipped him! Dean showed me into the living room. Dennis had already relaxed on the couch and was listening to Charlie's music. So Dean and I joined them as a couple of the girls served us sandwiches and coffee. It was like the girls were slaves and the men were kings meant to be served. There was this big chunk of hashish on the coffee table. As we smoked it and listened to Manson's love songs, I began to see why people looked up to Charlie. As he smiled at me, it seemed he could see right into me. It was like love filled the air. I left that night on cloud nine. I'm sure the hash had a great deal to do with it, but I couldn't believe what had just happened and couldn't wait to come back. Sure enough, Dennis asked me to come back anytime. I don't know if I was more impressed with Charlie or Dennis. [Manson] was much different, back then, than he is today. If I met him back then, as he is today, I'd run from him, scared for my life. Back then, he was much younger, of course, with deceptive charisma. In my book, I think I described him as "always changing"; his movements, his appearance, his dress, becoming someone new everyday – rock star, guru, devil, son of God, even a child. He was a magician and a charmer. He was aware, almost catlike. His eyes were hypnotic, having the ability to psych you out immediately. I feel it was because of the drugs and the philosophies he had studied, but he was much more "aware" than we were.'

Manson's raps in 1968 and 1969 started to become angrier, more and more preoccupied with the forthcoming racial war that he called Helter Skelter. The Beatles' 'White Album', released in 1968, was interpreted by the Family – mostly, allegedly, by Paul Watkins rather than Manson himself – as being prophetic of the tribulation ahead.

After *Sergeant Pepper's Lonely Hearts Club Band*, an album that had involved the band, the London Symphony Orchestra and producer George Martin in a Herculean effort to push back the frontiers of pop music, The Beatles made a conscious decision to return to a more basic set of songs not linked by any grandiose concept. The plain white cover and the fact that the title is eponymous has often been interpreted as a statement of minimalist intent after the crowded Pop Art cover of its predecessor, designed by artist Peter Blake, and the almost Dadaist title. In fact, according to plans for the 'White Album' before it was released, *The Beatles* was to be anything but minimalist white. Paul had wanted to include an elaborate booklet, which became the lyric-poster-and-photos idea. The cover concept was originally to have an illustration showing the band's heads carved into a mountainside, similar to Mount Rushmore but overlooking a seascape. Also, the album was recorded partly under the working title *A Doll's House*.

Many of the songs on the record were written while the band were studying meditation with the Maharishi in India. They had only brought acoustic guitars with them, so this more simple and stripped-down approach is reflected in the songs.

After the heavy-duty psychedelic experimentation on 'Tomorrow Never Knows' (on 1966's *Revolver*) and on *Sergeant Pepper's Lonely Hearts Club Band*, the opening track on *The Beatles* is like a step back to classic R&B. 'Back In The USSR' (a nod to Chuck Berry's 'Back In The USA') was a stark, hard-rock number.

The album was ahead of its time in that it spelled the end of the band's involvement with acid, difficult musical experiments and flirtations with the artistic avant-garde. Psychedelia had reached its peak worldwide, but *The Beatles* pointed to a new direction, back to a kind of sanity that was to give rise to country rock, to the heavy, amplified blues that became known as heavy metal and to the folksier boom of solo singer/songwriters at the close of the decade. 'Glass Onion' and 'Revolution 9' continued the band's experimentation, though this was to be where it ended; subsequent releases *Abbey Road* and *Let It Be* found the band returning to a classic simplicity.

George Harrison's 'Piggies' – a childish (in every sense) stab at bourgeois society – was to have appalling resonances with the LaBianca murders the following year: 'Everywhere there's lots of piggies/Living piggy lives/You can see them out for dinner/With their piggy wives/Clutching forks and knives to eat their bacon.' This is arguably the only song that was not misinterpreted by the Family: Harrison's intention was to sneer at the unenlightened collar-and-tie saps, latching on to the counter-culture's personification of them as 'pigs'.

'Helter Skelter', unambiguously about the fairground ride, could also be interpreted as being about acid and McCartney growing tired ness of 'going back to the top of the slide' repeatedly. In *Musician* magazine in 1985, McCartney said, 'Pete Townshend in *Melody Maker* said The Who had some track that was the loudest, the most raucous rock 'n' roll, the dirtiest thing they'd ever done. It made me think, "Right. Got to do it." I like that kind of geeing up. And we decided to do the loudest, nastiest, sweatiest rock number we could. That was "Helter Skelter".'

Charles 'Tex' Watson recalls, 'I ran from Manson on December 1, 1968, the day we listened to the "White Album" together. That day he began to formulate part of his philosophy from The Beatles, because to him their music confirmed his black-white revolution theory. For the next three months, while I was away from the Family, he brainwashed the hardcore Family members with this madness. So much so that, when I was drawn back to the Family at the end of February, all they could talk about was Helter Skelter coming down fast. To them, I was ignorant and blind and had a lot of catching up to do. I didn't know what they were talking about. My head was spinning from all this new insight.

'Not only did Manson believe his philosophy with strong conviction, but also he took pride in it. He didn't tell us where he was borrowing it from, but to him The Beatles were confirming all he believed.

'When the Scripture spoke of four angels, Charlie saw The Beatles-prophets bringing the word of Helter Skelter and preparing the way for Christ (Manson) to lead the chosen people away to safety. The avenging locusts that are mentioned were also a reference to the rock group, he said, since locusts and "beetles" were virtually the same. In the King James version that Charlie used, these locusts are described in verses seven and eight as having faces like men but the hair of women, and it seemed to be a clear description of The Beatles' long hair, while the "breastplates of iron" were their electric guitars. The fire and brimstone recorded as pouring from the mouths of the horses in verse 17 were, to Charlie, the symbolic power of The Beatles' music to ignite Helter Skelter.

'As for the "seal of God" on the foreheads of some men that keeps them safe from the plagues of the angels (verse four), Charlie never explained what it was, but he made it clear that he would be able to see it, and it would divide those who were for him from those who were against him and who would thus die. He also found references to the dune buggies we were gathering and to the motorcycle gangs he was trying to recruit into the Family in the passage's descriptions of "horses prepared unto battle" and horsemen that would roam the Earth, spreading destruction. As for the one-third of mankind that the writings say will be destroyed, Charlie interpreted them as the white race, wiped out in Helter Skelter for "worship of idols of gold, silver, bronze, stone and wood" (verse 20) – cars, houses and money, according to Charlie.

'Finally, and most importantly, there was a fifth angel given the key to the shaft leading down into the Abyss, the Bottomless Pit. Charlie himself was the fifth angel, he taught us, and he would lead us, his chosen, into the safety of that Pit. Although he never told us (perhaps he didn't know), the translation of this angel's name – Abaddon in the Hebrew, Apollyon in the Greek – is "destroyer".

'In no way do The Beatles share responsibility for the murders. Their music was misinterpreted by Manson and developed into a false teaching.'

Manson was not alone in misinterpreting The Beatles. In fact, it was a favourite pastime for bored kids in the 1960s, as illustrated by the persistent 'Paul is dead' rumour.

In 1969 an American disc jockey, Russ Gibb on Detroit station WKNR-FM, received an anonymous phone call claiming that Paul McCartney had been killed in a car crash. It claimed that the record company was trying to cover this up because it thought this would hurt sales, but the band were sending clues in their music and the clues were in the hidden messages wedged in at the end of 'Strawberry Fields Forever', where John was supposed to be chanting, 'I buried Paul'. (He was in fact singing, 'Cranberry sauce'.)

The rumour spread across the Atlantic, and Apple Records in London was deluged with phone calls from fans. Although they were reassured that Paul was in perfect health, the story grew until fans were interpreting 'clues' in everything The Beatles did. The sleeve of Paul's military uniform on the cover of *Sergeant Pepper's Lonely Hearts Club Band* had the letters OPD, which meant Officially Pronounced Dead. (It was actually given to him by the Ontario Police Department.) Paul is wearing a black carnation in the finale of the *Magical Mystery Tour* film. On the cover of *Abbey Road*, Paul is the only member of the band walking across the zebra crossing barefoot and the number plate of the Volkswagen Beetle in the background is 28 IF, which was reputed to mean that Paul would have been 28, had he lived. The 'stupid bloody Tuesday man' from Lennon's 'I Am The Walrus' was supposedly a reference made to the car crash in which he had died. The guitar made out of flowers on the *Sergeant Pepper's Lonely Hearts Club Band* sleeve was a wreath that spelled 'Paul' and in the inside cover photo where Paul has his back to the camera is a sign that he is dead. The cut-out behind Paul in the photo on the front has his hand raised above his head, which represents the Indian symbol of death.

The rumours are absurd – if McCartney had died, sales would have rocketed – but in the climate of paranoia, they were not unusual. Fans of Bob Dylan would examine his every lyric for evidence of clandestine communication. One underground newspaper claimed that 'Sad Eyed Lady Of The Lowlands' from *Blonde On Blonde* contained the truth behind the Kennedy assassinations.

The fertile ground that is teenage rumour has always given rise to these stories. As a kid, I remember ruining my copy of Led Zeppelin's untitled album 'IV (Four Symbols)' because people swore blind that there was a backwards message at the end of 'Stairway To Heaven' that said, 'My sweet Satan.' As discussed earlier, such 'backward-masked' Satanic-message rumours were taken seriously enough by American courts in the 1980s, when Judas Priest and Ozzy Osbourne were put on trial.

Manson's belief system, incoherent at best, was constantly changing, depending on whom he was talking to or what frame of mind he was in. The guts of his philosophy – that we are living in the 'end times' and part of the 'chosen' – is actually rather commonplace for apocalyptic sects that even pre-date Christianity. Groups like the Essenes, dissident Jews who lived out in the desert in Qumraan, believed that the world was about to end and that we lived in the 'last days' and that they alone would be spared. Even the Jesus of the Gospel of Mark – the earliest of the four Gospels and the one that retains most of the 'source book' known as Q – portrays a Jesus proclaiming that the kingdom (or reign) of God was at hand; he expected the world to change drastically in his own lifetime. Early Christian sects believed that the return of Christ was imminent, not an event that would take place in a distant, unknowable future.

This thread runs through some of the most destructive and revolutionary sects and cults, such as the Anabaptists in 16th-century Germany and the Free Spirit Movement, or Ranters, in revolutionary England. The flowering of fundamentalist Christianity in the 19th and 20th centuries produced a bewildering variety of 'end times' groups, from the comparatively harmless Jehovah's Witnesses (whose prophecies for the end have come and gone several times over) to much more dangerous and murderous groups like Manson's. The interpretation of the Book of Revelation in the light of contemporary events was actually a long tradition within American Christian fundamentalism; a popular magazine at the time called *The Plain Truth* was distributed free of charge through supermarkets, news-stands and, significantly, in prisons, and was full of articles about current events in the light of biblical prophecy. The core belief of the magazine and its founder, Herbert W Armstrong, was that the end of the world was imminent, though their Armageddon involved the more conventional nuclear superpower confrontation in the Middle East, which in the light of the Six-Day War was not entirely unrealistic. In the mid-1960s, it claimed a readership of hundreds of millions worldwide.

Much of the Helter Skelter philosophy seems to have come about after a visit to the Barker ranch in 1968. While out in Death Valley, Manson heard a story from a local prospector, a jumbled version of a Hopi Indian creation myth that involved the human race emerging from an 'inner world' below the surface of the world. According to the myth, the entrance to this world was located somewhere in Death Valley. Death Valley is riddled with caves and there had long been stories about a cavern vast enough to contain an entire city with an underground river called the Amargosa flowing into it.

The idea of an inner Earth populated by 'the gods', or at least an advanced race, was actually a very old and persistent one; fictional depictions in Jules Verne's *Journey To The Centre Of The Earth*, Edgar Rice Burroughs' *Pellucidar* and Edward Bulwer Lytton's forgotten Victorian sci-fi classic *The Coming Race* (reputedly a novel much admired by Hitler) had helped to popularise the notion. But occultists like the Theosophists and the Thule Society in Germany held that there really was an inner world. The Nazis – particularly Rudolf Hess and Heinrich Himmler – were also convinced of its existence.

In the 1940s and 1950s, the pulp magazine *Amazing Stories* ran a series of articles based on the 'revelations' of a man named Richard Shaver about malevolent inner-Earth dwellers called the Deros who were tormenting him with a telepathic ray. Surprisingly, Shaver's words, rather than being dismissed as the ravings of an obvious schizophrenic, struck a chord with the public. Before UFOs and alien abductions, people believed in advanced races – the survivors of Atlantis, Lemuria and Mu – living under the ground. Again, this was a mass-market magazine, and if Manson had not actually read any of the 'Shaver mystery stories', it's reasonable to assume that he had heard at least some of the hollow-Earth myths recounted by someone else.

Manson was convinced that there was a world under Death Valley and sent Family members out into the desert in dune buggies to search for the entrance to this vast cavern. Just over the state line in Nevada, he discovered the Devil's Hole, an opening in the base of a cave filled with water, which extended hundreds of feet below the ground. He believed that the water was a door placed there by the inner-Earth dwellers to keep the surface dwellers out. Manson thought he was being sent visions of the world under the ground, which was a paradise of milk and honey, overflowing with chocolate fountains. He ordered Ruth Morehouse and Steve Grogan to swim down as far as they could (the water actually gets far too hot to bear the farther down you go). They tried sinking a rock attached to rope. Then Manson decided he would try to get a contractor to come and drain the water. They would then attach a truck to a winch with hundreds of feet of special gold-laced rope to lower it to the bottom, a sort of escalator to hell. As Helter Skelter broke out and the blacks enslaved or slaughtered the remaining whites, Manson planned a mass flight to the Devil's Hole with his followers – who by this time would number the requisite 144,000 – and slide down the golden rope into the land below to wait out the end of civilisation as we know it on the surface. He planned to raise money for the forthcoming Armageddon by sending the girls out to work as topless go-go dancers and prostitutes.

At his trial, Manson denied this: 'There's been a lot of talk about a bottomless pit. I found a hole in the desert that goes down to a river that runs north underground, and I call it a bottomless pit, because where could a river be going north underground? You could even put a boat on it. So I covered it up and I hid it and I called it "the Devil's Hole" and we all laugh and we joke about it. You could call it a Family joke about the bottomless pit. How many people could you hide down in this hole?'

Even after he was in jail, his followers on the outside continued to visit Devil's Hole (on 'hole patrol') to find the hidden opening into this underground world. Remaining Family members came to believe that there was some sort of occult conspiracy in effect to conceal this secret entrance.

In a recent posting in *Reptilian Research* (the e-zine of notorious cult kook David Icke, another would-be son of God or son of man), there is this description of Devil's Hole: 'The pool connects to a vast underground lake, the bottom of which has not been probed. A bottomless pit! In it swims an endangered species of tiny prehistoric pupfish found nowhere else on Earth. Biologists believe that the pool may be connected underground to other small pools of pupfish located hundreds of miles away. UFO experts believe that Devil's Hole is connected to the underground caverns located beneath Area 51. Purportedly, reptilian-type aliens live in Devil's Hole and have emerged now and again.'

There had always been a racist dimension to Charlie and those around him – at one point a biker called Danny DeCarlo, a member of the Straight Satans outlaw motorcycle club, was hanging around the Spahn ranch and Manson berated him for listening to jazz, which was black music – but in that poisonous summer of 1968 it took on a more ferocious dimension. The love and peace of the previous year was giving way to violence and bloodshed.

A fresh wave of assassinations rocked America: Robert Kennedy, who may well have won the Democratic nomination for the presidential election on an anti-war ticket, was gunned down in Seattle by a gunman who acted as though brainwashed, and Martin Luther King was murdered by white racist gunman James Earl Ray. A new militancy was growing in America and in the counter-culture; frustrated at the continuing war in Vietnam, the anti-war movement – hitherto based on the non-violent principles of Martin Luther King and the civil-rights movement – started to fragment.

As well as the violence that followed the assassination of Martin Luther King, there was actually some serious tension between the white hippy children and the black communities. Occasionally, this would result in actual confrontation. Hippies, feeling themselves to be victimised by 'the man', would make outrageous statements: 'We're the new niggers!' The black communities resented the fact that white kids were coming into their neighbourhoods to buy drugs, giving a boost to a trade that they found unwelcome. They also resented the patronising attitudes of these middle-class children 'dropping out' for a brief adventure in poverty when they themselves had to work hard at dead-end jobs to put food on the table, who had no choice in whether they were part of the world outside the American dream. Crucially, there was a feeling that these draft-dodgers were being dealt with leniently; white college drop-outs went over the border into Canada or to Europe. This was not an option for young black men, who were disproportionately represented in the armed forces.

The fighting in Vietnam intensified. On the night of 31 January 1968, 70,000 North Vietnamese soldiers and Viet Cong guerrillas launched the Tet Offensive, surging into more than 100 towns and cities in South Vietnam, including the capital, Saigon. It proved to be one of the greatest campaigns in military history. It shocked the American military, who until that point had been able to convince politicians and public alike that they were winning the war. US public opinion was probably most affected by the infamous incident at Mylai, where American soldiers massacred 100 peasants, women and children among them.

By January 1969 there were nearly 542,000 American troops in Vietnam with no obvious way home and no prospect of achieving their aim of preventing a communist takeover of South Vietnam.

The Students for a Democratic Society (SDS) fractured into the Action Faction (which later formed the nucleus of America's first far-left terrorist group, the Weathermen, named after a line from Bob Dylan's 'Subterranean Homesick Blues' – 'You don't need a weatherman to know which way the wind blows') and protests against the war started to become violent. In 1967, at the March on Washington against the war, hippies had stuck flowers in the barrels of the rifles pointed at them by National Guardsmen. In 1968, inspired by the rising of French students that had almost led to a popular Marxist uprising in May, many abandoned non-violence as a dead end. The Yippies – the Youth International Party, formed by Abbie Hoffman, Anita Hoffman, Jerry Rubin and Paul Krassner – put a pig called Pigasus up for President (sadly, it was defeated by Republican candidate Richard Nixon). At the Democratic Party National Convention, the anti-war protest that they staged resulted in a police riot, with Chicago police firing tear gas and randomly beating anyone who was there.

The music, too, had become more strident and angry. The Beatles recorded 'Revolution' and 'Revolution 9' on their 'White Album', although in fact John Lennon was actually questioning the new militants ('When you go carrying pictures of Chairman Mao/You ain't gonna make it with anyone anyhow') while The Rolling Stones recorded 'Street-Fighting Man' (though their street-fighting consisted mostly of running away from the tax man) and The Doors had a hit with 'Five To One', a call to arms in the guise of a bubblegum pop song, based on the demographic bombshell that the population under 30 outnumbered those over by a ratio of five to one: 'The old get old/And the young get stronger/May take a week/And it may take longer/They got the guns/But we got the numbers/Gonna win, yeah/We're takin' over/Come on!' In Detroit, a radical proto-heavy-metal band called The MC5 (short for Motor City Five) released their debut album *Kick Out The Jams*. Allied to the White Panther Party, a Diggers/Yippie-like collective inspired by the Black Panthers, The MC5's brand of feedback-drenched blue-collar rock 'n' roll was almost the ultimate expression of the revolutionary feeling among American youth that year. The album opened with an incendiary monologue by Brother JC Crawford: 'Brothers and sisters! The time has come for each and every one of you to decide whether you are gonna be part of the problem or whether you are gonna be part of the solution! You must choose, brothers, you must choose! It takes five seconds. Five seconds of decision. Five seconds to realise your purpose here on the planet!'

Black America's voice, too, had grown more confident; James Brown emerged as a figure as significant on the entertainment scene as Martin Luther King and Malcolm X had been in politics.

Concurrent with this, a conservative mood was also growing, a reaction against the free love and long hair – the voters who had put Richard Nixon in the White House were the polar opposite of the hippies, the Yippies and the student left. As well as a sneaking feeling that this was a bunch of no-good communist sympathisers seeking to undermine the American way of life (serious conservative

commentators suggested straight-faced that The Beatles, *Rowan &
Martin's Laugh-In* and nudity in the movies was all part of a
monstrous plot to bring down the USA), there were those who actually
felt that civilisation itself was in crisis. In many ways, Manson's
apocalyptic raps were only a distorted version of the same message
preached in churches and on the fringes of the Republican Party and
myriad right-wing groups like the John Birch Society, the Posse
Committatus and the Minutemen.

The reactionaries had their chart-toppers, too: Staff Sergeant Barry
Saddler's 'The Ballad Of The Green Berets' (theme to the John Wayne
film *The Green Berets*), an unapologetic celebration of American
military involvement in Southeast Asia, reached Number One in the
Top 40, as did 'An Open Letter To My Teenage Son' by Victor
Lundberg III, a comical (in retrospect) monologue by a crusty old
conservative with 'The Battle Hymn Of The Republic' swelling in the
background as he delivers the punchline: 'If you burn your draft card
then also burn your birth certificate, for from that day forth I have no
son!' And then there was the reactionary anthem to end them all: Merle
Haggard's 'I'm Proud To Be An Okie From Muskogee' ('We don't make
a party out of lovin'/We like holdin' hands and pitchin' woo/We don't
let our hair grow long and shaggy/Like the hippies out in San Francisco
do') was a hit that year, though many have suggested that Merle's
tongue was firmly in his cheek.

America had not been so polarised between two factions since its
Civil War. Even before the Manson murders, the paranoia on both sides
was reaching a crescendo. Manson was not the only person who
predicted an imminent race war between black and white America. The
roots of America's militia movement can be traced to this time, with
weekend survivalists and assorted white supremacists arming themselves
and preparing for an all-out war with the blacks. Fascist groups like the
Liberty Lobby, the Minutemen and a revived Ku Klux Klan were all
rumoured to be arming in readiness for a black uprising. Hippy paranoia
consisted of urban myths about government concentration camps being
constructed in the Midwest to house hundreds of thousands of political
prisoners in a fascist crackdown on all dissenters.

As 1968 turned to 1969, Manson became increasingly frustrated that his music wasn't getting him anywhere and turned back to crime to support the Family; as well as petty theft, he had re-established contact with some old money-earning career thieves from prison. He had been involved in a confrontation with a black drug dealer and had apparently shot him. Manson missed but was convinced that he had killed him and that his victim was connected to the Black Panthers, who would come after him for revenge. The Family was also dealing drugs through the Spahn ranch, though it was mostly marijuana, LSD and mescaline as opposed to hard drugs like heroin or cocaine. The Spahn ranch became renowned among the LA set as a place where you could go at weekends, score some weed and kick back with the Family.

There's some suggestion that at this time Manson also approached a hanger-on around the Family with a proposal to kill either Terry Melcher, Gregg Jakobson or both for $5,000. Both men had angered him because his demos had gone nowhere. Gregg Jakobson was involved in pitching a film about 'love communes' and had shot some footage of the Family at the Spahn ranch. The film seems to have been intended as a titillating documentary with lots of naked hippies involved in group sex and free love, one of the many soft-porn 'documentaries' that did good business in the adult theatres. Manson was furious. He felt that it should be about his music and that he should talk about Helter Skelter.

Melcher had been out at Spahn to hear Manson and the girls perform new songs. It was, by all accounts, a mess, with the Family joining in on kazoos, whistles and all singing along. Melcher knew that he really didn't want to take things any further with Manson but, like most LA music and movie professionals, saying no straight out was problematic. He smiled and nodded, and said that it was 'nice'. He gave Manson $50 – all the cash that he had in his wallet – to buy hay for the horses.

Susan Atkins claimed in her confession that Manson had ordered the Family to go to the house at Cielo Drive and kill everyone inside because he was angry at Melcher, but Manson and, more importantly, Charles 'Tex' Watson were well aware that he was no longer there.

At Christmas, Melcher and his girlfriend Candice Bergen moved out of the house on Cielo Drive. Manson encountered Melcher subsequently and may even have visited him at his new address. While Gregg Jakobson was initially enamoured of Manson and the girls and even considered joining them, Melcher was starting to become wary of them, as indeed was Dennis Wilson.

The new tenants of the house on Cielo Drive were Roman Polanski and his wife, actress Sharon Tate. Polanski and Tate were in many ways everything that Manson aspired to be. They knew The Beatles and socialised with them in London. Robert Kennedy had dined with Sharon Tate and Roman Polanski on the night of his death. They were part of the hip elite; wealthy and ambitious – Roman dressed in smart Nehru jackets and Sharon in her mini-skirt and boots – they were the epitome of the new Hollywood glamour. When they moved into the house, Polanski was riding high on the success of his film *Rosemary's Baby*, although the follow-up, *The Fearless Vampire Killers* (aka *Dance Of The Vampires*), had fared less well. He was respected as an artist and for the fact that he was hot, in commercial terms.

Sharon was more famous for being Polanski's wife than for her acting. She had appeared in lots of TV shows – the notoriously awful comedy *Petticoat Junction*, *The Beverly Hillbillies* and *The Man From UNCLE*, among others – and was definitely on the way up. She had appeared in the strange British cult film *Eye Of the Devil* in 1966, along with David Niven, Donald Pleasence, John Le Mesurier and David Hemmings (*Blow-Up*), playing a witch, seemingly in a trance throughout. Set in rural France, *Eye Of the Devil* is about a pagan religion that has survived into the 20th century. When the grape harvest fails, David Niven's French aristocrat character has to leave Paris and return to his home village to be ritually sacrificed in order to ensure that the rain will come and save the crop. It is a poor film, shoddily made, but with an intriguing theme (one taken up by the far superior *The Wicker Man* a few years later). Tate, dressed in black polo neck and jeans with an amulet around her neck, plays one of two creepy siblings (Hemmings plays her brother) who are in some way integral to this pagan cult in a way that is never really explained.

There are the usual 'underground' rumours from those too dumb to see that a film is a fictional story and not some 'truth' made public for the initiates to decipher, that Sharon Tate actually was a witch and that this film is in some way connected to the murders. There are also stories that Tate was inducted into a witch cult on the set of *Rosemary's Baby* and may even have been initiated into the Church of Satan by Anton LaVey, who was a technical adviser on the film. LaVey greatly admired the film, which portrayed Satanists as being cool, moneyed and intelligent, unlike the tabloid depiction of them as drug-addled numbskulls dancing naked around a campfire. Accounts of the film say that LaVey got on well with everyone and made a number of recruits among the crew and cast. Regardless of the truth of these stories, it's a giant leap to conclude that Sharon Tate was somehow complicit in her own murder.

Some writers have gone even further in suggesting a link between *Rosemary's Baby* and the assassination of John Lennon outside the Dakota Building in 1980. They make much of the fact that Lennon's killer was aware of the Manson–Polanski–Beatles connection and actually spotted actress Mia Farrow – who played Rosemary in the film – leaving the building as he waited outside, reading his copy of *The Catcher In The Rye* and waiting for the former Beatle to appear.

Apart from her role in *The Fearless Vampire Killers* and appearances in cheesy comedies like *Don't Make Waves* and the dreadful James Bond spoof *The Wrecking Crew*, starring Dean Martin, she is best known for her appearance in *The Valley Of The Dolls*, still something of a camp classic today. A would-be exposé of the dark side of Hollywood – the booze, pills and broken lives beneath the glamour – Sharon's role in the film was that of Jennifer, a sex symbol torn between the money that she could earn and humiliation at the way in which she allowed herself to be used. All that Jennifer wants is a man to love her and to have a child. Hardly a feminist classic. Sharon's performance was at least as good as those of her more heavyweight co-stars Patty Duke and Susan Hayward.

A few miles away, in Death Valley, Manson now grew angrier and angrier and more and more frustrated. Two years out of prison and he now had power, status and the respect of a growing circle of sycophants who, more and more, came to regard his word as law, who would carry out any act he commanded, no matter how ludicrous. The group had accrued a number of guns, including machine guns. Danny DeCarlo, leader of the Straight Satans motorcycle club, maintained the arsenal and also provided additional protection for Manson, who felt that the other men at the ranch – Bruce Davis, Paul Watkins, Bobby Beausoleil and Charles Watson – were not reliable when it came to meting out physical violence. They were, after all, love children, the wimpy children of the middle class, while DeCarlo was a blue-collar outlaw who was more than able to take care of himself. In return, DeCarlo had all of his meals provided for him and access to all of the girls whenever he felt like having sex. 'It was better than mother's milk,' he recalled. At one point, the rest of the Straight Satans rode out to the ranch prepared to free their leader, whom they believed had been kidnapped and was being held there against his will.

At this time, Manson also meted out beatings to the girls if they disobeyed him. There was no room for debate. The Family had a stern authority figure as its father. He preached to them about Helter Skelter, a mish-mash of interpretations of the Book of Revelation, the sort of paranoid fantasies that were common currency on the paranoid right, and possibly some first-hand knowledge of black revolutionary groups picked up in prison when Manson would have been in close proximity to members of organisations like the Nation of Islam (who are still active recruiters in American jails) but also the United Slaves. The United Slaves was a violent nationalist rival to the Black Panthers, though one that was thoroughly penetrated and compromised by the FBI from the start. Although it was a tiny group, it espoused black separatism and a racial war against the whites and was involved in the murder of rival Black Panthers, whom it deemed not sufficiently revolutionary. The Nation of Islam, although also a separatist group, advocated violence only for defence, while the Black Panthers was essentially a socialist group and was prepared to involve white and mixed racial groups in pursuit of its aims.

As with all microfactions of both right and left, United Slaves founder Ron Karenga (aka Dr Maulana Karenga) had vast dreams of a forthcoming black revolution that would lead to the creation of an Africanised America.

Manson claimed first-hand knowledge of black revolutionary groups arming and planning their day of carnage. He said that the blacks would win and overthrow the whites, slaughtering all of the men, raping the women – impregnating them with 'mongrel' children – until the race was completely eliminated. The only survivors would be the Manson followers, for he was the angel with the key to the bottomless pit. But once the blacks had won and slaughtered all the whites, Manson said, things would quickly fall apart because they would be too stupid to run things: the machines would break down, they would not be able to grow crops, there would be starvation. That, he said, would be the point at which they would come to him, Charles Manson, and ask him to take over and run things. Manson said he would accept, and his first act would be to say 'Back to the cotton fields, niggers.'

Like all prophets of doom, Manson could not wait for Helter Skelter to happen. Just as a lot of Christian fundamentalists, like the Reverend Jerry Falwell and Pat Robertson, revel in the idea of the 'end times' because they will get to see Jesus, as well as having the satisfaction of seeing all the smart-arse atheists who sneered at them cast into the lake of fire along with all the other sinners, Manson more and more came to believe that Helter Skelter was what would fulfil him. Despite his firm conviction that behind every door in Watts, Oakland and south-central LA the black families were busy oiling rifles and plotting their insurrection, the reality was that black militants and moderates alike were only demanding to take their rightful place in the mainstream of American society while the black nationalists were looking for ways to separate themselves from white America rather than overthrow or destroy it.

Manson's idea became more convoluted: the white fear of the blacks would cause a backlash, a pogrom that would be resisted by blacks. But this, too, was unlikely; outside of a network of disorganised fringe groups, the challenge to the prevailing racism of the past 200 years was actually starting to have some impact. Groups like the Ku Klux Klan started to look like a tawdry joke and their membership fell dramatically in the 1960s. The idea of actually provoking this conflict by going out and slaughtering affluent middle-class white people but leaving clues that would point to black militants must have occurred to Manson at this time, although it took another killing to bring this plot to fruition.

10 The Valley Of Death

'Neither repented they of their murders, nor of their sorceries,
nor of their fornication, nor of their thefts'
– *Revelation 9:21*

Gary Hinman, a rock musician, Buddhist, teacher and drug dealer, was
introduced to Manson through Bobby Beausoleil in 1967. Manson had
actually lived with him at his house for a while before Hinman became
uncomfortable and asked Manson to leave. Some erroneous reports
and books have claimed that the reason why Hinman became the first
'victim of the Manson Family' was because he rejected them.
Regardless, he actually was interested in Manson's philosophy, as well
as in the willing, half-naked girls who surrounded him, and far from
rejecting them, he kept in contact and engaged in drug deals, and it was
this that resulted in his death.

Bobby Beausoleil felt that Hinman owed him money for drugs:
'This motorcycle club [the Straight Satans] wanted to party and they
had some money which they wanted to use to score some psychedelics.
I told them I knew a guy in Topanga Canyon and that I could score for
them. The guy I knew was Gary Hinman. They wanted LSD or
mescaline or something along those lines – I don't think they really had
a whole lot of experience in that. So I turned over $1,000 for 1,000 hits
of mescaline from Gary Hinman and took it to the bike club. I figured
it was a successful deal, and I never thought Gary to be the kind of guy
who would bother selling something that wasn't good or wasn't what
it was purported to be. I thought maybe I would have been invited to
the party, but I wasn't! The transaction occurred at the Spahn ranch,
and the next day they came back and wanted their money back, saying

that the mescaline had turned out to be bunk. I had to take them at their word... So I had to go to Gary's to try to get the money back. Before I rode over to Gary's, one of the Straight Satans, Danny DeCarlo, put a gun in my hand and told me, "If he doesn't want to co-operate, here's what you do: you hit him with the gun and..." – now, I was in no way prepared for this! Apart from a little target shooting with a .22 as a kid, I'd never had a gun in my hand. I was not inclined whatsoever toward guns. I was way out of my element, I didn't know what the fuck I was doing. Bruce Davis – who was eventually convicted as an accessory to the crime, although he actually didn't do anything – drove me over to Gary's and dropped me off. He was a friend of Danny's, and he knew what was going on, but he wasn't going to get involved – it was up to me. Also, two of the girls that hung out at the ranch had wanted to come. They didn't know what was going on at that point. I didn't think it was going to be any big deal to get the money back, so I said, sure, they could come along.'

According to the prosecution, Manson sent Susan Atkins and Mary Brunner with him to Hinman's house to collect, though Beausoleil denies that it happened that way: 'They were both friends of Gary's to begin with. Everybody in the area, Manson included, knew Gary. Gary was part of the Topanga Canyon subculture, and Charlie and his people had lived there for a year and a half, so they all knew each other. Some of the girls had even stayed with Gary. In fact, one of the girls that went with me, Mary Brunner, lived with Gary for a time. The girls had wanted to know where I was going, and I said, "Over to Gary's house." They asked, "Can we come, too?" That's all it was – their initial involvement was quite innocent.' Hinman protested that he had no cash and signed over the ownership of his two cars to Beausoleil while one of the girls held a gun on him. Beausoleil then searched the house for money. Hinman, meanwhile, overpowered one of the girls and took the gun from her. Bobby Beausoleil then returned and started pistol-whipping Hinman with the loaded gun, which went off. According to the official version of the story, they then stabbed him repeatedly.

Beausoleil panicked. He then wrote 'POLITICAL PIGGIE' on the

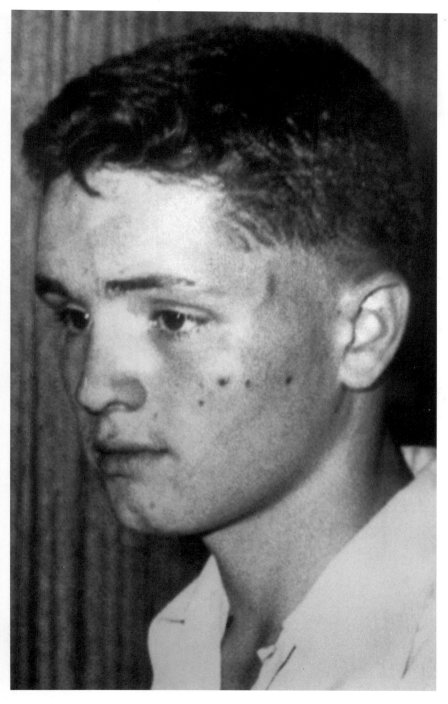

Charles Manson at 14 years old, when he lived in Indianapolis. When this photograph was taken, he had just been released from a juvenile home

Anton Szandor LaVey of the First Satanic Church is assisted by his wife, Diane, as they go through a Satanic ceremony

The Diggers' 'Death of a Hippie' funeral procession in Haight-Ashbury. Bobby Beausoleil was in attendance

Charles Manson at his 1986 parole hearing

The Beach Boys in 1968, on tour to promote their new single, 'Bluebirds Over The Mountain'. The B-side was 'Never Learn Not To Love', written by Charles Manson

An abandoned cabin at the Spahn Ranch, where Manson and his gang holed up

Beach Boys drummer Dennis Wilson

Sharon Tate at London Airport in 1966

An LAPD officer stands in front of a car containing the sheet-covered body of one of the five persons found dead in and around the home of Sharon Tate. Abigail Folger was found on the lawn under trees on the far left

Charles Manson arrives at Inyo County Courthouse in Independence, California, for a preliminary hearing on charges of arson and receiving stolen goods. He wasn't a suspect in the Tate/LaBianca killings at the time that this picture was taken

Charles Manson entering court in LA

Sandra Good, 31 (left), and Lynette 'Squeaky' Fromme (right) in 'Family photo'

Susan Denise Atkins (left) and Patricia Krenwinkel (2nd from right) arrive in court with Manson

Charles Manson in court looking youthful and fresh-faced, unlike the stereotyped images we have of him

Leslie Van Houten arriving at her retrial in LA for the LaBianca murders

Charles 'Tex' Watson arriving in court for his arraignment on charges of conspiracy and murder in the Tate/LaBianca slayings. Watson was arraigned on the charges, but further psychiatric examinations were ordered

Manson girls share a joke – Susan Atkins (left), Patricia Krenwinkel and Leslie Van Houten (right) are led toward the courtroom where they would be sentenced to death

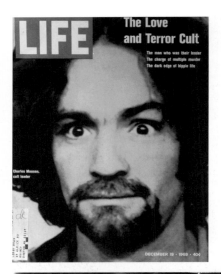

The cover of the December 1969 issue of *Life* magazine fixed the image of Manson as a hypnotic manipulator in the public mind

The *Life* magazine story was the definitive account of the Family until Bugliosi and Ed Sanders wrote their books

Los Angeles prosecutor Vincent Bugliosi as he leaves the courtroom during Manson's trial

Terry Melcher, 27-year-old son of actress Doris Day, at the Los Angeles County grand jury probe into the Sharon Tate murder case

Lynette 'Squeaky' Fromme shown leaving the courthouse after her first hearing on the charge of attempting to assassinate President Gerald Ford

Manson in front of the Parole Board, 1992

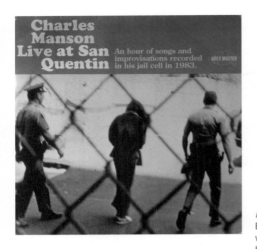

Manson Live At San Quentin parodies The Beach Boys' Pet Sounds album. The tapes were recorded in Manson's cell and had to be smuggled out of prison

'Lie' was released by Phil Kaufman soon after the trial and later on cult label ESP-Disk

wall in Hinman's blood in an attempt to make the killing look like the work of the Black Panthers. (The word *pig* as an insulting term for the police or members of the establishment had been in common currency throughout the counter-culture in 1968 and 1969, though its origins were in the Black Panther slogan 'Off the pig!') A few days later he was arrested driving Hinman's Toyota in San Jose. He told police that the Black Panthers had killed Hinman and that he, Beausoleil, had arrived while Hinman was dying. He then told them that the dying man had told him that he wanted him to have the car, signed it over and gave him the keys as his dying act. The fact that the knife used to kill Hinman was still on the back seat of the car rather undermined the plausibility of this story. Beausoleil was held at LA County Prison, made his phone call to Manson at the Spahn ranch and told him that he had been arrested but that he hadn't told the police anything.

According to Beausoleil, however, what actually happened is that Manson and Bruce Davis arrived at Hinman's house after he had managed to conclude things amicably, Hinman having agreed to sign over the two vehicles – a Fiat with a Toyota engine and a Volkswagen bus – to him. Manson then took out a sword that had been given to him by Danny DeCarlo and slashed Hinman across the face, saying, 'That's how to be a man!' Beausoleil then tried to stitch up the wound in Hinman's face, but it was not helping. Hinman wanted to go to the hospital, which Beausoleil knew would then entail police involvement, and in his panic, as the situation spiralled out of control, he then killed Hinman.

One version of events casts Manson as a mind-controlling mastermind, a puppet-master sending his obedient servants out to do his business. The other shows Manson acting like a thug and messing up a situation that had already been resolved.

It is at this point that conjecture as to the actual motives and reasons for the spate of killings gets hazy and confused. Bugliosi's theory – that Manson wanted to spark a race war – is not incompatible with the suggestion that Manson sent his followers out to commit a series of copycat murders to draw suspicion away from

Bobby, to give police the impression that the 'real' killer was still at large. He believed that, by killing the Hollywood wealthy, he would be showing the way to black militants, who were incapable of doing anything unless a white man showed them how. By stealing wallets and credit cards from the victims and dumping them in black neighbourhoods, where they would be found and hopefully used, Manson would point the finger at his imaginary movement of LA Mau Maus. He also believed that the backlash from the whites would spark off the race war.

We should remember that these are not exactly master criminals; Manson was at best a petty thief. Also, the copious quantities of acid, combined with a desert environment in which people were entering into a shared belief that was mostly fantasy and paranoia in equal measure, did not exactly help anyone to think through all of the consequences of their actions.

Beausoleil was arrested on 6 August. On 8 August, Charlie told Tex Watson to go and break into a house and kill anyone inside. 'Don't forget to leave a sign,' he said.

Again it is unclear whether Manson wanted to kill Terry Melcher – he was actually aware that he was no longer a resident of Cielo Drive – or to send him a message. Bugliosi suggests that they chose the house simply because they knew the layout and the route to it, and because it was in a quiet and secluded locale where they could be reasonably certain that they would not be disturbed.

Tex Watson, Susan Atkins, Patricia Krenwinkel and Linda Kasabian set off up Benedict Canyon Road with Manson's words 'Now is the time for Helter Skelter' ringing in their ears.

Roman Polanski was in Europe scouting locations for a forthcoming film. Sharon Tate, eight months pregnant with their first child (which she and Roman planned to name Paul if a boy) was not alone at the house on Cielo Drive. Friends of Roman's – Abigail 'Gibby' Folger, heiress to the coffee fortune, and Wojiceich (Voytek) Frykowski, film buff and confidant of Polanski's from Poland – were also in residence, ostensibly to look after Sharon. It has been rumoured over the years that Frykowski had taken nude photographs of women by the pool at the residence while Sharon was in Europe. Jay Sebring, former boyfriend of Sharon Tate before her marriage to Roman, enjoyed an international reputation for his hair-styling salons. He was the sort of character that Warren Beatty's role in the 1970s comedy film *Shampoo* was based on: hip and heterosexual in a world where hairdressers were presumed to be gay. Sebring's customers included Frank Sinatra, Peter Lawford, George Peppard, Paul Newman and Steve McQueen; he was a friend of Bruce Lee and studied martial arts at his 'kung fu' school. Sebring was also known as a 'candyman', a supplier of illegal substances to the Hollywood hip. So was Frykowski. On the night of the killing, Frykowski had secured a batch of MDA (ecstasy), which was a comparatively unknown drug at that time. Everyone apart from Sharon was loved up.

Abigail went to bed while Frykowski fell asleep on the living-room couch, listening to the stereo. Sharon and Jay went to her bedroom and smoked a joint.

Tex and the girls drove up to the house wearing black clothes, as Charlie had ordered them to do. Tex did most of the talking in the car on the way up the hill, explaining that the house had been chosen because he had been there before, with Charlie and Dennis Wilson, and he knew the layout. He also said that Manson had been up and had been treated disrespectfully by the new residents. Actually, Watson knew the house very well indeed; after Melcher moved out of 10050 Cielo Drive, but before the Polanskis moved in, Gregg Jakobson had arranged for Dean and Ruth Ann Morehouse to live there briefly. Tex Watson had visited them there at least three times.

Steven Earl Parent, 18 years old, was working at two jobs and saving for college. His friend William Garretson was a groundskeeper at the Polanski/Tate residence on Cielo Drive. His body was the first one that the police found the next day.

As his car slid down the driveway, Watson jumped out. One of the girls heard a voice say, 'Please don't hurt me. I won't say anything.' Then there were four gunshots.

They then walked up to the house, past the garage. It was a muggy night – still unbearably hot, even after dark – and a lot of the windows had been left open. Watson climbed in through one and unlocked the front door. Frykowski, lying on the couch, woke up as the four black-clad hippies entered, groggily asking them who they were and what they were doing there.

'I am the Devil and I'm here to do the Devil's business,' Watson replied. 'Where's your money?'

Watson ordered one of the girls to tie up Frykowski with the nylon cord they had brought with them. Susan wandered through the house, past the room in which Abigail Folger was reading a book. According to Atkins, the two smiled at each other. Next she saw Tate and Sebring and thought, 'Wow, what beautiful people.'

They were ordered at knife point into the living room. Sebring, angry that they were abusing pregnant Sharon, shouted at Watson 'Can't you see she's pregnant?' Watson shot him. They then took everyone's money; even though they had just shot Sebring, there was still a feeling that this was just a robbery. They were ordered to lie down on the floor. Watson tied Sharon to Sebring. Then he told them he was going to kill all of them and started wildly stabbing Sebring. He ordered Atkins to kill Frykowski, which she did. Frykowski fought back but Watson hit him over the head with a gun butt. 'He was full of blood,' she said and claimed that she had stabbed Frykowski three or four times: 'He was bleeding and he ran to the front part, and would you believe that he was there hollering, "Help! Help! Somebody please help me," and nobody came. Then we finished him off.' She then tied the cord around Sharon Tate's throat. Sharon begged for her life but Atkins replied, 'Woman, I have no mercy for you.'

Sharon sobbed that she only wanted to have her baby. Tex then ordered her to kill Sharon. Atkins says that she saw Sharon as being no more human than as a store mannequin.

When asked if killing Sharon Tate bothered her at all, Atkins answered, 'I thought you understood. I loved her, and in order for me to kill her, I was killing part of myself when I killed her.' This is an echo of Manson: 'If you kill a human being, you're just killing part of yourself; it has no meaning. Death is psychosomatic.'

Susan had wanted to cut out Sharon's baby, but there wasn't

enough time. She had also wanted to take out all the victims' eyes and squash them against the walls and cut off and mutilate all of their fingers, but they didn't have the chance.

Susan said she saw that there was Sharon's blood on her hand and she tasted it. 'Wow, what a trip! To taste death, and yet give life.'

She thought about how proud Charlie would be if she cut the baby from Sharon's womb and presented it to him. Then she went and got a towel, dipped it in Sharon's blood, and wrote a message on the door.

Back at the ranch, Charlie ordered the girls to clean any traces of blood from the car and to check it thoroughly, inside and out. Then, in the bunk room, Tex recounted the night's events: 'Boy, it sure was Helter Skelter.'

Charlie told everyone to go to bed and get some sleep and not to talk about what had happened to anyone.

On the morning of 8 August, Winifred Chapman, who worked as a maid at the Polanski house, ran screaming out onto the road: 'There's bodies and blood all over the place!'

Parent was found in his Rambler with one stab wound (inflicted as he defended himself) and four gunshot wounds, which had led to his death. The wheels of the car were turned as though he had made one last desperate attempt to escape. Just inside the door lay Frykowski's body, having been stabbed and shot. Under a fir tree 20 yards down the lawn lay the body of Abigail Folger, dressed in a nightgown, curled up and covered in blood. Inside lay the bodies of Sharon Tate and Jay Sebring. They were connected by a nylon cord wrapped around their necks and thrown over a beam in the house. Sebring had been shot. Inside the front door, the word *Pig* had been written in blood. LA police are hardened to all sorts of crime, but this was something way out of the ordinary.

William Garretson, the groundskeeper, was arrested and charged with five counts of murder. In a state of shock, he kept repeating that he had heard nothing and seen nothing. Garretson had slept through the murders.

A wave of horror spread throughout Hollywood and the city of Los Angeles as news of the murders broke.

What Joan Didion wrote in her essay 'The White Album: A Chronicle Of Survival In The '60s' (from her 1979 collection of writings) helped define California as the paranoia capital of the world: 'On August 9 I was sitting in the shallow end of my sister-in-law's swimming pool in Beverly Hills when she received a telephone call from a friend who had just heard about the murders at Sharon Tate Polanski's home. I also remember this and I wish I did not: I remember that no one was surprised.'

Paramount Pictures producer Peter Bart, quoted in *Easy Riders, Raging Bulls,* said, 'Roman was the most brilliant man, the best read, most cultured director I have ever met in my life. But in those days people who were close to Roman had a tendency to die.'

There was a lot of knowing shaking of heads. Rumours spread that Sharon was a student of voodoo, that she had attended a Black Mass at Jay Sebring's home. Then there was speculation about the state of Sharon and Roman's marriage, the fact that ex-boyfriend Sebring was with her on the night of her death. It was almost as if her 'immorality' led to her death. One detective, interviewed by *Life* magazine, said, 'You wouldn't believe how weird these people were. If you live like that, what do you expect?' Or, as one of the neighbours on Cielo Drive told reporters, 'Live freaky, die freaky.'

Stories spread like wildfire through the film-and-music community. A few months earlier, Polanski had tried to get Warren Beatty to take over the lease on the house. Steve McQueen, who was supposed to have been at the house on Cielo Drive on the night of the murders, started to carry a loaded gun with him at all times. Gun ownership boomed. Others in the neighbourhood bought attack dogs. Within days, people like producer Robert Towne, who lived on Hutton Drive, quite near to Cielo Drive, locked up and moved. But it was only the beginning.

In London, Roman Polanski received the news and flew back on the first flight to LA, crying all the way. He was met by two cops at the airport, who questioned him relentlessly. Roman suspected a lot of his own friends. Despite his marriage and the fact that Sharon was pregnant, he had been having affairs all through the summer of 1969. He had recently slept with Michelle Phillips of The Mamas And Papas and briefly suspected that her husband and bandmate John Phillips, whom he alleged had threatened him with a meat cleaver, might actually be responsible.

'Mary [Brunner] and I were in jail the night of the murders,' Manson Family member Sandra Good recalled, 'and we picked up the paper and Mary said, "Right on," and I said "Wow, they finally did it."'

In fact, most of the others at the Spahn ranch were not aware at the time that they had had any involvement in the killings. Atkins and Kasabian learned the next day who the victims had been when they saw news reports on TV.

That night, Manson told Atkins, Leslie Van Houten, Tex Watson, Patricia Krenwinkel and Steve 'Clem' Grogan to get a change of clothing and meet him in the bunkhouse.

At around the same time, Rosemary and Leno LaBianca were returning to LA from a weekend away. Their boat in tow, they stopped at the Chevron station on Hillhurst for gas and a newspaper. Rosemary commented on the front-page story about the Tate murders of the previous night. They arrived at their Silverlake home, 3301 Waverly Drive.

The Manson group went out in the same car – borrowed from a ranch hand at the Spahn – and drove around. Then they stopped. Manson got out of the car.

A while later, he returned. He started telling them what they had done wrong: Tex had let the people know that they were going to be killed. That was wrong. It caused panic. He, Charlie, had the people all tied up inside. He had reassured them that he was just there to rob the place. Then he told the others, 'Paint a picture more gruesome than anyone has ever seen.'

The group went inside and did just that. The LaBiancas were stabbed repeatedly. The word *War* was carved on Leno LaBianca's stomach and a fork stuck in his abdomen. Rosemary was stabbed 41 times. Evidence showed that she was stabbed long after she was dead.

The killers wrote 'Rise', 'Death to all pigs' and 'Healter Skelter' [*sic*] in the victims' blood on the walls. Then they all took showers and changed their clothes inside the house. Patricia Krenwinkel was fascinated by the fork in Leno's gut and kept touching it and watching it wobble backwards and forwards. As they were leaving, the LaBiancas' dog entered the house. They were surprised at how friendly it was and went into the kitchen to feed it before going out to the car.

The 'disconnected' behaviour of the killers has been wrongly ascribed to LSD. In fact, according to Watson, he was actually using crystal meth on the night of the murders: 'I was on methamphetamines. When I tell people that, they say, "I knew it!" It's commonly called "speed, the drug of violence" by users, and even the police, who use the term "cranker violence". Crystal meth was blamed by one national magazine for ending San Francisco's psychedelic scene in 1969, by turning the Haight from weeds and beads to crystals and pistols. Those on the stuff tend to be very erratic and violent. They do crazy and stupid things, including murder, like I did. The choice to take this or any drug only ends in destruction and death. Methamphetamines, or speed, affects the central nervous system. It made me feel alert and self-confident. On the other hand, it caused me to feel jittery and irritable. It made my speech unclear. Afterwards, I felt let down and depressed. What I remember most is that my emotions were dulled. I realise now that I was medicating my emotional pain, and as a result the feelings of others meant nothing. I only took meth for a month, but in that short period of time it took me over the edge. I believe it was a major contributing factor in my crime. I had been using it constantly for three weeks before the crime. During the murders, I felt like a mechanical man, a programmed machine out of control, like a malfunctioned robot unable to stop the brutality. It was like being on another planet; electricity filled the air. I was without restraint, empowered by the drug and without my normal inhibitions and personhood.'

Manson then ordered them all to drive towards Venice and stop at a gas station. He gave Susan Atkins the wallet stolen from Rosemary LaBianca and told her to leave it in the rest room in the hope that whoever found it would start using the credit cards and implicate themselves in the killings.

Leno and Rosemary LaBianca were discovered by their son, daughter and daughter's boyfriend. The men went further into the house and the young woman stayed behind in the kitchen. The men found the body of Leno and immediately called the police.

The Los Angeles Police Department, called to the scene of the Tate slaughter, did not immediately make any connection to the killing of Gary Hinman, despite the 'clues' left by the killers. Worse, because the LaBianca murder actually came under the jurisdiction of the Los Angeles Sheriff's Department – a separate agency with responsibility for policing Los Angeles County but not the city itself – the two departments did not initially share enough information to link the crimes.

At a press conference a few days after the second murders, LAPD inspector KJ McCauley told reporters, 'I don't see any connection between [the Tate] murder and the others. They're too widely removed. I just don't see any connection.' This, despite the fact that the Sheriff's Department had already told the LAPD about the writing on the wall at the LaBianca residence. They had also pointed out a possible link to the Hinman slaying in July, which the LAPD disregarded.

The two cases were worked separately. Also, the LAPD made several important procedural errors. According to Bugliosi in his book *Helter Skelter*, one officer noticed that there was blood on the button that operated the electric gates in the driveway to the house: 'Officer DeRosa, who was charged with securing and protecting the scene until investigating officers arrived, now pressed the button himself, successfully opening the gate but also creating a superimposure that obliterated any print that may have been there.'

According to Ed Sanders in *The Family*, the gun used in the murders was discovered by a boy in Los Angeles about two weeks later: 'The boy was careful not to touch the revolver to protect fingerprints. The police smudged it up and filed it away, the chambers of the weapon containing seven spent shells and two live bullets.'

Shortly after the murders, back at the Spahn ranch word about what had been done spread throughout the group living there, even those who were not involved. There was a smirking acknowledgement about the killings. Danny DeCarlo, the Straight Satans leader who later became the prosecution's star witness against Manson, says that he asked Steve 'Clem' Grogan what he had been up to. Grogan smiled and said, 'We got some piggies.' Even Manson wanted some recognition for his work, screaming at one ranch hand, 'You son of a bitch, don't you know that I'm the one who is doing all these killings?' Ultimately, the fact that the Family were so proud of their crimes would be their undoing.

They compiled a death list of other 'pigs' that they were going to get. According to Susan Atkins, the targets included Elizabeth Taylor and Richard Burton (who were then an item), Frank Sinatra, Tom Jones, Yul Brynner and Steve McQueen. She had planned to carve the words *helter skelter* on Elizabeth Taylor's face with a red-hot knife and then gouge out her eyes. Then she would castrate Richard Burton and put his penis along with Elizabeth Taylor's eyes in a bottle and mail it to Eddie Fisher (Taylor's ex-husband). Sinatra was to be skinned alive while he listened to his own music. The Family would then make purses out of his skin and sell them in hippy shops. Tom Jones would have his throat slit, but only after being forced to have sex with Susan Atkins (aka Sexy Sadie).

This may have been pure fantasy; while it was easy to get access to kill seemingly random, comparatively obscure victims, A-list celebrities had tight security even when there weren't homicidal hippies creeping around the Hollywood Hills. Just as this horror show was about to get under way, a veritable army of police and LA Sheriff's deputies arrived at the Spahn ranch to arrest Manson and his followers on 16 August, a week after the slaughters. Acting on a tip-off that a car-theft ring was operating in the area, centred on Manson's group, they had a search warrant and made 26 arrests, including those of Manson, various Family members and ranch hands. Finding no hard evidence and having the warrant valid only for the day that the raid took place, they were forced to release everyone.

When they returned to the Spahn ranch, Manson was furious. The main suspect for snitching to the authorities was a ranch hand called Donald 'Shorty' Shea. Manson disliked Shea, who was also unpopular with other Family members because he was a drunk. Manson surmised that Shea knew too much about their activities and at the very least would get them evicted. Manson, his lieutenant Bruce Davis and Tex Watson killed Shea. Thanks to Ed Sanders' book and the boasts of one of the killers, it was popularly believed for years that Manson beheaded

Shea with a sword. It was only when his body was recovered in 1990, after Steve 'Clem' Grogan had led authorities to the site of Shea's burial in an attempt to get a more favourable parole hearing, that it was found to be intact. He had spread this story, he claimed, on Manson's instructions, to make the killing seem more terrible, to spread fear among everyone living at the Spahn ranch.

The situation was becoming unmanageable so Manson moved his group out into Death Valley, to the more remote and isolated Barker ranch and Myers ranch. The Family spread out in camps, building dugouts and lookout posts. They accrued more guns, more stolen dune buggies, more cars and more knives and other weapons in preparation for Helter Skelter.

Life in Death Valley was markedly less comfortable than at Spahn. A change came over Manson; any gentleness was gone. He had transformed into an angry and wrathful father. He told the followers that they were a democratic set-up and everyone had a voice; it just so happened that he was acting on instructions from God.

Charlie told his minions to let scorpions crawl on them: 'You have to learn from them. They are the same as you. We're all here together.' One ranch hand who had settled in the Barker ranch recalls seeing Manson hypnotising rattlesnakes as though he had power over them.

The women were treated like dirt and the dogs were treated special. Charlie would say, 'Don't treat the dogs like people. Treat the dogs like dogs. They are better than people.' The dogs would eat first, then the men would eat the dog left-overs and the women would eat last.

Although Patricia Krenwinkel was the only Family member who allegedly showed any remorse at the time, others fled the scene. Charles Watson, who was still boasting of his involvement, returned to Texas. While there, he tormented his mother by telling her about how he had been involved in the murders. She did not believe him and thought it was mental illness brought on by his obvious drug use. Linda Kasabian and Mary Brunner also fled back to their parents.

On 19 September, a park ranger discovered a burnt-out vehicle and suspected arson. A few days later, a group of ragged hippies in a Toyota was picked up and questioned but later released. The vehicle was registered to Gail Beausoleil, wife of Bobby, incarcerated for the murder of Hinman. A local miner swore out a complaint about the half-naked hippies in Goler Wash indulging in sex orgies and drugs. A raid involving park rangers and the California Highway Patrol was arranged, a warrant was granted and their were targets identified.

The ranches were raided and everyone was taken to headquarters in Independence and booked on suspicion of arson. Manson was discovered hiding in a cupboard and was led away in chains. Some members who had slipped away a few hours before the raid were picked up trying to hitchhike away from the scene.

While in prison in Independence on theft charges, the girls insisted on going naked. Forced to wear dresses, they raised them up above their heads in the exercise yard. Manson, in his cell, would yip like a coyote and the girls would respond.

Having made a link to the Hinman murder, Susan Atkins readily confessed her involvement after another Family member pointed the finger at her and was taken to a women's prison in Los Angeles. Susan Atkins was placed in the Sybil Brand Institute. Her bed was next to that of a former call girl named Ronnie Howard. Another inmate, Virginia Graham, was a close friend of Ronnie's. Susan acted strangely, dancing and singing, laughing inappropriately. She also talked incessantly about her lover Charlie, who was Jesus Christ, and how he was going to lead her to a hole in the Earth in Death Valley where there was an underground civilisation. She told Virginia Graham about her involvement in the murders, describing them in lurid and gleeful detail. Virginia Graham told Ronnie Howard and, at first, they were incredulous. She described the death list and their gory plan for the Burtons. Ronnie Howard tried to get permission to go to the LAPD but was denied, even though the woman who denied her permission was actually dating one of the detectives investigating the Tate murder. Virginia Graham was transferred to another prison and was also unable to get permission to talk to the police. Finally, on 17 November 1969, two LAPD homicide detectives came to Sybil Brand to interview Ronnie Howard. After they interviewed her, they had her moved for her own safety into an isolation unit.

Susan Atkins agreed to co-operate with the prosecution in return for leniency – a guarantee that she would not be sentenced to death.

Watson was arrested in Texas and, on 18 November 1969, 35-year-old Deputy District Attorney Vincent T Bugliosi was assigned the Tate/LaBianca murder cases. Not only did he need to prove that members of the Manson Family were responsible for the Tate and LaBianca murders but he also had to prove that Charles Manson had ordered them to do it. He had to prove that Manson had masterminded the killings, which was a difficult task. They could place Manson as an accessory to the LaBianca killing, because he had gone to the house and tied them up, but there was no evidence that Manson had actually killed anyone.

The impact on the city of Los Angeles, the Hollywood set and the counter-culture worldwide was profound; 1969 had been the year of the high-water mark of the hippies, at Yasgur's Farm in upstate New York at the end of August 1969, about three weeks after the Tate/LaBianca murders but before Manson was named as the perpetrator. Woodstock, the legendary free concert that attracted half a million people to a muddy field with all of the top bands of the day – Joan Baez, The Band, Blood, Sweat And Tears, The Paul Butterfield Blues Band, Canned Heat, Joe Cocker, Country Joe And The Fish, Creedence Clearwater Revival, Crosby, Stills, Nash And Young, The Grateful Dead, Arlo Guthrie, Tim Hardin, Richie Havens, Jimi Hendrix, The Incredible String Band, Janis Joplin, Jefferson Airplane, Melanie, Mountain, Santana, John Sebastian, Ravi Shankar, Sha Na Na, Sly And The Family Stone, Ten Years After, The Who, Johnny Winter – and enormous quantities of LSD and marijuana, was the culmination of everything that had gone on in San Francisco and worldwide. It was a coming together of a new nation based on peace, love and good music. It seemed like a new and better world might still emerge from the love generation.

Although it was a disaster – the promoters had expected 100,000 people, but most of the 450,000 who arrived did not pay, perpetual rain turned the site into a swamp and emergency food and blankets had to be helicoptered in – it was a symbol of hippydom.

Arnold Skolnick, the artist who designed the Woodstock poster, said, 'Something was tapped, a nerve in this country, and everybody just came.' Woodstock came to symbolise all that was right and good about the hippy movement but also that the movement was to be short-lived. In December, The Rolling Stones staged a free concert at a race track in Altamont, California. The Stones didn't want any establishment 'pigs' on the site, so they employed the Hell's Angels motorcycle club to provide security. Altamont turned ugly when members of the Hell's Angels attacked and killed a man near the stage where The Rolling Stones were performing. It was the anti-Woodstock. News about Manson was out and things didn't look quite so rosy for the longhairs.

In *Easy Riders, Raging Bulls*, Peter Biskind writes, 'Intimidating automatic gates that had heretofore been beneath contempt in the Age of Aquarius became *de rigueur*. People scrambled to get on the I-almost-got-killed bandwagon. "If half the people who were supposed to be there that night had gone, it would have rivalled Jonestown," says [Buck] Henry. It was as if people wanted to have been part of it, slaughtered like animals for some dark purpose of their own. This wasn't death at the hands of the "pigs", as *Bonnie And Clyde*, *The Wild Bunch* and *Easy Rider* had fantasised it; it was a much better, more frightening script: Manson was themselves, a hippy, the essence of the '60s. If Hollywood was the forbidden planet, he was the monster from the id... [Buck Henry:] "To me it was the defining event of our time. It affected everybody's work, it affected the way people thought about other people." Manson wanted [Dennis] Hopper to star in a film version of his life. Hopper didn't want to meet him, because Sebring was a good friend of his, but curiosity finally triumphed over scruple.'

Hopper, co-star and director of 1969's surprise movie hit *Easy Rider*, assumed that Manson had seen the film and wanted him because of his hippy-cool cachet. As it turned out, when Hopper visited Manson in jail, he had actually seen him as a guest star in an early 1960s TV show called *The Defenders* (a drama about court-appointed public defenders) where Hopper's character had killed his father because he beat up his mother. According to Peter Biskind, 'Manson missed his calling. It was inspired casting – he should have been a producer – but Hopper never did do the movie.'

There was palpable shock in Haight-Ashbury and in the hippy

hangouts around Sunset Strip. The hostility that they had always got from cops and straights now took on a new dimension; as well as hostility, they were actually feared.

The 19 December 1969 cover of *Life* magazine featured a chilling cover shot of Manson, a UPI agency shot taken at his arraignment hearing, black-eyed and staring into the void, and the story inside was the first detailed look that America got at 'the dark edge of hippy life'.

For the LA newspapers, the Manson Family was bread and butter and, as the whole horror show unfolded in the courtroom, the *LA Times* mixed its revulsion with a fascination with the lurid details.

Some elements in the counter-culture were openly celebrating Manson as an icon. The underground magazine *Tuesday's Child* – a rival to the more successful *Rolling Stone* – splashed Manson over its front cover with the headline 'Charles Manson: Man Of The Year' and a grovelling feature about the killings. The Weathermen, the radical terrorist faction of the SDS (which has the dubious distinction of having bombed the Pentagon before Al Qu'eda), also celebrated Manson. 'Dig it! Manson killed those pigs, then they ate dinner in the same room with them, then they shoved a fork into a victim's stomach,' said Bernardine Dohrn, one of the leaders of the movement and one-time star of the FBI's Most Wanted list who spent years in hiding to avoid charges of inciting riots and conspiring to bomb police stations and other government buildings. In December 1969, the SDS Weathermen faction staged a National War Council in Flint, Michigan, and toasted Manson by repeatedly stabbing three fingers in the air, symbolising the forks '…that "Comrade Manson" and his girlfriends had plunged into his victims' entrails'.

On 5 December 1969, Susan Atkins testified before Los Angeles County Grand Jury. She was still enamoured by the Family's acts and spelled out in loving detail for several hours the details of the killings, affectionately describing how Manson had masterminded them. Indictments were issued for Manson, Atkins, Watson, Kasabian and Krenwinkel for seven counts of murder and one of conspiracy to commit murder.

11 The Day Of Judgement

'History will be kind to me for I intend to write it.'
— *Winston Churchill*

The trial opened in July 1970 and was the first event for which the term *media circus* seemed truly appropriate. Manson and his followers assumed crucifixion poses and asked the court, 'Why don't you just kill us now?'

Presiding over the trial was Judge William Older. There were over five weeks of jury selections and pre-trial motions before Bugliosi opened the case for the people. Manson had requested that he be allowed to defend himself, a motion denied by the judge. In the end he was defended by Irving Kanarek, an attorney with a reputation as a pedantic and obstructive fighter who wore down judges and juries by a relentless barrage of points, digressions and irrelevances. The LA District Attorney's office at one point petitioned the State Supreme Court to order a competency hearing for Kanarek, though this was denied. Manson, Atkins, Kasabian and Krenwinkel arrived in court with their attorneys. (Watson was still fighting extradition from Texas.) Manson had carved an X on his forehead with a razor.

His followers handed out a statement from Manson that read, 'Your courtroom is man's game. Love is my judge. No man or lawyer is speaking for me. I speak for myself. I am not allowed to speak with words so I have spoken with the mark I will be wearing on my forehead.'

Manson's followers, such as Ruth Ann Morehouse, Lynette 'Squeaky' Fromme and Sandra Good, all gathered outside the courtroom, 'performing' for the reporters and TV cameras. Throughout the trial they kept the vigil, sitting in circles, singing, dancing, sometimes sitting in the public gallery and giggling during a particularly gruesome piece of evidence. They came with babies and revelled in the tabloid press's description of them as 'Satan's slaves'.

Inside the court, Bugliosi made his opening statement: 'A question you ladies and gentlemen will probably ask yourselves at some point during this trial, and we expect the evidence to answer that question for you, is this: "What kind of a diabolical mind would contemplate or conceive of these seven murders? What kind of mind would want to have seven human beings brutally murdered?" We expect the evidence at this trial to answer that question and show that defendant Charles Manson owned that diabolical mind. Charles Manson, who the evidence will show at times had the infinite humility, as it were, to refer to himself as Jesus Christ. Evidence at this trial will show defendant Manson to be a vagrant wanderer, a frustrated singer/guitarist, a pseudo-philosopher, but, most of all, the evidence will conclusively prove that Charles Manson is a killer who cleverly masqueraded behind the common image of a hippy, that of being peace loving...'

With the exception of Leslie Van Houten's attorney, Maxwell Keith, the defence arguments were bizarre and half-hearted, attacking the testimony of witnesses like Danny DeCarlo and Virginia Graham. Maxwell Keith argued that his client had not actually killed anyone, merely stabbed Rosemary LaBianca after she was already dead: 'As repugnant as you may feel this is, nobody in the world can be guilty of murder or conspiracy to commit murder who stabs somebody after they are already dead. I'm sure that desecrating somebody that is dead is a crime in this state, but she is not charged with that.'

The first witness called by the prosecution was Sharon's father, Paul Tate. He had been a lieutenant-colonel in US Army Intelligence and had had a long and distinguished career. He had resigned after the murders and spent months conducting his own investigation, growing his hair long and wearing psychedelic clothes, trawling through the anti-establishment world from which he rightly believed his daughter's killers had sprang.

The story of Paul Tate delving through the underworld was later the inspiration behind a film called *Hardcore*, directed by Paul

Schraeder, whose other screen credits included the scripts for *Taxi Driver* and *Patty Hearst*.

There were rumours that Tate had sworn to kill Manson; the bailiffs made a point of frisking him thoroughly before he entered the courtroom, as though they fully expected him to be carrying a loaded weapon, which he would pull out and use to gun down Manson. It may also have been a bit of psychological warfare by the prosecution in an attempt to unnerve Manson. But Tate's appearance was undramatic. He confirmed that the photos shown were of his daughter, Folger, Sebring and Frykowski, and confirmed that the last time he had seen her alive was on 20 July 1969, when he had visited Cielo Drive to watch the moon landing.

Susan Atkins withdrew her co-operation after having testified to the Grand Jury. Linda Kasabian's lawyer managed to cut her a deal for immunity in return for her testimony against her former associates and lover. As she was sworn in, Manson's appointed attorney, Kanarek, stood: 'Objection, Your Honour, on the grounds this witness is not competent and she is insane!'

Bugliosi was furious: 'Wait a minute, Your Honour. I move to strike that, and I ask the Court to find him in contempt for gross misconduct. This is unbelievable on his part!'

'There is no question about it, your conduct is outrageous,' the judge agreed.

The cross-examination began with Bugliosi asking Kasabian, 'Linda, you realise that you are presently charged with seven counts of murder and one count of conspiracy to commit murder?'

'Yes,' she replied.

Kanarek again stood up, this time motioning for a mistrial. This was to continue throughout the cross-examination of Kasabian until, finally, the judge lost patience, cited him for contempt of court and ordered him to spend the night locked up in the county jail.

Later in the trial, Manson asked if he could cross-examine a witness: Los Angeles Sheriff's Office detective Paul Whiteley. 'No you may not,' said the judge.

Manson replied, 'You are going to use this courtroom to kill me?

May I examine him, Your Honour? I am going to fight for my life one way or another. You should let me do it with words.'

'If you don't stop, I will have to have you removed,' said the judge.

'I will have you removed if you don't stop. I have a little system of my own,' said Manson.

With a pencil clutched in his right hand, Manson suddenly leapt over the counsel table in the direction of Judge Older. He landed just a few feet from the bench, falling on one knee. As he was struggling to his feet, the bailiff leapt too, landing on Manson's back. Manson's arms were pinned and he was dragged out of court shouting, 'In the name of Christian justice, someone should cut your head off!' Atkins, Krenwinkel and Van Houten then stood and began chanting in Latin.

Older, a veteran of the Second World War, said, 'If he had taken one more step, I would have done something to defend myself.'

The trial dragged on, occasionally erupting into farce. On 3 August, President Richard Nixon berated the media for their 'glorification' of criminals: 'The coverage of the Charles Manson case is front page every day in the papers. It usually got a couple of minutes in the evening news. Here is a man who was guilty, directly or indirectly, of eight murders, yet here is a man who, as far as the coverage is concerned, appeared to be a glamorous figure.'

Nixon did not qualify his statement with 'allegedly'.

The next day the papers all picked up on the story. The *LA Times* splashed the banner headline 'MANSON GUILTY, NIXON DECLARES' across its front page. The White House press office tried to smooth over Nixon's gaffe. Nixon issued a statement: 'I have been informed that my comment in Denver regarding the Tate murder trial in Los Angeles may continue to be misunderstood despite the unequivocal statement made at the time by my press secretary. The last thing I would do is prejudice the legal rights of any person, in any circumstances. To set the record straight, I do not now and did not intend to speculate as to whether the Tate defendants are guilty, in fact or not. As the facts in the case have not yet been presented, the defendants should be presumed to be innocent at this stage of the trial.'

But the damage was done. Although newspapers were banned from the courtroom and the jury were held in seclusion at a hotel away from the press, radio and television, one of the defence attorneys picked up a confiscated paper, he claimed, to read the sports pages. Somehow it found its way to the defendants. Manson produced a copy of the *LA Times*, held it up for the jury to see, and smiled. Atkins, Krenwinkel and Van Houten stood up and said in perfect unison, 'Your Honour, the President said we are guilty, so why go on with the trial?'

There was almost a declaration of a mistrial and proceedings were held up as every single person on the jury had to be polled and cross-examined to find out if they had been prejudiced by the headline.

At one point, Manson complained to the judge that he was not being given a chance to defend himself in his own words. On 19 November, the judge removed the jury – fearful that Manson might 'hypnotise them into believing that he was innocent' – and asked if he had anything to say. Manson said, 'Yes, I do,' and delivered a self-justifying monologue that took nearly three hours, involving a recess being called. As an insight into Manson's power as an orator, a transcript of the sort of raps he would deliver to his followers in Haight-Ashbury, in the Spahn ranch and deep in Death Valley, it is unsurpassed. He employs repetition, speaking in rhythms, making his points as a series of pithy epithets.

He denied that he was a racist, that he had invented Helter Skelter: 'You invent stories, and everybody thinks what they do, and then they project it from the witness stand on the defendant, as if that is what he did. For example, with Danny DeCarlo's testimony. He said that I hate black men, and he said that we thought alike, that him and I was a lot alike in our thinking. But actually all I ever did with Danny DeCarlo or any other human being was reflect himself back at himself. If he said he did not like the black man, I would say, "OK." I had better sense than tell him I did not dislike the black man. I just listened to him and I would react to his statement, so consequently he would drink another beer and walk off and pat me on the back and he would say to himself, "Charlie thinks like I do." But actually he does not know how Charlie thinks because Charlie has never projected himself.'

He returned over and over to this theme, that he is a reflection. He also denied that Helter Skelter was anything to do with race war: 'Like, Helter Skelter is a nightclub. Helter Skelter means confusion. Literally. It doesn't mean any war with anyone. It doesn't mean that those people are going to kill other people. It only means what it means. Helter Skelter is confusion. Confusion is coming down fast. If you don't see the confusion coming down fast around you, you can call it what you wish. It is not my conspiracy. It is not my music. I hear what it relates. It says, "Rise!" It says, "Kill!" Why blame it on me? I didn't write the music. I am not the person who projected it into your social consciousness, that sanity that you projected into your social consciousness, today. You put so much into the newspaper and then you expect people to believe what is going on. I say back to the facts again.

'You made me a monster and I have to live with that the rest of my life because I cannot fight this case. If I could fight this case and I could present this case, I would take that monster back and I would take that fear back. Then you could find something else to put your fear on, because it's all your fear.

'You look for something to project it on and you pick a little old scroungy nobody who eats out of a garbage can, that nobody wants, that was kicked out of the penitentiary, that has been dragged through every hellhole you can think of, and you drag him up and put him into a courtroom.

'You expect to break me? Impossible! You broke me years ago. You killed me years ago. I sat in a cell and the guy opened the door and he said, "You want out?"

'I looked at him and I said, "Do you want out?" You are in jail, all of you, and your whole procedure. The procedure that is on you is worse than the procedure that is on me. I like it in there.

'I like it in there – it's peaceful. I just don't like coming to the courtroom. I would like to get this over with as soon as possible. And I'm sure everyone else would like to get it over with, too.

'Without being able to prepare a case, without being able to confront the witnesses and to bring out the emotions, and to bring out the reasons why witnesses say what they say, and why this hideous thing has developed into the trauma that it's moved into, would take a bigger courtroom and it would take a bigger public, a bigger press, because you all, as big as you are, know what you are as I know what you are, and I like you anyway. I don't want to keep rehashing the same things over. There are so many things that you can get into, Your Honour, that I have no thoughts on. It is hard to think when you really don't care too much one way or the other.'

He summed up by saying, 'Prison's in your mind... Can't you see I'm free?'

It was hypnotic – Manson employed many of the techniques that are taught to salesmen in neuro-linguistic programming seminars today, something with its roots in the murky pseudo-psychology of Scientology, EST and the pseudo-psychological self-improvement in which Manson was steeped.

Finally, on 13 January 1971, Bugliosi began his summing up for the people: 'On the hot summer night of August 8, 1969, Charles Manson, the Mephistophelian guru who raped and bastardised the minds of all those who gave their selves so totally to him sent out from the fires of hell at Spahn ranch three heartless, bloodthirsty robots and – unfortunately for him – one human being...Linda Kasabian. The photographs of the victims show the world how Watson, Atkins and Krenwinkel carried out Charles Manson's mission of murder. What resulted was perhaps the most horror-filled hour of savage murder and human slaughter in the recorded annals of crime. As the defenceless victims begged and screamed out into the night, their lifeblood gushed out of their bodies...forming rivers of gore. Krenwinkel would gladly have swum in that river of blood, and with orgasmic ecstasy on [her face] Susan Atkins, the vampire, actually tasted Sharon Tate's blood...

'The very next night, Leslie Van Houten joined the group of murderers, and it was poor Leno and Rosemary LaBianca who were brutally butchered to death to satisfy Charles Manson's homicidal madness... The prosecution put on a monumental amount of evidence against these defendants, much of it scientific, all of it conclusively proving that these defendants committed these murders. Based on the evidence that came from that witness stand, not only isn't there any reasonable doubt of their guilt, which is our only burden, there is absolutely no doubt whatsoever of their guilt. Ladies and gentlemen, the prosecution did its job in gathering and presenting the evidence. The witnesses did their job by taking that witness stand and testifying under oath. Now you are the last link in the chain of justice.

'Ladies and gentlemen of the jury, Sharon Tate...Abigail Folger...Voytek Frykowski...Jay Sebring...Steven Parent...Leno LaBianca...Rosemary LaBianca...are not here with us now in this courtroom, but from their graves they cry out for justice. Justice can only be served by coming back to this courtroom with a verdict of guilty. You have been an exemplary jury. The plaintiff at this trial is the people of the state of California. I have all the confidence in the world that you will not let them down.'

On Monday 25 January, the jury returned to a courtroom packed with reporters, spectators, and the friends and relatives of the dead: 'We the jury in the above suited action find the defendant Charles Manson guilty of murder, in violation of the penal code 187, a felony, and we further find it to be murder in the first degree.'

Manson got angry: 'You are all guilty! We weren't able to put on a defence, old man! And you won't forget it for a long time.'

Manson was sentenced to death, as were his co-defendants.

Manson always maintained his innocence and claimed that he was denied a fair trial with the right to defend himself. Subsequent interviews and statements have reiterated his belief that he has no responsibility for the killings. 'I had some friends who killed some people,' he said bitterly.

At his 1992 parole hearing, Manson said, 'I was never on the scene where anyone was killed. I think the law says you can only keep me 17 years or 18 years if I was never on the scene when anyone was killed. I was never on the crime scene of anything.

'The closest I came to the crime scene is I cut Hinman's ear off in a fight over some money because the Frenchman [Bobby Beausoleil] – he wouldn't pay the Frenchman and I told him, why don't he be a man about himself and pay his debts? And we had a fight.

'So to... In order to hook me up to that, they say, "Well, they tortured the dude three days." I was gone from that scene of that crime for three days. I was never on the scene of any crime. I never told anyone directly to do, to go anywhere and do anything.

'I always said – and mostly it come from the witness stand – I said, like, "You know what to do. You have a brain of your own. Don't ask me what to do, I've just got out of prison. I don't know what's going on out here." I hadn't been out of jail long enough to really get a perspective of what was happening.

'I just was released from McNeil Island and I was in Mexico City prison before that and I was in Terminal Island before that, so I really wasn't up on the 1960s as much as you all make me out to be. I had just got out of prison.

'Most of those people, I – like Kasabian, I knew her two weeks. I had seen her two or three times around the ranch. I had never even been with the broad, man, that much, you know. People came around me because I played a lot of music and I was fairly free and open because I really didn't know, honestly.

'Everyone says that I was the leader of those people, but I was actually the follower of the children because, like, I never grew up. I've been in jail most of this time, so I stayed in the minds of the children. And I'm pretty much a street person so violence is no new thing to me. And people getting hurt around me is no new thing.

'I've lived in prison all my life. That happens all the time. I've always walked on a line. In Ohio, Kentucky, Indiana, all across this country. Cook County jail, Chicago, it's always about fighting. That's part of everyday life where I live, you know?

'So, a lot of the things that people were doing were just their own little episodes that they get involved in and they looked at me like I was something like a friend or a brother or a father or someone that understood, because I learned in prison that you can't really tell anyone anything because everybody's got their own perspective. And all you can do is reflect people back at themselves and let them make up their own mind about things.

'So, when Beausoleil come to me with, could I be a brother? I told him, "Certainly," you know? So we were, like, in a little brotherhood together, like we didn't lie to each other.

'And whatever he said do, I would do. And whatever I said do, he would do.

'But as far as lining up someone for some kind of Helter Skelter trip, you know, that's the district attorney's motive. That's the only thing he could find for a motive to throw up on top of all that confusion he had. There was no such thing in my mind as Helter Skelter. Helter Skelter was a song and it was a nightclub – we opened up a little after-hours nightclub to make some money and play some music and do some dancing and singing and play some stuff to make some money for dune buggies to go out in the desert. And we called the club Helter Skelter. It was a Helter Skelter club because we would be there and when the cops would come – we'd all melt into other dimensions because it wasn't licensed to be anything in particular. And that was kind of like a speakeasy back in the moonshine days behind the movie set.

'And I'm an outlaw. That's – they're right there, you know, and I'm a gangster and I'm bad and I'm all the things that I want to be. I'm pretty free within myself. I cut people and I shoot them and I do whatever I have to do to survive in the world I live in. But that has nothing to do with me breaking the line.'

Bobby Beausoleil, in an interview with writer Michael Moynihan, also casts doubt on the Helter Skelter motive: 'I guess, because I know the truth, to me that explanation seems ridiculously simplified. How can anybody not see through that? Murder by Beatles records – this is what happens if you listen to Beatles records and take LSD!? What could be a more blatant attempt to discredit the youth movement of the '60s than that? To use that theory as the basis of convicting these people stretches credibility to the breaking point. You know, one thing I've learned from all this is that the truth is coloured by the light. All of those books that were written about those events – Bugliosi's, Ed Sanders' and others – have a certain thread of factual truth, these collections of "facts". I suppose these chronological recordings of events that happened are reasonably accurate in terms of these facts, but the real truth of it does not come through those books. It's not in those facts. Knowing the people and knowing more or less what actually had happened, and then seeing how it's represented, is... I've learned how history is written, and it makes all of history suspect.'

The Beatles, who were friends of the Polanskis, were horrified, though in an interview in December 1970 John Lennon seemed almost to sympathise with Manson: 'I don't know what I thought when it happened. I just think a lot of the things he says are true, that he is a child of the state, made by us, and he took their children in when nobody else would, is what he did. Of course, he's cracked, all right.'

Lennon's ambivalence was reflected across the counter-culture. The idea that Manson was a 'plot' by the government to discredit the movement took root at that time, with many underground magazines almost refusing to believe what had gone down in the courtroom.

Speaking about the killings in an interview at the end of the 1970s, shortly before his own death, Lennon dismissed Manson and his followers as crank obsessives: 'It has nothing to do with me. It's like that guy, Son of Sam, who was having these talks with the dog. Manson was just an extreme version of the people who came up with the "Paul is dead" thing or who figured out that the initials to "Lucy In The Sky With Diamonds" were LSD and concluded I was writing about acid.'

Ringo said in *Anthology*, 'It was upsetting. I mean, I knew Roman Polanski and Sharon Tate and – God – it was a rough time. It stopped everyone in their tracks because suddenly all this violence came in the middle of all this love and peace and psychedelia. It was pretty miserable, actually, and everybody got really insecure – not just us, not just the rockers, but everyone in LA felt, "Oh God, it can happen to anybody." Thank God they caught the bugger.'

The reaction was swift. Hippies were demonised in the press, not merely as drug users and as kooky anti-establishment clowns who needed to take a bath. Assaults on hippies increased: right-wing, blue-collar, 'hard-hat' types who would taunt longhairs mercilessly in the past now perceived them as an actual threat. Urban legends about vicious killer hippies began to circulate, about longhairs giving kids who came to their house for Hallowe'en trick or treating candy laced with LSD (in another version it was apples with razor blades or with needles impregnated in their flesh). In LA, the rumour spread that Manson was only the tip of the iceberg and that there was in fact a huge army of disciples waiting for the word to continue the slaughter.

The details of the celebrity 'death list' were leaked to an underground newspaper and then to the mainstream press, heightening still further the already spiralling paranoia. Both the film hipsters and the rock 'n' rollers were beset seemingly on all sides by hostile hippies and squares who actually perceived them to be part of the hippy problem.

Dennis Wilson, still shocked by how close he had come to being a victim and thankful that he had only been taken for money, suddenly found himself *persona non grata* in certain circles. Even Roman Polanski, still viewed with suspicion of complicity, found it hard to get work; after directing his best ever film the multi-award-winning *Chinatown* in the wake of the murders, he actually experienced hostility from Hollywood and had problems getting suitable projects. His moody and bloody screen version of *Macbeth* – financed by associates at *Playboy* magazine and filmed in England – was met with a certain amount of embarrassment when it opened in the USA. Polanski was later to be hounded out of America after allegations of statutory rape were brought against him and there is no doubt in the minds of some that it was because people actually blamed him for his wife's death in some way.

A young English rock band called Black Sabbath, touring the USA for the first time after having released a successful eponymous debut album that melded heavy-electric blues riffs to 'Satanic' lyrics, found that, on the one hand, they were treated with revulsion by one sector of the audience, who wanted to distance themselves from the sleaze of the Manson trials, and that on the other they were starting to attract nutters who claimed to be part of the Family. The band then took to wearing large, prominent crucifixes at all times, popularly to 'ward off evil'.

One night in 1970, Jim Morrison of The Doors got drunk in LA – as he was wont to do – and fell asleep in someone's doorway. When the lady of the house opened the door to get her newspaper the next morning, she mistook him for Charles Manson (presuming him to have escaped from jail), an easy mistake to make as Jim at that time sported wild, raggy hair and a full-face beard. Morrison awoke to find himself surrounded by armed LAPD officers, who arrested him for public drunkenness.

Morrison was fortunate that he was not shot where he lay (his appointment with the reaper was still some weeks off). All over the affluent suburbs of Bel Air, Beverly Hills and Laurel Canyon, home-owners bought security gates and handguns to defend themselves and their property. Vigilante groups skulked around the Hollywood Hills, no doubt in the hope of catching some long-haired psychopath in the act.

The death sentences passed against Manson seemed like a beginning and not an end.

More was to come. Charles Watson was extradited from Texas to stand trial. Steve 'Clem' Grogan and Bruce Davis were also to be tried for their part in killing Donald 'Shorty' Shea, a case unusual in the history of California law because they had not recovered a body.

Davis, a cross carved on his head in imitation of Manson, walked barefoot to the court, declaring, 'I have come to free my father.'

Barbara Hoyt, a peripheral member of the Family, allegedly heard Susan Atkins tell Ruth Ann Morehouse that Sharon Tate had been the last to die because she had to see the others butchered first. When she arrived with them, Manson told her they had already left. Morehouse told Hoyt that she knew of ten other murders. She fled the Barker ranch just before the raid. The Family later contacted her and offered her a free trip to Hawaii if she didn't testify. She agreed and flew out to Honolulu with Ruth Ann Morehouse, under fake names with cash and stolen credit cards, and stayed in the penthouse suite of the Hilton Hawaiian Village Hotel. Hoyt then decided to return to LA. Morehouse bought her a hamburger and laced it with ten tabs of LSD – known as a 'weirdburger' – then left her. Hoyt entered a nightmare trip and started running until she collapsed and was taken to hospital. Her father brought her back to LA. That same day, they received death threats. Hoyt testified in September 1970 that Atkins had called her to the back house at Spahn and asked her to bring three sets of dark clothes to the front ranch on 8 August 1969, the night of the Tate murders.

Morehouse and four others were arraigned on charges of conspiracy to prevent and dissuade a witness from attending a trial. Morehouse was released because she was nearly nine months pregnant, and she fled to Nevada. She was never extradited and remains at liberty to this day.

Hoyt also told police that Morehouse had told her in Hawaii that Leslie Van Houten had only six months to live for co-operating with the prosecution. Ronald Hughes, the attorney who represented Leslie Van Houten during the murder trial, mysteriously disappeared and was found murdered months later.

Threats were made against witnesses. Judge Older was assigned a bodyguard, as were some of the jurors in Manson's trial and those of Grogan, Davis and Charles Watson. A new trial was ordered for Bobby Beausoleil in the light of the revelations after Tate/LaBianca.

A few months after the sentence was passed, Mary Brunner, Catherine Share and several men associated with the Manson Family were arrested after a shoot-out with police at an LA gun store. The group had planned to steal weapons in order to hijack a Boeing 747, killing one passenger every hour until Manson, Atkins, Van Houten, Krenwinkel and Watson were released. Brunner and Share were sent to the California Institution for Women to join their female Family associates. Mary completely dissociated herself from Manson and was paroled after ten years.

Just as Manson and the Family were a product of the 1960s, so they continued to cast a shadow over the 1970s. While there is no evidence of a vast Satanic conspiracy, there were at least 100 or so associates who were involved in the Family in one capacity or another. Many simply dropped out of the counter-culture and carved out comparatively normal lives away from the glare of publicity, returning to whatever career path they had chosen. Ella Jo Bailey, who along with Lynette Fromme had connected Dennis Wilson with the Family, dropped out of sight after learning of the Hinman murder. Ruth Ann Morehouse is still a wanted felon, although she apparently lives a normal middle-class life in an unnamed location. (In how many small towns in America is the local schoolmistress or respectable housewife a former Manson devotee?) Some met tragic ends; others remained loyal and even recruited new Family members throughout the decade. Sandra Good was imprisoned for ten years for conspiracy to send threatening letters to corporate executives warning that 'something bad' would befall them unless their corporations changed their polluting ways. Her friend and associate Lynette 'Squeaky' Fromme rivalled even Charlie for notoriety when she tried to shoot President Gerald Ford in Sacramento. She used a Colt automatic. It was loaded with four bullets, but there was no bullet in the chamber ready to be fired. To shoot the gun, Fromme would first have had to pull back the slide on top of the pistol, thus forcing a bullet from the clip up into the chamber. After the first shot was fired, the next bullet would have been automatically fed into the chamber. Had she succeeded she would have been the first woman to assassinate an American president.

As a weird footnote, a mere few weeks after Fromme's attempt, a second woman – Sara Jane Moore, a 45-year-old leftist – attempted to shoot Ford, this time in front of the St Francis Hotel in San Francisco. The bumbling, accidental President was becoming adept at dodging female would-be assassins. Moore ended up incarcerated alongside Fromme and the two hissed at each other like cats whenever they met. There was absolutely no suggestion that there was a Manson connection.

In the mid-1970s, a radical leftist group called the Symbionese Liberation Army kidnapped heiress Patricia Hearst – granddaughter of William Randolph Hearst, the billionaire newspaper baron – and held her to ransom. Hearst joined with her kidnappers and after her capture by the FBI claimed that she had been brainwashed. There were eerie echoes of the Manson case – a paranoia that a nice, middle-class girl could be converted into a gun-wielding outlaw after a few weeks – which, along with the mass suicide of the People's Temple in Jonestown, Guyana, sent waves of terror through American society.

Edward George's 1997 book, *Taming The Beast: Charles Manson's Life Behind Bars*, is an essential and readable account by Manson's prison counsellor, cataloguing the doings of Manson in the various prisons in which George worked and Manson was incarcerated. George is alternately fond of Manson and protective towards him but harbours no illusions about his capacity for evil. Manson emerges as a manipulative, occasionally aggressive and poisonous character, yet with a great capacity to charm. George gives short shrift to the idea that he is some sort of mind-controlling demon but warns that he thrives on sowing seeds of disunity, tearing people up and remaking them in his own order for the hell of it, if they allow him to. He ends with a warning about white supremacists approaching Manson to be their leader.

He also writes about Manson's time in San Quentin – where he was sent in 1971 to await execution – which was a demoralising experience. He was placed in the general population of the prison and found that his 'raps' held no power over the other surly cons. Bobby Beausoleil, defending Manson, ended up having his jaw broken by a violent con on the yard. Manson boasted when he was sent away that there was 'lots of sex, lots of drugs' in prison and that he would be OK. A few months after he was sent there, he was eventually 'punked' by another violent and aggressive inmate, a member of the Aryan Brotherhood, who took him as his prison 'wife'. While Manson was afforded some protection from the violent gangs that dominate prison life, his submissive position must have galled him.

He was temporarily sent to the California Medical Facility, where he returned to his more threatening ways, and when he was transferred to Folsom Prison, Sacramento, he told a guard that he had despatched a 'hit squad' of his followers to assassinate President Nixon, a threat that the Secret Service took seriously. A hunger strike followed, but after he received little press coverage or sympathy, he managed to get himself transferred to the CMF again by flooding and burning his cell.

In 1972, the state of California abolished the death penalty and Manson's sentence was commuted to life imprisonment. Manson himself was placed in solitary confinement or protective custody as rumours circulated of 'contracts' by everyone from Hollywood friends of Sharon Tate's, the Mafia, black radicals and even Weathermen leftists embarrassed at how he had discredited 'the movement'. But, more importantly in the American prison system, the way to make your reputation is to kill somebody, and who better to choose than a superstar murderer?

★

So, is there any correlation between the Manson, the music and the murders? While accepting that the killings were not directed against Terry Melcher, and that, in a terrible way, the fact that Sharon Tate and her friends were in the house was nothing personal, there does seem to have been a point in 1969 when Manson realised that the music was going nowhere, when the race-war raps became more earnest.

Neil Young recalls, 'When you listen to his songs, a lot of them were about "getting" somebody or getting back at them.' Certainly the title 'Cease To Exist' is ominous in the light of the killings, though it is not about murder, it is about loss of ego, a theme Manson harped on about in his raps and in his songs.

'Submission is a gift/Go on give it to your brother' may have been, as he claimed, written to heal the ongoing rift in the Beach Boys camp, but it also describes the ritualised mutual submission of guru and follower prevalent in most religions, if not all. It's a theme he returns to in 'Mechanical Man' – the idea that we are robots with programmed identities: 'I see you out there Joe/And you think your name is Joe/I see you out there Sam/And you think your name is Sam/You ain't Joe, you ain't Sam/You just am.' There are no individuals, everyone is everybody else, we are all connected in an infinite soul – it was a favourite hippy theme borrowed from Buddhism and filtered through the acid culture.

At the Spahn ranch, one of the games that Manson and his friends played was washing each other's feet, something that had biblical connotations (Mary Magdalene washed the feet of Christ) but was also an act of submission.

Much more ominous is 'Sick City', in which Manson sings, 'Restless as the wind/This town is killin' me/Got to put an end/To this restless misery/I'm just one of those restless people/Who can never seem to be satisfied with livin'/'Cause sick old sick sick sick old sick city/It may be too late for me to say goodbye/And it may be too late/To watch the sick old city die'.

It's apocalyptic, but in the song it isn't Manson who is going to kill the 'sick city' and its people who 'just sit/Watch TV and drink your beer'. He's just going to watch or walk away. Is it about the retreat to the desert from LA?

Many of Manson's songs are about his real-life experiences. 'Garbage Dump' describes the fact that, while at the Spahn ranch, Manson and the girls got by through making 'garbage runs' to rake through the bins outside local stores: 'There's a market basket and a A&P/I don't care if the box boys are starin' at me/I don't even care who wins the war/I'll be in them cans behind my favorite store/Garbage dump oh garbage dump'.

Meanwhile, 'Big Iron Door' is pretty self-explanatory: 'Clang bang clang/Clang bang clang bang clang/The judge said to me, "Now boy/You've had it"'.

The link between the music and the murders is more convoluted. Manson and Bobby Beausoleil were allies in the sense that they both wanted to make it in music, Beausoleil more than Manson. Beausoleil was living at the Spahn ranch in 1969 in the hope that they could still do something. Manson was talking about recording his 'desert music' and Beausoleil was constantly trying to make that happen. The drug deals that Beausoleil got involved in were to bring in money to buy equipment, to get the band up and running. It was a drug deal gone wrong that led to the killing of Gary Hinman. The Tate/LaBianca murders were carried out ostensibly to throw suspicion off Beausoleil, who had been arrested for killing Hinman.

12 Jailhouse Rock

'And when at last I find you, your song will fill the air.
Sing it loud so I can hear you, make it easy to be near you,
For the things you do endear you to me. You know I will'
*– From 'I Will', written and sung by Paul McCartney,
included on the 1968 album* The Beatles.

Thirty years on, Manson has become an almost mainstream figure. His albums are available in high-street megastores and he is now officially part of the pantheon of icons that your average teenage metalhead would regard as 'cool'.

A movie project about Charles Manson, starring Johnny Depp, was recently mooted. Depp turned down the role of Manson after reading a script based on Ed Sanders' 1972 book, *The Family*. Despite the fact that he had worked for Polanski on his very poor modern horror film *The Ninth Gate*, Depp, who collects Manson memorabilia, did not turn down the role out of sympathy with his colleague. Depp thought that the 1976 TV mini-series *Helter Skelter* told the whole story. 'There was no point in doing it again,' he said. Actor Steve Railsback, who starred in the mini-series, saw his career nosedive after he played Manson. Depp, whose screen roles have included maverick 1960s gonzo journalist Dr Hunter S Thompson (in *Fear And Loathing In Las Vegas*) and whose purchase of Jack Kerouac's overcoat for several thousand dollars at an auction in the early 1990s had other beat luminaries like William Burroughs looking through their wardrobes for similar items to unload, no doubt sees Manson as just another 1960s figure, a piece of subcultural history.

Producer Don Murphy, who worked with Depp on *From Hell*,

bought songs performed by Manson for the soundtrack and experienced significant difficulty in casting the movie, which had already attracted negative attention from the press, concerned that Manson's music would be aired 'for the first time' (according to Britain's *Sunday Times*) on the soundtrack.

Other Manson film projects in the past have come to naught. There was talk of Oliver Stone making a Manson film, adding him to his gallery of 1960s icons such as JFK, Nixon and Jim Morrison, though the furore that surrounded his *Natural Born Killers* put paid to that.

In 1999, *PopSmear* magazine staged a photographic reconstruction of the murders using a whole host of LA subcultural luminaries including Tool lead singer Maynard James Keenan (who appeared in the pics as Manson), Dictators singer Handsome Dick Manitoba (Leno LaBianca) and various other members of low-level underground bands. It also ran a successful exhibition of the photos in LA. Meanwhile, other actors, such as Crispin Glover (who has a musical career and whose 1989 album, snappily titled *THE BIG PROBLEM does not = the solution. The Solution = LET IT BE*, included a barely listenable cover of Manson's 'Never Say Never To Always'), go one louder than Depp in their obsession with Charlie.

But it is in metal that we find Manson's most ardent adherents. Rob Zombie, former White Zombie vocalist, appears onstage with an X carved on his forehead in imitation of Manson, cultivating a personal style that recalls Manson now – rangy with straggly hair and a beard, fixing his black piercing eyes on the camera. If you look at photos of Manson from the arrest and trial, or more recent shots of him in prison, you could almost imagine that he was some mate of Ozzy Osbourne's.

When the average listener hears Charles Manson's music for the first time, they are usually surprised. Instead of the expected heavy metal or screaming punk that some people expect, given his status as a T-shirt emblem for the disaffected, his songs are folky, gentle and even whimsical. Those who know a little bit about Manson often expect there to be a heavy Beach Boys or Beatles influence, a sort of adjunct to the 'White Album' or *Pet Sounds*. It is not. If there is a precedent, it is Hank Williams, Bob Dylan or Donovan. If circumstances were different, Manson could have developed along similar musical lines to Elektra/Asylum artists like Tim Buckley, Fred Neil and James Taylor. And, despite the assertion of Dennis Wilson that Manson was not actually a very talented musician, the evidence on record, whether we like to admit it or not, is not the work of a complete no-hoper.

The idea that Manson ordered his followers to go on a killing spree because he failed as a rock 'n' roll star is absurd and contrary to all of the evidence. If anything, Manson failed to make it as a rock 'n' roll star because he lacked the single-minded determination that is necessary – has always been necessary – to wade through the waist-deep bullshit of the music industry and to stay focused on the songs and keep the dream alive. How could Manson dedicate himself to the serious hard graft of composing, performing, recording and maintaining enthusiasm in the face of adverse reactions from people with power when all along he believed that he was the fifth angel given the key to the pit, the future ruler of the world who was both Christ and Lucifer? Most rock 'n' roll stars suspect that they are Christ incarnate and that their shit tastes sweet, but few are as convinced as Manson was that he was a man of destiny. And when you believe that, how can you possibly play on the bill at the local Battle of the Bands?

In many ways, Manson was already a rock 'n' roll star. He was living the life of a 1960s pop potentate – surrounded by half-naked girls willing to do anything he told them, enjoying a free-flowing torrent of drugs, hanging out with other rock stars like Dennis Wilson, enjoying the fanatical adulation of people who came to visit – without actually doing all the other tedious stuff like writing and recording songs, touring, doing TV appearances and press interviews.

In an interview with *Outer Shell* magazine, Lynette 'Squeaky' Fromme told writer Roy Harper, 'He was successful within his own judgement but he was not willing to make the bargain required for financial success, and that's the first and most important requirement before the industry is willing to handle an artist. Many musicians will say they don't care about the money yet they must commit themselves to appear at given times and places and to produce what sells, whether they believe in it or not. It depends on contracts.'

For somebody who failed as a musician, there's a surprising amount of Manson material available in shops, on the Internet and through mail-order retailers. *Lie*, the album comprising the demos that Manson recorded for Capitol at its studios in Van Nuys, California, in 1968 with Gregg Jakobson and Dennis Wilson producing, has rarely been unavailable since its release by Awareness in 1970, the ESP-DISK reissue and the subsequent CD reissues by Grey Matter in the mid-1990s. It's estimated that if these were 'legitimate' releases then they would qualify Manson for a gold disc (500,000 copies sold worldwide).

Manson was unhappy with the release. In his interview with John Gilmore in *Garbage People*, he said, 'All the good music was stolen. What's there is a couple of years old. I've written hundreds of songs since then. I've been writing a lot since I've been in jail. I never really dug recording. You know, all those things pointing at you. Gregg would say, "Come down to the studio, you know, and we'll tape some things." So I went. You get into the studio and, you know, it's hard to sing into microphones. Giant phallus symbols pointing at you. All my latent tendencies... [laughs and mimics giving a blowjob] My relationship to music is completely subliminal. It just flows through me.'

Reviews of the album that appeared in the underground press after its release at the height of the trial were damning: 'Trite...lightweight folk-pop...mediocre...coffee-shop strummer.'

Phil Kaufman, a legendary music business figure who has been, in his time, a 'nanny' for The Rolling Stones during their American tours (his brief for Mick Jagger was, 'Look after him, get him to the studio on time, get his medicine, keep him fed, keep him out of trouble'), road manager for country star Emmylou Harris and blues diva Etta James, as well as the man who stole the corpse of ex-Byrd and country-rock pioneer Gram Parsons and burned him on a funeral pyre, met Manson in Terminal Island. Kaufman was serving time for a drug deal that went wrong and got to know Manson because of a shared interest in music. Kaufman was Manson's link to the music business and it was his name that got him into Universal's studios to record his first demos.

Kaufman was in contact with Manson after his release in 1967 and was a regular visitor to the home of Harold True, who lived next door to the LaBiancas, when Manson and the Family partied there regularly. In his autobiography, *Road Mangler Deluxe*, he remembers Manson and the girls fondly: 'I don't think [Manson] ever did physically murder anyone. He planted the seeds and other people did it. I looked after some of the girls after Charlie's arrest because I didn't think any of them were guilty. When I looked at the papers and read the names of the perpetrators and their accomplices, I realised that I'd had sex with every one of those murderesses.'

Kaufman released the Van Nuys demo tapes under the title *Lie* on Awareness Records, his label formed solely to put out the album. Soon his house became a magnet for Family members and wannabe Family members, some of whom blamed him for the lack of success that the album enjoyed. (In fact, it was difficult to distribute the record because a significant independent network did not exist and many retailers did not want to stock a record by a murderer.) Kaufman still apparently owns the rights to the songs on the album.

Subsequent to his imprisonment, albums like *The Manson Family Sings The Songs Of Charles Manson*, recorded in LA in 1970 and featuring Steve 'Clem' Grogan on vocals and Family members Catherine 'Gypsy' Share, Ruth Ann Morehouse, Lynette 'Squeaky' Fromme and Sandra Good on backing vocals, were rushed out to cash in on the continuing interest in Manson during the trial and his supposed value as a counter-culture icon.

Manson also recorded several albums of material in prison, including *Charles Manson Live At San Quentin* and *Way Of The Wolf* (recorded in the maximum-security prison in Vacaville Medical Facility, where Manson was incarcerated in the mid-1980s), which were actually smuggled out on cassette tape. These albums have also been released on Grey Matter – a label that specialises in 'transgressive' releases like recordings of the People's Temple Choir, including Jim Jones's rantings as they committed mass suicide – as well as on White Devil Records, a Seattle-based independent label that, as well as releasing material by Manson has also put out material by Blood Axis (the band formed by

Church of Satan member and author Michael Moynihan) and rare recordings of Theatre of the Absurd dramatist Antonin Artaud.

In an interview with the *New York Press*'s Joe S Harrington in 2002, ESP-DISK founder Bernard Stollman recalled the circumstances under which he came to release Manson's music: 'Charles Manson had been convicted of complicity in the massacre in Beverly Hills. I believed that the media treatment of the case was intended by our government to discredit the hippy movement and in that manner counteract the growing anti-war climate in the United States. I came across an LP on Awareness Records by Manson and I was impressed by his songs and delivery. Phil Kaufman, road manager for Etta James and Emmylou Harris, is the author of an autobiography, *Road Mangler Deluxe*, in which he describes how he met Manson while both were in prison. Manson asked him to put the record out. Kaufman released it, and then freaked because his house had been surrounded by Manson followers with knives. So he brought it to me at my invitation, and ESP reissued it. Our distributors and dealers then refused to handle it. ESP folded in 1974, paid off its creditors and the record masters were placed in safe deposit boxes, where they remained for 17 years.'

ESP-DISK was a seminal New York art/free jazz label that, in its brief lifetime, released remarkable records by Albert Ayler, William Burroughs, Ornette Coleman, Sun Ra, Charles Tyler, The New York Art Quartet, The Godz, Pearls Before Swine, Pharoah Sanders, The Holy Modal Rounders and Patty Waters. Ironically, another band on the label was The Fugs, led by American beat poet Ed Sanders, whose 1971 book *The Family* did more to establish Manson as an icon of evil than any other. 'I thought originally that they might be innocent, but I learned that they were very, very guilty,' Sanders told *Goblin* magazine in 2000. 'There was sympathy for them in the underground at that time and I wanted to tell the story in a way that would lessen the sympathy. There was some danger. I haven't gotten any – knock on wood – threats in some time, but Manson still sends me hostile postcards. I think he's a fan of mine.'

When Sanders landed a contract to write his Manson book, it led to the (temporary) demise of the band just as Manson's album had led to the demise of the label.

The Fugs were one of the unique voices in American music in the 1960s. The forerunners of everything from punk rock to folk rock, their deranged, bawdy verses pre-dated Frank Zappa And The Mothers Of Invention. Their hardcore political commitment and gleeful troublemaking pre-dated The MC5. Their openly gay and bisexual membership at a time when rock was resolutely heterosexual pre-dated David Bowie. Formed in 1964 by Sanders and fellow beat poet Tuli Kupferberg in New York, The Fugs grew out of the civil-rights movement. According to Kupferberg, 'The Fugs were about dope and fucking and any kind of mind liberation that didn't kill you or damage your internal organs.' They could barely play instruments, their voices were awful and their lyrics were often scatological and childish, yet there was an undeniable genius about them. They were more the heirs of Lenny Bruce than anything to do with conventional rock 'n' roll. In an odd way, their deliberately amateurish jams sound not unlike some of the music on *The Family Sing The Songs Of Charles Manson*, though The Fugs were never entirely as po-faced and serious. Ed Sanders beat Manson to the cover of *Life* magazine by two years after their involvement with the anti-war marches on Washington and their attempt – along with Allen Ginsberg and the San Francisco Diggers – to level the Pentagon. There's a case for saying that, after he was jailed, there were elements in the American establishment that regarded Sanders as a bigger threat than Manson.

Lie is an album bought almost exclusively by people in 'the underground', whose other interests are usually industrial music, extreme performance art or black-and-white 16mm films of plastic-surgery operations. It's a kind of smirking 'fuck you' to the straight world that wouldn't understand. Had Manson not been convicted of murder, there is no way that these people would be in any way interested in his music, no more than they would admit to owning a Peter, Paul And Mary or Cat Stevens record.

Manson is usually found in the racks beside luminaries such as

David Koresh and GG Allin. Koresh, the cult leader of the Branch Davidians, who perished when the FBI and ATF stormed their compound at Waco, Texas, had ambitions to be a progressive rock star and recorded an album's worth of rather tedious biblical rock. Allin is celebrated in the underground for being 'real' while other punk rock stars were pussies who used fake blood. Allin would regularly insult and assault his audience, slash himself with razors and broken glass and actually urinate or defecate onstage. He died of an overdose, robbing fans of his long-promised onstage suicide. Allin covered Manson's 'Garbage Dump', along with originals such as 'Legalise Murder', 'I Wanna Rape You', 'I Kill Everything I Fuck' and 'Kill Thy Father, Rape Thy Mother', though, like Manson, the actual quality of the music was of secondary concern to fans who went along to watch a freak show.

It would be convenient if Manson was a mere no-talent like Koresh and Allin, but the truth is that *Lie* shows a competent grasp of songwriting and includes at least two genuinely excellent songs – 'Look At Your Game Girl' and 'Cease To Exist' – and others that, with work, could also have been great. The music – to detach it from any other layers of meaning – is as good as many first albums by contemporary folk-rock artists.

In her interview for *Outer Shell*, Lynette 'Squeaky' Fromme described Manson's influences: 'He grew up in the '30s with Hank Williams; the first who was, he tells me, originally called "Luke the Drifter" – Lefty Frizell; Frankie Laine; and he always mentions Bing Crosby. Charlie's got a fine voice with three or four comfortable octaves, but he generally only sings soft, beautiful songs in soft, beautiful places. He can sing "Begin The Beguine" going up three octaves on the guitar and on my spine, but he doesn't like to sing old or over-used stuff that is not in now.'

'Look At Your Game Girl' is certainly in the tradition of 1950s and 1960s loung' music like 'Begin The Beguine' rather than anything from the contemporary 1960s California hippy scene. Delivered in a gentle folksy voice that betrays his Arkansas roots, the listener may be surprised by the warmth of his singing, a comforting tone that's reminiscent of James Taylor. It certainly doesn't sound like the work of a gibbering psychopathic madman. Lyrically, the song reflects Manson's idea that life is a game in which we are unwilling or unknowing players: 'What a mad delusion/Livin' in that confusion/Frustration and doubt/Can you ever live without the game?/The sad, sad game/Mad game'. These may not be wholly original sentiments: eastern religion has always preached that life is a veil of illusion, though its theme could equally have been lifted from the Moody Blues song 'Simple Game': 'As time goes by, you will see that we're going to be free/You and me, we'll touch the sky, can you see in your mind's eye/That we are one, we're all the same/And life is just a simple game'. Had the Brummy easy-listening progressive dinosaurs gone on a killing spree, no doubt close analysis would reveal that their manifesto was contained in these banal lyrics. The only similar song on the album is the plaintive 'Eyes Of A Dreamer': 'Take nothing from nothing brother/And it's all just the same/For the loser is the winner/And there ain't no blame/Except the end of the game'.

'Cease To Exist' is perhaps the most disturbing of Manson's songs and the one that some listeners believe gives them the feeling that this is the work of a killer. (In fairness, it is nowhere near as weird as The Beach Boys' version on 20/20, with its background chanting and odd signature changes.) Manson claimed that he wrote the song for The Beach Boys, who were going through a fraught artistic and emotional crisis in the wake of the failed *Smile* sessions. The band were on poor terms with each other, ridden with factions trying to control the group while the leader huddled in his room or played piano in his sandpit. 'Dennis [Wilson] has a true soul, but his brothers couldn't accept it,' Manson said. 'He would go over to Brian's house and put his arms around his brothers and they would say, "Gee, Dennis, cut it out!" You know, they could not accept it.'

The Beach Boys did accept the song, however. Dennis Wilson changed the title to 'Never Learn Not To Love', another line from the song, and the line 'Cease to exist' became 'Cease to resist'. Recording took place on 11 September 1968 (a gift for conspiracy-theory buffs), with Dennis taking lead vocals. The track begins with an eerie sound – a cymbal recorded backwards and played forwards – with the lyrics changed around slightly from Manson's version. It opens with 'Cease to resist, come on say you love me/Give up your world, come on and be with me/I'm your kind, I'm your kind, and I see'. For all that they have washed their hands of Manson in the intervening years, as we have already seen they thought well enough of the song to use it on the B-side of their single 'Bluebirds Over The Mountain', released in December 1968. The record failed to dent the Top 40; Manson argued that, if they had left his song as it was and released it as the A-side, it would have sold millions. That is debatable; 20/20, along with *Friends* and the follow-up, *Sunflower*, represented a nadir for The Beach Boys, both commercially and artistically. In comparison to the new wave of American bands – The Byrds, Jefferson Airplane, The Doors – they seemed a little too quaint, a little too Eisenhower era to the counter-culture kids. Since Brian Wilson had not delivered the expected work of genius that was to have been *Smile*, even critics and fans sympathetic to the band felt that they had gone into reverse mode. Perhaps if Manson had delivered his song to them only two years before, he may actually have enjoyed the mass success he felt he deserved.

The song is about giving up control, losing your ego: 'Submission is a gift/Go on give it to your brother/Love and understanding/Is for one another'. 'Cease To Exist', despite the finality and negativity of the title, again borrows from eastern concepts of ego loss, the idea that we are all one, connected, and that our individuality is an illusion. As an idea, it was not so far from the Maharishi (whom The Beach Boys had visited and eventually rejected) and countless other gurus. He takes up the theme again in 'Ego' – 'And they call it your subconscious/Remember Freud/In the front is your computer/And I call him/Old ego is a too-much thing/Old ego is a too-much thing/He'll make you fool yourself/You'll think you're somebody else' – and again in 'Mechanical Man': 'I see you out there Joe/And you think your name is Joe/I see you out there Sam/And you think your name is Sam/You ain't Joe, you ain't Sam/You just am'.

Manson was attempting to use his songs to spread his philosophy, his idea of the Infinite Soul, that we are all one being therefore there is no life or death, no property or ownership.

In an interview with Manson included in the book *Death Trip*, attributed to 'Johnny Satan' and published by Death Valley Books in 1994, he says of the song, 'Ego is the man, the male image. Ego is the phallic symbol, the helmet, the gun. The man behind the gun, the mind behind the man behind the gun. My philosophy is that Ego is the thinking mind. The mind you scheme with, make war with. They shoved all the love in the back, hid it away. Ego is like "I'm going to war with my ego stick".'

He expands on the line 'Your heart's a pumpin'/Your paranoia's a-jumpin' ': 'Paranoia is just a kind of awareness and awareness is just a form of love. Paranoia is the other side of love. Once you give in to paranoia, it ceases to exist.'

Other songs are like straightforward prison blues reminiscent of Lightnin' Hopkins, Robert Johnson or Leadbelly on one hand and country stars like Hank Williams, Johnny Cash and Jimmy Rodgers on the other. 'Big Iron Door', about his prison experiences, sounds like an updated cowboy song: 'Clang bang clang/Went the big iron door/They put me in a cell/With a concrete floor/Nine other men in that cell with me/Moaning their date with destiny'. Later work, written when Manson was incarcerated after the murders, goes right back to these hillbilly roots. It's like a reflection of what happened in the music scene outside. After the mania of psychedelia, artists like The Byrds, The Grateful Dead and The Band rediscovered the simplicity of the folk, blues and country music of blue-collar America and forged a more downhome sound that returned to the very heart of American music.

But there is a forgotten Manson band, a rock 'n' roll band that he formed with Bobby Beausoleil, of which there are no known recordings. The Milky Way, by all accounts, was much closer to the psychedelic mainstream of late-1960s LA rock. In Michael Moynihan's 1998 interview for *Seconds* magazine, Beausoleil tells of their collaboration: 'At one point I had these notices put up advertising myself as a guitar player for hire and I got a call from a band called The Milky Way who wanted me to play guitar for a gig.

It turned out to be a little band that Manson was in. Charlie Manson was the lead singer. They had a gig at the Topanga Canyon Corral, which was the only nightclub in Topanga – it was actually a beer bar. I played with them and it was really pretty easy; I just improvised along with them. I think Charlie wrote most of the lyrics. It was kind of garage-band stuff, not particularly inspiring or inspired. The best thing, though, was Charlie and his singing and his kind of Dylan-esque sounding lyrics. At that time I didn't listen to them too closely, but when I did, I liked them. I liked the songs. They were relevant for what was happening then, and because of that I wanted to work with him and get him into the studio. Instrumentally, he strummed a guitar – that was his style. He strummed a guitar and he strummed it well, I will say that. He provided a good rhythmic foundation for his own music. He could have been a really good drummer, had he gone that way. But playing with him from my point of view, as an instrumentalist, came very natural. I found it really easy to do interesting things instrumentally around what he was doing, to enhance the delivery of his songs. I had a bass clarinet, left over from The Magick Powerhouse Of Oz, and I'd gotten to where I'd played it a lot – I used to just go out and sit by a creek and play the thing. I really liked the earthy, resonant timbre of the instrument, that kind of throaty sound. I wasn't by any stretch of the imagination a good woodwind player, and I wouldn't advertise myself as one, but I could play alright and I was able to apply my improvisational ability from the guitar to this instrument. So, to keep the Corral gig from getting too boring, I took the thing along with me one night and just got up to the mic and played a solo on it. As the solo progressed, I took the instrument apart and kept playing the pieces of it as I did until I was down to a mouthpiece. It was good, though – a lot of people really enjoyed it and got a kick out of it. That was a highlight of the Milky Way performances at the Corral. The band didn't do anything; it fell apart. The gig at the Corral didn't go that well. The people who showed up weren't interested in drinking the beer, which is of course what the proprietors wanted. As far as I know, those gigs were the end of the band... I wasn't going to be getting paid. I did get a little bit of money from the Corral, but there was no point in me playing with the band. I hadn't been asked to become a member of the band in the first place, and I wouldn't have been interested if they did ask. I was just sitting in; I was a hired guitar. I did find Manson's songs and his delivery of them to be interesting. I didn't get in depth with them at that point, but I did meet him again a month or two later and went down and visited with him down across from the Spiral Staircase house, where they had the bus parked across the street.'

One fan of the band was Neil Young, recently departed from The Buffalo Springfield, building his own solo career. Young recalled that the gigs he saw were 'interesting', that he was impressed by the poetic quality of Manson's words and the improvisational nature of the music. 'He had this kind of music that nobody else was doing,' said Young in an interview quoted in Sylvie Simmons' book *Neil Young: Reflections In Broken Glass*. 'He would sit down with a guitar and start playing and making up stuff, different every time. Musically, I thought he was very unique. I thought he really had something crazy, something great. He was like a living poet.'

Young actually tried to get Manson a deal with Reprise Records – which would have made him a labelmate of Frank Sinatra, one of the names on the infamous death list – and gave him a motorcycle as a present. Young later wrote 'Revolution Blues' on his bleak 1978 album *On The Beach*, inspired by visions of Manson's ragged dune-buggy attack battalions rolling down Laurel Canyon to slaughter the rock elite in which he, Neil Young, now found himself.

Although few people will admit to it now, there were many other people besides Neil Young, Phil Kaufman, Gregg Jakobson, Dennis Wilson and Terry Melcher who gave Manson a helping hand and believed in his music. In his two years flitting between LA, San Francisco, Death Valley and San Diego, Manson is supposed to have casually met with various members of garage band The Seeds, The Mamas And The Papas (John Phillips had heard the demos and Mama Cass was allegedly a regular visitor to the Spiral Staircase in Topanga Canyon) and It's A Beautiful Day, whose leader, David LaFlamme, was a friend and one-time Orkustra bandmate of Bobby Beausoleil's. Since the LA rock fraternity was a close-knit community, it is feasible to assume that while he was living at Dennis Wilson's house on Sunset Boulevard, many many bands and artists would have come into contact with Manson and the Family.

Given the amount of talentless clowns who were able to release records at this time (trawl through the countless 'Pebbles' and 'Nuggetts' series of psychedelic compilation albums and the number of acid-rock bands releasing material between 1966 and 1968 seems to expand the more you search), it's rather remarkable that Manson never actually had the opportunity to release a record at this time. He may not have been the greatest artist ever to grace LA, but he was better than, say, The Mom's Boys, The Mushrooms, The Weeds, The Positively 13 O'Clock, The Hobbits or any of the other one-hit and no-hit wonders whose acid-baked bubblegum is the detritus in which the true psychedelic aficionado wallows.

In fact, there's a great deal of doubt as to whether Manson was actually serious about a music career himself. According to Beausoleil, it was he who was instrumental in getting Manson into the recording studio to do the songs that featured on *Lie*: 'I would stop...and try again to get Charlie into the studio, trying to get him to focus on doing something, but he saw that whole music industry thing as part of the establishment, the authoritarian principles that he was in conflict with, so it was very difficult to get him to focus on any kind of professional aspirations, which I still continued to have. I saw great potential in recording him or in seeing his music recorded. I thought what he was saying was relevant and I wanted it to be heard. At one point in time, I did get him into the studio. I'd met Dennis Wilson, and Manson had met him independently. It was through a mutual friend of myself and Charlie's...Gregg Jakobson, that I met Dennis. Dennis tried to do the same thing, to get Charlie into the studio. Gregg Jakobson had done so, too – he saw that same potential. Gregg and I eventually did get him to the studio a couple of times. The first time was just a complete disaster. We had a nice little studio set up, ready to at least record a demo of his stuff, and he dragged his whole entourage down along with him, and he had them singing background sounds and playing tambourine. They were sort of humming in the background. You just can't do a good recording like that! I tried to tell him, "You know, if you want to add this, we can always overdub," but it wasn't working.'

Those Manson vocal sessions were produced by Dennis Wilson with Gregg Jakobson. The session sheets have never turned up (apparently, they were deliberately buried), but it is likely that it was mostly session players on the tracks, though there is a persistent rumour among Beach Boys aficionados that Carl Wilson may have been part of the session.

As an aside, although Dennis Wilson is the Beach Boy most associated with Manson, there were individuals who recall meeting Manson accompanied by Brian Wilson and Mike Love where Dennis was not present, though since these meetings took place in and around Capitol Records while Manson was recording there and trying to obtain a record deal, it is not indicative of anything other than that they were acquaintances.

One backing singer recalled meeting Brian, Terry Melcher and an 'ordinary looking' hippy in the corridors at Capitol in 1968. Brian – not Dennis – said that he was going to do something with 'this guy's' songs. The percussionist who played on these sessions also played on some of The Monkees' tracks, which is as close as Manson got to them!

Manson's first recording sessions – made at Universal – resurfaced in the 1990s on an album called *Charles Manson Unplugged 9/11/67 Volume 1 – The Psychedelic Soul Of Charles Manson* (satirising the 1990s fashion for bands like Nirvana, Neil Young and Kiss to record acoustic-only sessions for MTV) on Archer CAT Productions. Recorded on 11 September (that date again) in the same year that Manson was released from prison, the album includes some of the same songs that he later re-recorded and which appeared on *Lie*, but there are other songs there, too, like 'House Of Tomorrow', which starts with Manson rapping, 'Oh yeah, this will make me some money, this is a money song/This is for all the people fighting for peace, to get your freedom!' Then he laughs. The song itself betrays more of a Bob Dylan/Barry MacGuire influence typical of many of the mediocre imitators who clogged up the music scene at that time. More interesting is 'Run For

Fun', which seems to be structured in an unconventional way in the manner of 'After Bathing At Baxters' by Jefferson Airplane, a band that Manson would have been familiar with in the Haight-Ashbury. The lyrics are stream of consciousness and the song finishes with Manson laughing, 'If I can make myself nervous, I should be able to make myself un-nervous. It works both ways...' 'Close To Me' is a 1950s lounge ballad, a Johnny Mercer-style song with some intricate jazzy guitar licks. Manson finishes by explaining that he has a whole bunch of songs that other people could sing that he 'don't agree with' but he wrote them anyway. There follows a dialogue between the engineer/producer (who may or may not be Phil Kaufman) asking him to play some of the songs that he wrote in prison. Manson replies that they are sad songs. 'Groovy, let's have some sad songs,' replies the producer. Manson then plays three prison blues songs 'written by a friend of mine who robbed a bank and got caught'. 'She Done Turned Me In' is a jocular western-swing ditty while 'Twilight Blues' is a deep Ray Charles-like country-soul number and 'Your Daddy's Home' is more Hank Williams-influenced western blues.

The most revealing thing about the recordings is how unconfident Manson sounds, giggling nervously, forgetting songs, rapping nervously, trailing off in the middle of numbers. The songs here actually have more connection to the songs Manson later recorded in prison.

During the trial, ESP-DISK recorded and released *The Manson Family Sings The Songs Of Charles Manson*, a quickie cash-in featuring Steve Grogan on lead vocals with various Family girls on backing vocals, percussion, kazoos and shakers. *Crawdaddy!* magazine's review of the album was scathing: 'When [Hannah Arendt] witnessed Eichmann's performance in Jerusalem, she wrote, "A report on the banality of evil." Listening to this collection of zonked-out acid casualties strumming away at a camp-fire singalong, you know what she meant. This is banal in the proper sense of the term. Mediocre talentless hippies, an artefact that only a really sick puppy would want to own. Nasty people, shit record.'

It is an appalling record, typical of the sort of late-hippy cash-ins produced by straight labels desperate to make a buck on the folksy hippy craze, then in its terminal phase. The songs are reminiscent of cowboy songs, almost like Frankie Laine (whom Manson often cited as an influence) or The Mamas And The Papas taped live at a party when they were all stoned. There was little to no interest in this album and it sank without trace, showing up at record fairs as a curiosity item until it was reissued in the 1980s by Grey Matter.

There was little interest in Manson's music throughout the 1970s, though the case continued to exert fascination, encouraged by the publication of Ed Sanders' *The Family* in 1972 and *Helter Skelter*, the 1974 book by Vincent Bugliosi (with Curt Gentry), the most exhaustive study of the Manson trial to date. A TV film based on the book was shown in 1978 and given a limited cinema release in Europe as a double bill with *Patty*, based (loosely) on the Patty Hearst case. It was a dull, if occasionally sensationalist, rendering of the book starring Steve Railsback as Manson and with Susan Atkins played by Marilyn Burns, who also starred in the cult film *The Texas Chainsaw Massacre*.

The horror films post-Manson betray the real anxieties of the public in a way that a factual film or documentary could not. Tobe Hooper's *The Texas Chainsaw Massacre*, actually based on the Ed Gein case in 1950s Wisconsin, tapped into people's anxiety about Manson. In a plot that owes more to *Scooby Doo, Where Are You?*, a bunch of hip kids in a bus travelling through Texas pick up a deranged Manson-like hitchhiker. They end up in a slaughterhouse getting picked off one by one by the grotesque family of freaks who live there butchering humans in an orgy of motiveless mayhem. Fears of mind control were exploited in films like *The Parallax View* (a secret agency recruits brainwashed assassins – based on the conspiracies surrounding the death of Robert Kennedy) and *The Crazies* (US biological warfare experiment goes wrong and turns the inhabitants of a small American town into homicidal maniacs). Tobe Hooper's 1972 film *The Last House On The Left* (escaped convicts on killing spree) and Jeff Lieberman's 1977 cult classic *Blue Sunshine* were both inspired by Manson. *Blue Sunshine* in particular preys on the fears of the 'disco-era' yuppies, harking back to the 'sins' of the 1960s – a group of successful 1970s types suddenly become psychotic killers. Not only that, they become bald, giving them an astonishing resemblance to the pictures of the shaven-headed Manson girls at the trial. The cause is a batch of bad acid known as Blue Sunshine that they all ingested while at college in the 1960s.

In the wake of punk rock, Manson gained a new status as a cult icon. In the late 1970s and early 1980s, there was a worldwide psychedelic renaissance. Contemporary bands like the UK's Echo And The Bunnymen, The Teardrop Explodes and The Jesus And Mary Chain and US groups like The Rain Parade, The Dream Syndicate and REM sparked off a wave of interest in the more obscure and undiscovered corners of psychedelia. Manson was part of this rediscovery: bootleg cassettes of *Lie* circulated hand to hand or at record fairs; bands occasionally threw in a Manson cover – usually 'Cease To Exist' – as a smirking statement of outrage.

Psychic TV, on their seminal 1983 album *Dreams Less Sweet*, recorded a strange version of Manson's 'Never Say Never To Always' under the title 'Always Is Always'. PTV founder Genesis P Orridge claimed in the sleeve notes that the track 'destroys any ideas you may have about him', though how it does this is never really made clear. The band's 1984 single 'Roman P' – about Roman Polanski, husband of Sharon Tate – repeats the line 'Are you free?/Are you free?/Are you really, really, really, really free?' before going into the verse 'Sharon walks alone as your wife/Sharon is a life for a knife/Sharon's floating high up above/Sighing, crying, dying for love'. The band appeared on the artwork for the single wearing Manson T-shirts – all variations on the classic *Life/Lie* cover shot in a room daubed with bloodstains and the words 'Healter skelter' (with the K reversed) on the wall behind them.

Hardcore punk band Black Flag, featuring a newly recruited lead singer called Henry Rollins, advertised their 1981 gigs in LA as 'creepy crawls' (after a term used by the Manson Family for breaking into people's houses and rearranging their furniture), using flyers designed by comic artist Raymond Petibon. One featured a blonde girl telling an

X-carved-between-the-eyebrows Charles Manson 'You better be good, Charlie. It wasn't easy getting in here, you know'. The flyers' content – and their ubiquity on telephone poles and street walls – contributed to the band's already edgy, menacing mystique.

In an interview with Australian magazine *Juice* in 2001, Rollins spoke about the aborted plan to release a Manson album: 'Some Massachusetts lawyer contacted SST and Touch & Go and every other label and said, "Manson has these tapes he's been making – solo acoustic guitar and vocals." So I was all for it. I was, like, "Yeah, let's put it out. Fuck these people, man." But SST got these unbelievably scary death threats. It got full on enough to where they ran an article about it in the *LA Times*, and *60 Minutes* or somebody called and said, "We'd like to put Henry in a jail cell with Manson and have them interview each other." Nothing ever happened, but it was an interesting two weeks in 1984.' SST at that time was *the* premier American punk rock label, releasing material by Black Flag as well as Hüsker Dü, Mission Of Burmah and Dinosaur Jr. The acoustic album entitled *The Saints Are Hell On Earth* eventually turned up on TSOL in the late 1990s, though more Manson releases were to follow in the 1980s.

Manson recorded long improvised sets on the guitar, mixing his songs, spoken-word poetry and rambling raps with occasional cover versions of Hank Williams songs. There followed a slew of cassette bootlegs of Manson songs and spoken-word tracks smuggled out of various jails. The three most significant Manson prison albums are the ultra-rare *The Way Of The Wolf*, released on Pale Horse; *Charles Manson Live At San Quentin*; and *Commemoration*, released on Seattle label White Devil and which parodies a famous Nazi-era German stamp, with Manson's head in place of Hitler's.

The *Live At San Quentin* title parodies that of Johnny Cash's famous 1969 album *Live In San Quentin* (Manson also served time in Folsom Prison, scene of Cash's classic 'Folsom Prison Blues'), while the cover – a blurred monochrome photo of Manson in prison fatigues being led through the gates between two guards – parodies

The Beach Boys' *Pet Sounds*, using the same typography and colour scheme. Recorded in one take in his cell in 1983, the songs are increasingly bizarre internal monologues that probably make sense only to Manson. Free from any residual commercial instincts or compromises to try to make it in the music industry, these songs are his music in its purest form. Unstructured, the songs just flow into each other; he stops when he gets bored and plays something else, occasionally going off at a tangent. In the background can be heard the murmuring sounds of prison life – doors banging, raised voices, footsteps on metal – and at one point it sounds as if Manson is being threatened by another con.

The Way Of The Wolf, recorded in Vacaville in 1985, opens with 'Universal Law', which starts off like a gentle Kris Kristofferson rambling blues about how there is life in all things, before Manson starts rambling about 'cutting off his motherfucking head'. The whole album weaves between downhome folksiness, messages about the environment and terrifying threats. In 'ATWA: Message To The People Of The Earth/Computer Perfection', he strums his guitar and says, 'So I hope I get this tape out here to you/And that if I do I hope that you know that we have made contact with each other', then goes into a song about being 'back home in Kentucky': 'I can take them Indians and run back behind the still/Or move a little further down the track/Or give them a knife and tell them to stick it in your back… The bugs are mad/I got one spider that crawled on up through a guy's nose/Burrowed through on up/Ate through his brain/He started complaining about these headaches/He thought that there was a devil running in the night/I'm on the road again/Whoa, what's that mean?' What indeed?

Perhaps the strangest and most revealing insight into Manson's musical roots, including his thoughts on Elvis, tying the whole thing in with references to his deferred execution, playing music in 'the hole' (the Devil's Hole or the slang term for jail?) and prison rape is on 'Dream Train/My Oklahoma Angel Love' when he sings, 'When the day is done, I go to bed/I place my hands beneath my head/Close my eyes twilight blue/And board my dream train back home to you/Back to you Luke the Drifter, Hank Williams/There was a time/When I was lonely and I was up and down the lonesome highway/And Lefty Frizzell…ten years ago on a cold dark night/The scaffold was here in eternal light/Someone was killed somewhere in the county jail/And it was a jailhouse rock for some other jammer/Who was jamming some cock up somebody's nosehole/Now Elvis, the epitome of fake phony jive on freak/You made a laughing stock of country music/You took away my cowboy feet/You thought you had someone's heartbeat/But Lefty Frizzell and Hank Williams was riding that train/And then there was Woody Guthrie he used to sing/He'd sing them fools right to insane/Listening to the radio/My Oklahoma angel you know I know/We played the music down deep in the hole/You gave me just a little of your soul/And now left me down in the hole to get old/But it's all right, angel love/My Oklahoma angel love'.

Commemoration (subtitled 'Commemorating 60 Years Of Struggle Against Cowardice, Stupidity, And Lies', an allusion to Hitler's original and less snappy title for *Mein Kampf*), released by White Devil to celebrate Manson's 60th birthday in 1995, was recorded between 1982 and 1986 in Vacaville Prison. It is by far the bleakest of the three albums, mostly because, on the first two, Manson sounds quite insane, whereas on *Commemoration* he is lucid. Again, as with all of these albums, you cannot judge them purely on the merit or otherwise of the music; these are artefacts with much more meaning attached to them than any other record album. Yet, as with the material released on *Lie*, this is obviously the work of a talented man.

One wonders whether, if circumstances had been different, Manson would now be a major – or at least working – country performer. These songs aren't the work of a genius, as some of his defenders would have you believe, but they are competent. It's odd that the punks and art-vampires who have latched onto Manson as a figurehead would never in all seriousness listen to a record by Jimmy Buffett (of 'Margueritaville' fame), but this is what Manson sounds like. Put him in a plaid shirt and a stetson and he could be the truck drivers' favourite.

He can't resist one last swipe at the authorities, though. On the final track 'I'm Free Now', he sings, 'You couldn't get me killed, you motherfucking dogs!'

★

On Melrose Drive I visited a shop called The Third Eye. There is a mural painted on the front depicting a cowled figure with three glowing eyes clutching a locked book. It's a bit like something from a 1950s EC comic like *Tales From The Crypt*. The book has a huge question mark on the front. The shop sells clothes in the front – the sort of hippy tat you can buy at any such mart across the planet, screen-printed T-shirts, second-hand Levi's, vintage jackets – while in the back there is a bookshop-cum-herb store. The stench is pretty awful, like patchouli incense covering up the reek of a dead cat. One shelf is lined with New Orleans Voudoun products: John The Conqueror root incense as well as some wonderfully kitsch items like House Blessing aerosol sprays, Run Devil Run soap and washing-up liquid that will attract a husband. There are books with sickening new-age titles and pictures of dolphins and rainbows (*Unlocking The Goddess Within*, *Every Day Is Another Rainbow To Cross*), but also some meatier stuff such as (Church of Satan founder) Anton LaVey's biography, photocopied tracts by the Process Church of the Final Judgement and some profoundly subterranean publications on mind control. The two assistants are in their 20s and look like poster-children for the local piercing and tattoo parlours. A girl with peroxide hair formed into that terrible white person's equivalent of dreadlocks has, I notice, a tattoo of the Psychic TV symbol, which looks like a crucifix and a reverse Cross of Lorraine laid on top of each other (or, less prosaically, a TV aerial). PTV, as we have seen, are the band formed in the 1980s by Genesis P Orridge – performance artist, anarchist, occultist and psychedelic prankster. He was one of the co-creators of what came to be called industrial music in his first band, Throbbing Gristle, and had, at the time of my visit to that shop, recently been hounded out of the United Kingdom after a TV documentary (wrongly) accused him and his wife of being at the centre of a Satanic paedophile ring. Orridge, suffice to say, was one of the figures who were responsible in some way for my continued interest in Manson.

After striking up a conversation about PTV, Carrie, the assistant, informs me that she's really an actress and is currently trying to form a band. I tell her that I'm here doing research on Manson. She perks up.

'Oh, but that's the band I'm trying to form!' she tells me. 'We want to start a Manson tribute band, to recreate one of the shows that Manson and the Family did in the 1960s. Look…' She removes the dreadlocks and her head is completely shaved, like the photos of Manson followers Linda Kasabian, Leslie Van Houten and Susan Atkins during the trial. They were going to cut the letter X between their eyebrows. 'We want to call ourselves The Charles Manson Experience.'

I ask if they plan to finish the set by beheading a member of the audience.

'Oh, but you surely don't believe that Manson killed anybody?' She seems genuinely shocked. 'Manson never killed anyone. They couldn't find any proof that he killed anyone or planned the murders or ordered them.'

'You believe that he was framed?' I enquire.

'They needed a scapegoat; they needed somebody to blame. They wanted to destroy the 1960s, to quash the protest against the war, to silence anybody who wanted to opt out of their corporate society,' she says, a speech that she has obviously made several times and that is well rehearsed. 'Manson was a symbol. They used him to crack down on the whole movement.'

'They?'

'Nixon. Ronald Reagan. The LAPD. The establishment. The big corporations who want to keep people in line.'

'But Manson wasn't part of the anti-war movement, and politically, if he was anything, he was on the far right,' I say.

'Look at the way that the protests fizzled out after the trial. What's the best way to discredit somebody? Make out that they are a Nazi!'

Like all conspiracy theories, the Manson one involves firing an arrow and painting a target where it lands. This was not the first or the last time that this Manson-was-set-up conspiracy theory was put to me by somebody in a band who seemed otherwise smart enough to know better. Like all of the pop-occultery in the shop I had to wonder if this was something that Carrie really believed or if it was a pose, a way to be shocking and righteous at the same time, the way in which some people have adorned themselves in swastikas and claimed that they are wearing them because it was an ancient Vedic symbol of peace and good fortune.

In many ways, the whole new-age landscape of LA, with its countless varieties of mysticism and crank religions, food fads and where people believe that any number of alternative therapies from colonic irrigation (that's enemas!) to aromatherapy are equally as valid as mainstream medicine, is fertile ground for conspiracy theorists. If you believe that the smell of vanilla pods can be used to treat infertility, then you will have no problem believing anything. Most Americans (over half, according to a MORI poll in the mid-1990s) believe that there was a conspiracy to assassinate President John F Kennedy. The details of the conspiracy may vary – the Mafia, the military-industrial complex, the CIA, Fidel Castro – but it's only a short step from believing that your own government killed the president to believing that aliens regularly cross interstellar space to insert anal probes into people who live in trailer parks or that the moon landings were part of an elaborate con by NASA and the US government to gull the public out of billions of tax dollars. Or that Charles Manson is some misunderstood American hero, a political prisoner, jailed to silence The Truth.

Carrie, as well as being a big fan of Psychic TV, is also into other extreme industrial bands like Leatherstrip, X Marks The Pedwalk and Borghesia. I wonder aloud why somebody whose tastes run to this would be interested in the almost twee folkiness of Manson's music, particularly as she patently denies that he was a murderer. If Manson, then why not John Denver or Peter, Paul And Mary?

She shrugs. I'm annoying her by even questioning her.

I give Carrie an e-mail address that I proffer to people I want to keep at arm's length and she promises she'll let me know when her band get together to play their first gig. I'm still waiting...

Walk a little further along Melrose and pick a surfer/skater shop at random and the chances are you'll find an item of wearable Mansonabilia for sale. T-shirts showing Manson's eyes with the legend 'Charlie Don't Surf' seem to be popular, as does a rather tacky Hawaiian-style shirt with a repeat print of Manson – the famous picture from the cover of *Life* magazine's 'Love And Terror Cult' issue – in a sort of Andy Warhol's Marilyn Monroe style. There are no Jeffrey Dahmer, John Wayne Gacy or David 'Son of Sam' Berkowitz shirts for sale, no Hitler, Pol Pot or Idi Amin badges. It's as though Manson is just another piece of 1960s kitsch along with Ed 'Big Daddy' Roth hot-rod drawings, Beatles wigs and bell-bottom jeans.

At a café, I meet up with a guy called Billy Bee ('I guess 'cause I'm always buzzin' round!'), who is a friend of a friend several other friends removed. Billy is a self-styled professional '1960s person' who crops up occasionally as a pundit on documentaries about flower power. Billy, I'm warned, talks about a 70:30 ratio of bullshit:truth, but the 30 per cent that's true is pretty interesting.

He looks as if he's on the borderline between being a '1960s person' and a 'street person' – he wears a combat jacket with a map of Vietnam on the back and the legend 'I know when I die I'll go to Heaven because I've spent my time in Hell'.

I ask if he was in Vietnam. He tells me he was, with the 101st Airborne.

'Where were you stationed?' I ask.

'Khe Sanh, you know? It got really hairy down there,' he says, showing off a row of yellowing, rabbit-like teeth.

I discover later that this is bullshit ('Dude, he's never been to a Vietnamese restaurant, never mind Vietnam').

But he does produce a picture of himself with Charles Manson that I'm reasonably sure isn't faked.

'That's at Dennis Wilson's house, '68. That's Dennis.'

There is only one known picture of Manson at Dennis Wilson's house on Sunset Boulevard, a blurry shot of him sitting strumming an acoustic guitar. If these are genuine then it's exciting. I have to pay Billy $10 to look at them.

The photo of a young Billy and Dennis Wilson is like a document from another time. Dennis Wilson looks very out of it but very happy. It is taken in front of a swimming pool with a lot of girls lounging in the background. The Manson girls?

'Some,' Billy nods.

In the photo, Manson too looks young. He is less heavily bearded than most of the pictures you see of him where he looks like a crazed hillbilly. But there's still something about him that marks him out. It's maybe a look in the eye. He's not just one of the guys.

'He was a wizard, man,' says Billy. 'I'm not saying what he did was good, but at that time, if you could have heard him, you would have thought, "This guy knows. He's in tune with something." He could look at you and tell you stuff about yourself that you hardly knew. And for all that he was supposed to be such an evil tripper, he was a guy that you felt good to be around. You ask any of them and if they say that they didn't feel happy when Charlie came around, they're liars, man.'

Goodtime Charlie is a side of Manson that you don't expect to find, but it makes a certain kind of sense. If he was just some scary little creep, why would anyone – the women, Dennis Wilson – have wanted him around? There were plenty of other gurus, pimps, dope dealers and party leeches around.

Billy also produces photos of him with Jim Morrison, taken backstage at a show, possibly at the Whisky A Go Go. This raises a possibility that I have always wondered about. 'Did Manson and Morrison ever meet?'

'Sure. They all knew Charlie. Morrison, Dennis Wilson, Janis Joplin, Mama Cass... You see a pattern here?'

'Are you saying that Charles Manson had them killed?'

'And John Lennon, man. Think about that.'

'Tell me about how you met Manson,' I say, getting back to something where at least there might be a semblance of truth.

Billy launches into an anecdote involving The Grateful Dead, some acid that he was selling at the Matrix club in San Francisco before getting to the point that he sold Manson some LSD and travelled with the Family from San Francisco to LA some time in 1967.

'There were all these chicks who wanted to ball. We tripped all the way there and Charlie sat in the back and made everyone sing. Except it was kinda "Row Row Row Your Boat" kinda singing.'

Charles Manson the communal singer? You go looking for an evil genius and end up finding a Sunday school teacher.

Billy describes the gigs that Manson and the Family performed as being 'real special'. 'There was something about them. When it came together, when he sang. There was like electricity in the air. I truly believe that, if they had been signed and all that, Manson would be a guy who sold millions of records.'

It's the same argument that has been applied to Hitler: if he'd only been admitted to art school in Vienna, he'd have been a successful fine artist instead of Germany's 'saviour'. The truth, as we shall see, is a little more complicated; there are several schools of thought as to whether Manson's frustrations at trying to make it in the music business had any influence on the Tate/LaBianca murders. To say that he decided to try to spark off an apocalyptic race war because he couldn't get into the Top 40 is simplistic, to say the least, but it must have been no less frustrating for an intelligent and talented (though moderately) man like Manson to feel that he was getting the runaround from all of his music business contacts – Terry Melcher, Gregg Jakobson, Dennis Wilson and even Phil Kaufman, whom he had met in prison at Terminal Island and who had pointed him in the direction of Universal, where Manson recorded his first demos.

Billy Bee regales me with a few more anecdotes that, annoyingly, have a grain of truth in them somewhere before asking for $100 for his story. I tell him truthfully that I don't have $100. I give him another $10 and he seems happy. He offers me the photos for $200 and then tells me that CNN are also interested. He calls at my hotel the following day and offers to sell them to me for $10,000. I point out that if I couldn't give him $100 then $10,000 is pretty much out of the question.

The meeting piques my interest, however, as I think about how many of the bands I love from the late 1960s – The Byrds, The Buffalo Springfield, Frank Zappa And The Mothers Of Invention – actually came across Manson and the Family. How many of them partied with goodtime Charlie?

The conspiracy theorist sees patterns everywhere, and in rock 'n' roll it's possible to discern a vast web that connects Led Zeppelin, The Beatles, The Rolling Stones, Arthur Lee and Love, The Beach Boys, The Byrds and Gram Parsons, with Manson at the centre. The Led Zeppelin connection is through Manson associate Bobby Beausoleil, who composed the score for and appeared in the film *Lucifer Rising*, directed, as we have seen, by the brilliant underground director Kenneth Anger. Beausoleil played Lucifer in the original version of the film, though after he fell out with his lover, Anger, he stole most of the footage, which was reputedly buried in the desert by Charles Manson – another victim of the Family.

After Beausoleil was imprisoned, Zeppelin guitarist Jimmy Page was briefly involved in composing the music, though Anger and Beausoleil patched things up sufficiently for Beausoleil to eventually finish the score. Anger and Page's common ground was a shared interest in the great English magician Aleister Crowley. Like Manson, Crowley formed a commune of disciples to experiment in sex, drugs and magic. He and his devotees lived outrageous lives in Sicily in the 1920s until the puritanical Mussolini had them all deported. Crowley also dreamed of starting his own religion, called Thelema or Crowleyanity.

Anger was also friendly with The Rolling Stones and approached Mick Jagger with a proposal to play Lucifer in *Lucifer Rising*. Jagger refused, obviously wary of Anger. The film-maker then got Mick's brother, Chris, to appear in the film. Marianne Faithfull, then Jagger's girlfriend, appeared as Lilith. *Their Satanic Majesties Request* was influenced by Anger, and on the cover the band are portrayed dressed as stage wizards or magicians. The planet Mars is in the sky above them, a powerful occult symbol. Jagger renounced all connections with Satanism and the occult after the murder at Altamont, where the Stones headlined. Anger was irritated by the fact that Jagger took to wearing a heavy, jewelled crucifix and flirting with Christianity. (Jagger did, however, invite him to his wedding to Bianca. 'I'll wait for the divorce,' Anger replied waspishly.) Beausoleil was also briefly involved with an early incarnation of Arthur Lee's Love, which is strange given that Love was a band that featured both black and white musicians. Beausoleil made little secret of his racism, allegedly rising in the ranks of the notorious white supremacist prison gang the Aryan Brotherhood while in jail.

13 The Charles Manson Fan Club

'If you want to see the future,
Look into the eyes of your young, dancing children'
– *Jefferson Airplane, 'When The Earth Moves Again'*

Amanda is 30 and Josh is 28. They are both goths, dressed in a style that ill befits the summer-all-year beaches of Venice Beach. They are both serious Manson loyalists. Josh claims to be in touch with other Manson Family members, though he becomes cagey when pressed for names; he admits that he has written to Manson associate Sandra Good, the most public Manson loyalist, though claims a closer relationship to others who were never convicted of any crimes. Amanda proudly displays her tattoos. Her left arm bears a swastika with the word 'Rise' picked out in red while above it is a florid drawing of Manson based on the *Life* magazine cover.

They are also cagey about how they earn their living, though like many in the 'underground' I suspect that their lifestyle is subsidised by indulgent and wealthy parents. They have agreed to be interviewed to 'put right' some 'errors' I made in an article written for *Vox* magazine in 1995 about Manson and the re-release of his albums. As a result of this feature, as well as a politely worded and lengthy e-mail from them commenting on it, I received about 25 threats, all emanating from the same domain in the USA. These threats were sent to my personal account, leading me to believe that the source may have been someone known to me. I show the printouts to Josh and Amanda, who express shock and deny any knowledge of them. I joke that it doesn't matter, that it isn't as if Manson followers need to worry about getting a bad name.

AMANDA: I don't think it's anything that any one of us or anyone we know would do. It looks like somebody wants to discredit us.

TOMMY: Who would do that?

AMANDA: Who put Manson in prison? Who has lied and lied and lied about him for 25 years?

TOMMY: The California justice system? You tell me...

JOSH: The government of this country had consistently lied to the people about everything from the war in Vietnam to the systematic destruction of the planet. Does it really seem so strange that they would lie to cover up their mistakes?

TOMMY: Well, it seems weird that anyone in the US government would send me a bunch of death threats to discredit Manson followers. Tell me about Manson. You believe he was wrongly imprisoned?

AMANDA: He was denied a fair trial. He was not allowed to defend himself. His legal counsel was incompetent. The prosecutor even admits in his book that he suppressed evidence and testimony because it didn't fit in with his theory that Manson was some great criminal mastermind who sent all these brainwashed zombies out to do his crimes because he heard something in a Beatles song. They wanted him dead. He was sentenced to die. The worst thing he did was to slash Gary Hinman's ear with a sword.

TOMMY: But he was an accessory to murder. He tied up the LaBiancas...

AMANDA: But that doesn't make him a mastermind of murder. He went to rob them. It was other people who did the killing. If he had been anyone else, he would have been out on the streets years ago. But they need him as their scapegoat.

TOMMY: They?

JOSH: The corporations. The polluters. The bullshitters in Washington. The people who really run this country. They needed a symbol. They needed someone to use as a weapon against anyone who stands up to them. They wanted to shut up the voices who were speaking out about pollution, about war, about how fake the civilisation that they had created was. Manson was just the tip of the iceberg, but they locked him away to send a message to everyone else.

TOMMY: Hang on...they locked him away because of his involvement in the Tate/LaBianca murders...

JOSH: Look, we're not saying that nobody got killed. We're not saying that...

AMANDA: The real killers walked free.

TOMMY: The real killers?

AMANDA: Linda Kasabian. Got a new life, disappeared into the Witness Protection programme...

JOSH: Tex Watson was the guy who was there both nights, both killings. He was out of it on acid. Susan Atkins, too. These are the people who stabbed those people.

AMANDA: They keep saying that Charlie ordered the killings, but it's all on the testimony of, you know, two people who have become born-again Christians and a woman at the scene of the crime who got to disappear, got her freedom.

TOMMY: Isn't this a little like picking over the details of the Holocaust and arguing about whether Hitler knew because there's no paper document that says he ordered it? You do believe the Holocaust happened?

AMANDA: Of course.

TOMMY: You're saying that Manson had no knowledge of the murders?

AMANDA: He did after they happened.

JOSH: Look, they make this big fucking thing in this country about how everyone has the right to be tried by a jury and to receive justice. What justice did he receive? They wouldn't let him conduct his own defence. That's a right that's guaranteed by the sixth amendment to the Constitution. They wouldn't let him talk to the jury in case he convinced them that he wasn't guilty. Surely that's the point of a trial?

AMANDA: They thought he would hypnotise them. Does that seem likely to you?

TOMMY: No, but that's not really the point...

AMANDA: It is! It's exactly the point!

JOSH: He was denied something that is supposed to be the right of every citizen in this country. I mean, do you believe that everyone who is found guilty by the courts in this country is actually guilty?

TOMMY: There are miscarriages of justice everywhere. I believe Manson is guilty, however.

AMANDA: That's exactly the kind of closed-minded thinking that has landed him in a jail cell for a quarter of a century without hope of parole... He was denied the right to appeal. They were going to put him in the gas chamber and they wouldn't let him appeal.

JOSH: You believe he's guilty based on what? The Bugliosi book? The Ed Sanders book? The Susan Atkins book? These people all had something to gain by making him the scapegoat. That Helter Skelter fantasy...

TOMMY: OK, tell me your version of what happened in the Tate/LaBianca killings.

JOSH: They went to do a copycat killing to make it look like Bobby Beausoleil was innocent.

TOMMY: You admit Beausoleil was guilty?

JOSH: He admits it.

TOMMY: And Manson was unaware of the killings?

AMANDA: That isn't what he was tried for. Even if he had known about them, he was at best an accessory to murder and should have been released five, ten years ago. They said he masterminded the murders, that he was behind every detail and the people who carried them out were just like these robots carrying out his instructions.

JOSH: Tex Watson was the leader. He was the killer. Both times. He's the guy who should scare the shit out of everyone. Instead, he runs this church inside prison and everyone's real respectful of him – you know, poor Tex, too dumb and stoned to know what he was doing. But without all the Manson mind-control mumbo-jumbo and the Helter Skelter stuff, the prosecution didn't have a case. They ignored everything that didn't point a finger at

Manson. I mean, if he really believed all that Helter Skelter stuff then surely he was completely fucking insane and was therefore not fit to stand trial?

TOMMY: Well, surely if 'they' only wanted a hippy scapegoat, then Tex Watson would have done as well as anyone. What did 'they' have to gain by setting up this innocent guy…or this guy who was just around, an accessory after the fact or whatever…and setting him up as the brains behind the killings?

AMANDA: Manson was articulate. He was smart. He had a message. They wanted to shut him up.

TOMMY: What was his message?

AMANDA: Stop destroying the Earth. ATWA. Air, Trees, Water, Animals.

TOMMY: But in that case, why don't they target Greenpeace and Earth First?

AMANDA: They do!

JOSH: Manson's philosophy has a soul, a life and a mind. It's not just about economics; it's not about buying a nicer brand of detergent. He was saying that the way we live is wrong and that we need to change in order to survive. Not just change a little bit or drive cars with lead-free petrol but change everything, to become wild again. Get away from this [waves hand at LA in general], back to the way we're supposed to live.

TOMMY: How did you come in contact with Manson? His ideas?

AMANDA: When I was young, we lived around Laurel Canyon and I remember the murders on TV. My older sister knew some of the Manson... I'm loath to say 'Family' 'cause that's the label the media put on them. You know, there were people who hung around with Manson. Women, mostly. They were friends and they didn't all hang at the same time all the time. Anyway, my sister knew some people out at the Spahn ranch and would go out there sometimes – this was after they were all arrested, by the way – and she used to say, 'I can't believe this, they're being set up' when it came on TV. Anyway, when I got older I read the books and saw the movies and wanted to check it out for myself. I started to get interested in ecology and I've always been a vegetarian. Anyway, the more I found out about Manson, the more I realised that we had been lied to. And I'm not alone. I know people who think the same way.

JOSH: To me, Manson is a political prisoner in exactly the same way that Nelson Mandela is a political prisoner or Leonard Peltier [Native American activist jailed on a trumped-up murder charge] is a political prisoner. The American justice system is unwilling to admit that it made a mistake and I want to be here to keep pushing, keep reminding them. Manson has never taken the easy way out and said, 'Yeah, I did it. I brainwashed those hippies and made them go and kill those people but I'm real, real sorry.' He's always stood up for the truth all this time, even though they might parole him if he played the game. He's prepared to die in prison. That takes bravery.

TOMMY: And you feel no sympathy for the victims?

JOSH: Of course, but they weren't Manson's victims. It was Tex Watson who knew that house better than Manson. He had been there more often than Manson. But the prosecution conveniently left that out of their case because they wanted everything to point to Manson.

TOMMY: What do you think of Manson's music?

AMANDA: Well, it might surprise you but I'm not really a fan. I also really don't buy this idea that he was a frustrated rock star who went on a revenge killing spree against the music business...

TOMMY: Nor me.

JOSH: I think the songs are OK. He could have been big back then, I guess. I don't know that it's a great thing that Guns N'Roses are covering his stuff because he doesn't actually get to see any of the proceeds from that, so really they're just stealing from him.

TOMMY: What activities are you involved in?

AMANDA: Writing letters to the authorities drawing attention to his case...

JOSH: But mostly spreading the word and making contacts and getting involved with campaigns. Like, we are involved in the campaign against the Alaska oil pipeline.

AMANDA: I volunteer at an animal shelter.

TOMMY: Are you Nazis?

AMANDA: Of course not. That's the easiest way to discredit anyone, call them racists or Nazis.

TOMMY: What about the swastika? And don't tell me it's an ancient Vedic symbol of the sun.

AMANDA: Well, it is. Actually, I regret having had this done now. Not that I'm ashamed of it, but I have to spend all my time explaining it. People just focus right on it... I did it when I was younger and never really thought the whole thing through.

JOSH: I know what you're getting at. I'm not a Nazi or a racist, but it seems like there are these ideas that are ringfenced with danger signs and I'm not afraid to seek the truth, even if that means having some uncomfortable opinions.

There's still an aura surrounding Manson's name. The LAPD refused to talk to me about the case. Ditto prosecutor Vincent Bugliosi. It's as though they all expect the killings to begin again or something. Is it because after only 30 years it is all still too close to us? Probably. LA seems perversely proud of its other celebrated murders, like the Black Dahlia case. It's a city that produces a rich crop of crime fiction, from the novels of Raymond Chandler and James Ellroy, TV shows like *Dragnet*, *Adam 12* and *LA Law*, to *film noir* and the countless cop thrillers churned out in Hollywood's back yard. People you meet who have no involvement with real, actual crime seem to take a sort of macho pride in how tough and terrifying LA districts like Watts can be and the risks of life in the city of Angels.

Whether or not it's the whiff of danger that adds some spice to LA's comparatively sedate life, who can say? People will regale you with tales of how they survived the earthquake of 1994 or the riots or a mudslide or an out-of-control brush fire in the hills.

In the period following the Manson killings, a whole host of minor celebrities and aspiring celebrities told tales of how they were supposed to be at Sharon Tate's house the night of the murders or how their name was on the Manson Family's death list of actors, singers and politicians. Steve McQueen, one-time boyfriend of Sharon Tate, was supposed to be at the house on Cielo Drive on the fateful night but allegedly picked up a woman and changed his plans. *Valley Of The Dolls* author Jaqueline Susann was also supposed to be at the house. (Sharon Tate's best-known screen role is as the pill-popping Jennifer in the 1967 film of the novel.)

'The LAPD screwed up the actual investigation,' crime reporter Mark Lennox tells me. 'They're still sensitive about it after all these years. They got lucky with a jailhouse confession. Otherwise, Manson might have worked his way through all of those names on the list. Tom

Jones was on there, Liz Taylor, Richard Burton, Yul Brynner. I mean, Yul Brynner? What the hell was that about?'

At the time of the killings, Lennox worked for the *Hollywood Citizen News* and covered the initial investigations into the killings. 'They were saying all kinds of stuff, that they were mob-related killings because Leno LaBianca was an Italian-American. They said that they were carried out by the KGB because Roman Polanski had fled communist Poland. They said that it might be black radicals, which is exactly what Manson wanted people to think. They said that Jay Sebring was involved in some big-time drugs operation. But there was real fear at that time. It was a crazy time, anyway. The 1960s were a violent and ugly time in LA. You had riots, you had killings, you had rapes. You had the first stirrings from radical groups like the Black Panthers, the Weathermen and the Symbionese Liberation Army, just rumours that they were going to let off bombs or drop acid in the water supply. You had the Hell's Angels riding down Sunset like an invading army. You had all sorts of weirdness going on behind closed doors. You could believe that anything was possible. I remember that there was a guy who told me that there would be parties where they would have a girl, probably kidnapped in Mexico and drugged, and they would fuck her and then execute her while all these studio execs, these rich guys, stood around and watched. Now, whether that's true, I don't know. It's probably – I hope to God – one of those urban myths, like snuff movies, but at the time I thought, "Well, yeah, that could happen."'

The investigation that eventually led to the arrest and capture of Manson was meticulous and there is no doubt as to the guilt of everyone involved, but are we likely to find that there were many more killings? What about Bugliosi's figure of 35?

'Lots of people have gone missing in LA, all over California, in the past 30 years. Who knows? After Squeaky tried to shoot Gerald Ford, a whole lot of stories started doing the rounds – that the Family were all still out there creepy-crawling around. Don't forget that there were about 25 or 30 hardcore Family members but there were a lot of other associated hangers-on, people who drifted in and out of Spahn, people who had been listening to Manson since Haight-

Ashbury. And don't forget also that he receives letters in prison from all these kids telling him that they want to go and kill somebody for him and who should they kill? Most of them are just little dummies, but who knows who has actually gone out and killed somebody for Charlie? Ruth Ann Morehouse was never caught after she tried to dose a trial witness with acid. I think a lot of those people have probably grown up and are now shocked at what happened, but there are all these characters like Sandy Good who are sort of like the keepers of Charlie's flame. They're out there.'

Like many other Angelenos, and particularly those who document the city's secret history, Lennox seems to almost take a strange pride in the city's ugly side. 'People come here and they see where movie stars live,' he says. 'I look around and I see murder scenes. There's one on every corner.'

14 Down In The Valley So Deep

'Bleached by the sun and scorned by the moon,
  If I make it 'til tomorrow noon, I'm leaving
'Tween the horror of space and the terror of time,
My heart in crystal, down the line, I'm screaming'
          – *Blue Öyster Cult, 'Death Valley Nights'*

Deserts have been retreats for religious zealots, shamen and mystics probably since the beginning of time. One thinks of the Essenes in the hard-baked rocks and caves outside Jerusalem, racked by visions and through their ascetic life becoming fanatical, removed from the mainstream of civilisation. Or John the Divine, exiled to the island of Patmos, scribbling the poisonous text of Revelation in a fever. Or the Stylites, engaged in pointless acts of humility and abasement to God.

The Barker ranch can be reached only in a four-wheel-drive off-road vehicle. Just within the boundaries of Death Valley National Park, you pass abandoned mines and burnt-out cars, which may be decades old though they have not fully rusted away in the moistureless heat. Death Valley is the hottest, driest, lowest spot in North America. The Barker ranch is located in a rock- and boulder-filled valley near the top of the desert mountain range. Streams feed this little valley and provide much vegetation. It is surprisingly lush and green, like an oasis amid the bleak terrain around it. There is a small one-room guesthouse located to the side of the main house. There is also a primitive-style swimming pool made from cement and rock boulders towards the back of the property; it has an unappealing film of slime on its surface. There is actually a sign and an entry in the guide books that mark this out as the site where the Manson Family were finally captured. The local County Sheriff's Department and National Park law enforcers captured Manson and his group here in 1969. They wanted to prosecute the persons responsible for vandalising a portion of the National Park further north, unaware of any involvement in the Tate/LaBianca murders.

The Barker ranch is one of several locations that the Family used in 1968 and 1969. They built a track up here a few years ago, so it is actually easier to reach than it was in 1969. For me, as a London-based city boy, however, the journey, even in a four-wheel-drive SUV, still seems as arduous as a yomp across the Kalahari.

It is eerily quiet here and there is a real sense that you are in a wilderness, that if you got lost out here you would quite possibly never be found again. And unless somebody knew where to look, this would be the perfect place to hide.

I find it hard to breathe and drink a couple of two-litre bottles of mineral water within the space of about ten minutes. The idea of anyone actually living here seems quite implausible. The vegetation is sparse and the only evidence of human habitation apart from the desiccated and apparently abandoned dwellings are pieces of broken machinery and the hulks of abandoned cars, stripped of all and any useful parts and left here like the bones of dead cattle.

Somebody has set up little shrines around the Barker ranch, little circles of stones with what look like corn dollies in the centre. I'm not superstitious and pride myself on my rationality, but somehow I'm creeped out enough not to want to go near them, like someone who won't walk under a ladder. There is no 'bad vibe' about the place other than the one I have created in my own mind, but it is a relief to leave.

The Spahn ranch, where Manson and his followers hid out in 1969, is by contrast a comparatively short hop from the north of LA. As you drive along Iverson Road, you can see the spot where the movie-set ranch stood until it burned down during a brush fire in 1970. There's a 'For Sale' sign and a 'No Trespassing' sign. Somebody has scrawled 'Healter Skelter' in red paint – I hope – on the back of the former. At one time, it was owned by silent-film cowboy star and director William S Hart. The 511-acre ranch was a horse ranch that rented horses to the movie business. It was used as a set for Westerns, though latterly it has been used to shoot porn films such as *The Fabulous Bastard From Chicago*, *The Female Bunch*, *The Ramrodder* (in which Manson associate Bobby Beausoleil appeared) and *Hard On The Trail* (in which Manson Family victim Donald 'Shorty' Shea appeared).

Many of the ranches in the area were used in the filming of Western movies and TV series. I'm told that adjoining properties were used for shooting episodes of *Bonanza*, *Gunsmoke*, *Star Trek*, *Zorro*, *The Monroes*, *How The West Was Won*, *Dundee And The Culhane*, *The Big Valley* and *Have Gun Will Travel*, all TV shows that I remember vaguely from my childhood. As a result, the terrain is almost familiar: bleached pale-ochre rocks, sagebrush, a sky that is never anything but high-contrast blue. There are rattlesnakes here, and I am warned to be careful and not to sit down without looking. It's not the vast magnificent Western terrain of John Ford's *Stagecoach* or *The Searchers*, filmed in the more epic terrain of Monument Valley; it's the low-budget West. You feel somehow as though you're on the set of an episode of one of those cheesy 1960s TV Westerns like *Champion The Wonder Horse* – any minute you expect a bad actor on a horse to ride over the rocks and tell you that he's gonna 'head 'em off at the pass'.

There are still a lot of tourists from LA around who have come to look at the decaying sets – a new kind of ghost town. They ride horses and pretend to be cowboys like characters in the 1970s sci-fi film *Westworld*. Andy, my guide, a local journalist and something of an amateur historian of the great and the not-so-great days of Hollywood, points out where various shacks and buildings once stood, where Manson and the Family holed up at various times between 1968 and their eventual capture in 1969. 'If you knew what you were doing, you could hide out here forever,' says Andy. 'I've heard stories about survivalist types who have lived in Death Valley for years. There's everything here – food, water – if you know where to look and how to go about getting it.'

The Family used the Spahn ranch as a playground, a refuge from harassment at the hands of Californian law enforcement, a secluded community where they could live an idyllic existence, walking around without clothes, going on runs to nearby shops to rake through the garbage bins for food, taking acid in the vast privacy of the desert. This is where their plans were hatched – they were going to send out missionaries to set up similar communes up and down the Pacific coast. At one point, Bruce Davis even came to London. This is where the dream started to go bad.

The heat is a dry heat, so you don't get soaked in sweat the way you do in the interminable humidity and smog of LA itself, but after only a few hours I start to feel freaked out by the space, the light and the relentless sun.

Perhaps it's just my imagination and the overwrought feelings brought on by the fact that I am unused to this environment and am experiencing a profound culture shock, but I feel uneasy here, as though there are bad vibes in the air.

We drive back along Topanga Canyon road, past the house known as the Spiral Staircase, stopping off at a new-age bookstore and gift shop called The Spiral Staircase. It sells the usual monotonous selection of rainbow-fronted self-help tomes, UFO contactee screeds and offers signings of books on inner-child therapies and astrology.

The sales assistant is the more conventional new-age student kind, the sort of pretty cheerleader type who would probably have run off to join the Manson Family 30 years ago. She smilingly tells me that she is unaware of any connection between the Spiral Staircase shop and the occult centre of the same name.

Driving away, we pass a man – white, tanned like a lizard and possibly in his early 60s – wearing a white monk's robe, his long grey hair held in a headband and carrying a staff with a crescent moon at the top. He is leading a procession of ten or so girls and young boys wearing similar robes in red.

Andy, my driver, nonchalantly tells me that he's just one of many kooks you see up here. He doesn't even make a Manson connection, just another Heaven's Gate or Unarius crazy old coot with a few know-nothing kids who think he's a guru. Another shepherd of the lost and the lonely here in God's Western Eden.

15 The Manson Family: The Next Generation

'The days of digging Charles Manson are long gone.
It only shocks the sort of people who thought
the new U2 album was weird'

– Julian Cope

When Guns N'Roses released their collection of punk covers, *The Spaghetti Incident*, in 1993, the band was already in free-falling decline. Their debut album, *Appetite For Destruction*, had been released in July 1987 and included three Top Ten singles – 'Sweet Child O' Mine', 'Paradise City' and 'Welcome To The Jungle' – and went on to sell more than 20 million copies. Guns N'Roses were the ultimate white-trash metal band whose on-the-road penchant for drugs, groupies and hard living is the stuff of legends.

But in the wake of Nirvana's seminal *Nevermind* and the upsurge in new, vital rock bands like Pearl Jam, Guns N'Roses were starting to look ridiculous. In a small way, they were in the same position that the bloated 1970s rock dinosaurs found themselves in when confronted by angry, spiky-headed punks in the mid-1970s. Guns N'Roses had always thrived on controversy – at the Castle Donington Monsters of Rock festival in the UK, two fans were killed in the riotous crowd; 'One In A Million' from their 1988 'G N'R Lies' EP was both racist and homophobic – and their decision to cover a Charles Manson song on the album was calculated to win them maximum publicity. Axl Rose had performed in a Charles Manson T-shirt, revelling in the equation of them as two 'outlaw icons', but covering the song was to backfire on them.

Speaking to me in the mid-1990s after the furore had died down, Axl claimed – incredibly – that he was unaware that the song was by

Manson: 'I was played this track and I thought it was really good...really great. I'd never have guessed who it was. We decided we wanted to do it, and it was only then that I found out it was by Charles Manson.' Axl then refused to discuss the matter any further or give his opinions, claiming 'they're too easily misinterpreted'.

Patti Tate, sister of Sharon, was outraged and called for a boycott against Geffen, the band's label. Geffen issued a statement saying that they would have preferred the track not to have been on the album and accusing the band of poor judgement. Rose then issued a 1,000-word press release, trying to justify 'Look At Your Game Girl' as being of 'historical and musical' importance, lambasting the media for picking up on it, recalling his own violent childhood in Indiana, claiming that the song applied to a 'personal situation I happened to be in', calling Manson 'a sick individual', admitting that he enjoys the 'black humour' in wearing a Manson T-shirt onstage and claiming that Dennis Wilson of The Beach Boys wrote the song, anyway. He ended by complaining that people never pay enough attention to his charity work, such as dolphin conservation.

In the wake of Rose's endorsement, sales of Manson T-shirts boomed. The 'Charlie Don't Surf'/'Support Family Values' shirts from Zooport Riot Gear, California, were soon bootlegged all over the world. Stories appeared in the press that Manson had cut a deal where he received 10¢ on every T-shirt bearing his image sold. He also stood to earn at least $60,000 in royalties from the track on *The Spaghetti Incident*.

In the end, all mechanical royalties were paid to Bartek Frykowski, son of Voytek, then living in Lodz, Poland. The Voytek family had brought a civil suit against Manson, Watkins, Atkins and Krenwinkel in 1971. He petitioned the LA courts when his lawyer informed him of the Guns N'Roses controversy.

What was significant about Guns N'Roses was that they were not some underground punk band or some art-house goths who were going to be lucky to have sales in double figures; this was a mass-market album that you could buy in Wal-Mart. The track was left uncredited on the sleeve of the album.

There had been a long tradition in the 1980s of punk bands covering Manson songs. 'Sick City' almost became a punk standard. Boyd Rice, Satanist, fascist apologist, industrial music pioneer with his band NON, collector of Barbie dolls and number-one fan of Tiny Tim, performed a version of 'Sick City' backed by The Meat Puppets, a seminal 1980s UK punk band. Boyd wrote to Manson in prison and co-edited *The Manson Files* with Nicholas Schreck, another Satanist/ industrial music-maker. GG Allin also covered 'Sick City' and 'Garbage Dump', at one time with various members of Sonic Youth and Dinosaur Jr backing him.

Kitsch band Red Kross covered 'Cease To Exist' as a hidden track on their album *Born Innocent*. In an interview with *Trenchmouth Supermodel* magazine in 1993, Jeff McDonald of the band said, 'Well, this was kind of before there was any kind of Charles Manson revival. Now it's very hip in the rock 'n' roll scene to be a Charles Manson fan. We were kind of pioneers. It was very tongue in cheek. It was basically a way to bum out our parents. We were very heavily into this Charles Manson thing and we wanted to do "Cease To Exist" because we would do it in our garage and it sounded really good. In one of the last sessions of *Born Innocent*, we just started jamming it and it ended up good enough to go on record. When we had finished it, we heard that there were still Charles Manson loyalists out and Rodney Bingenheimer actually used to know the Manson Family and he said, "Well, you know, those people are kind of a little bit unbalanced and you don't really want to mess with them." So we kind of thought, "Well, let's just put it on as a bonus track with no listing." We thought it would be interesting and mysterious.'

Evan Dando of The Lemonheads has made several links to Manson. *Creator*, the band's 1988 album, has a cover of Manson's 'Home Is Where You're Happy' as well as a song called 'Clang Bang Clang', the alternate title for Manson's 'Big Iron Door'. There's also a Manson photo and various thank-yous to infamous Family members on the sleeve credits. *Lovey*, the Lemonheads' breakthrough album, has a track called 'Ballarat', which is reportedly about Manson. In an interview with a Scottish fanzine, Dando admitted his interest: 'I've been interested in Manson for a long time. I'm still just really interested in it, you know? There's just something about it.'

Cult Californian band The Brian Jonestown Massacre acknowledge Manson as a musical influence along with Bob Dylan and Syd Barrett, even 'collaborating' on a rewrite of Manson's 'Arkansas', titled 'Arkansas Revisited', on their 2000 album *Bringing It All Back Home Again*.

All of the above bands use Manson as a shortcut to shock value but wash their hands of any suggestion that they in any way endorse what he stands for. It's the sick thrill again.

Even songs that are anti-Manson cannot help but trade on the glamour with which he invests them. New York art-rock band Sonic Youth recorded a song called 'Death Valley '69' (also called 'Spahn Ranch Drive') on their classic 1985 album *Bad Moon Rising*. The words are oblique, starting with 'Coming down/Sadie, I love it/Now now now/Death valley '69'. The song is obviously about Manson (Sadie being the nickname of Susan Atkins) and the Tate murders. Later in the song, Lydia Lunch, guest vocalist on the track, sings, 'She started to holler/I didn't wanna/I didn't wanna/I didn't wanna/I didn't wanna/But she started to holler/So I had to hit it/Hit it/Hit it/Hit it', which alludes to Susan Atkins killing Sharon Tate. The song isn't exactly saying 'go and kill', but the title alone sounds like a cool manifesto.

Other art projects include John Moran's opera *The Manson Family*, which made its debut at New York City Lincoln Center's 'Serious Fun!' series in July 1990. It was the fourth opera by Moran, a composer who mixes popular with avant-garde music, creating his operas from 'collage sounds' (ie electronically treated sounds), using spoken as well as sung libretti and dealing with contemporary subjects. The recording featured Iggy Pop as Vincent Bugliosi and Terre Roche as Lynette 'Squeaky' Fromme, with Paige Snell as Susan Atkins (a role she originated onstage) and the composer himself as Manson. Moran used cut-ups, pastiche and samples of The Beatles' 'White Album'. The album was panned by critics for its music but also because it was felt that Moran reserved judgement on Manson.

Other artists have flirted with the Manson connection but rejected it.

Trent Reznor of Nine Inch Nails, mentor to Marilyn Manson, once voted one of the most influential figures of his generation by *Time* magazine, moved into the house at Cielo Drive while he was in Los Angeles working on his seminal album *The Downward Spiral*. Like all of his work, it is dark, obsessed with the bleak side of humanity. Yet his stay in Cielo Drive was also an epiphany. In an interview in the March 1997 issue of *Rolling Stone*, he said, 'There's a part of me that is intrigued by that. For example, I loved the Hannibal Lecter character in *The Silence Of The Lambs*. The last person I want to see get hurt in that story is him. And I think, "Why do I look at him as a hero figure?" Because you respect him. Because he represents everything you wish you could be in a lawless, moral-less society. I allow myself to think, "Yeah, if I could kill people without reprimand, maybe I would, you know?" I hate myself for thinking that, but there's an appeal to the idea, because it is a true freedom. Is it wrong? Yeah. But is there an appeal to that? Yeah. It's the ultimate taboo.

'My awakening about all that stuff came from meeting Sharon Tate's sister. While I was working on *The Downward Spiral*, I was living in the house where Sharon Tate was killed. Then one day I met her sister. It was a random thing, just a brief encounter. And she said, "Are you exploiting my sister's death by living in her house?" For the first time, the whole thing kind of slapped me in the face. I said, "No, it's just sort of my own interest in American folklore. I'm in this place where a weird part of history occurred." I guess it never really struck me before, but it did then. She lost her sister from a senseless, ignorant situation that I don't want to support. When she was talking to me, I realised for the first time, "What if it was my sister?" I thought, "Fuck Charlie Manson." I don't want to be looked at as a guy who supports serial-killer bullshit.

'I went home and cried that night. It made me see there's another side to things, you know? It's one thing to go around with your dick swinging in the wind, acting like it doesn't matter. But when you understand the repercussions that are felt…that's what sobered me up, realising that what balances out the appeal of the lawlessness and the lack of morality and the whole thing is the other end of it, the victims who don't deserve that.'

★

But in the wake of Marilyn Manson's endorsement of his namesake, there is a new breed of bands who *do* support Manson, who are not in any 'cult' ghetto.

Phil Anselmo of Pantera, as well as sporting a 'Charlie Don't Surf' T-shirt and affecting a personal style reminiscent of Manson, wearing a blue denim prison shirt with the nametag 'Manson' and Charlie's prison number stencilled on it, also wrote a song called 'Creepy Crawl', which appears on the debut album by his side project Superjoint Ritual.

Anselmo was ambivalent about Manson when I spoke to him: 'Actually I'm more interested in him as a very interesting study in human psychology. When you think about what really went down, what happened, why he's behind bars, it all makes for very fucking interesting food for thought. True crime always interests me very much.'

When pushed, Anselmo admits that his association with Manson was for shock value and not because of any genuine admiration: 'I've said the same thing to my mother and she said to me, "Well if there was a guy on the streets who you knew about who sent some of his friends to kill your sister, how would you feel about that?", and that stopped me in my tracks because I thought to myself, "Well, I'd want to kill that motherfucker, too." But without being there and without knowing hands-on what really happened, because there's so many different versions of the story floating around, I guess none of us will ever truly know what went on. In my eyes, looking at a bunch of young adults who should very much have the sensibility to make up their own minds and do just what they planned to do, I don't think anyone controls anyone else. I think that's a little absurd. To say, "Charlie made me do it" – well, that brings to mind the old adage "Well, if someone asks you to jump off a bridge, are you gonna do it?" No telling, with that mixture of LSD. It was the times, the 1960s, the drug culture. If you look back to the time from the middle 1960s to the middle 1970s, it seemed like everybody wanted to have this Jesus Christ figure to look to. Even in the 1980s, with David Koresh, people were dying to have this Jesus Christ role model to follow.'

Like their nu metal contemporaries Korn, Limp Bizkit and Snot, System Of A Down sound as white-bread American as apple pie and drive-by shootings. Vocalist Serj Tankian and drummer John Dolmayan were both born in Lebanon and bassist Shavo Odadjian was born in Armenia. The band mixes Middle Eastern, Native American, Armenian and tribal rhythms in a forceful and engaging melting pot of metal. Formed in the mid-1990s, System Of A Down went into the studio towards the end of the decade with legendary producer Rick Rubin to cut their self-titled debut. The album sold well, despite the fact that there were no obvious singles and it received minimal radio and TV exposure. Slots on the Family Values 1999 tour and Metallica's Summer Sanitarium tour in 2000 brought the band to the attention of a generation of malcontents. Like their contemporaries, they are powered by a dynamo of anger and frustration. But Korn's anger is largely apolitical. System Of A Down have a well-thought-out political edge, which has led to comparisons with The Dead Kennedys. *Toxicity* – also produced by Rubin – is one of the albums, along with releases by Staind and Slipknot, that saw metal dominate the charts in 2001, and such bands take their place in rock's premier league in 2002.

Yet one of the songs on the album, 'ATWA', is a song defending Charles Manson. The lyrics don't say a great deal: 'Hey you, see me, pictures crazy/All the world I've seen before me passing by/I've got nothing to gain, to lose/All the world I've seen before me passing by/You don't care about how I feel/I don't feel it any more'. In interviews, the band have aligned themselves to Sandra Good/Manson's ATWA organisation: 'Our band was formed on strong opinions,' guitarist Daron Malakian told *USA Today* in October 2001, pointing out that, while the band is solidly opposed to murder, it wanted to spotlight Manson as an 'important figure in the environmental movement'. 'We're trying to open the door a little wider and show another side,' he said. In the liner notes of *Toxicity*, they thank Manson 'for his inspiration and honesty'.

It's odd that a band who seem in other ways to be politically astute should align themselves with a racist like Manson, but the ecology movement as a whole has some odious antecedents, such as the Nazi 'blood and soil' philosopher Walter Darre.

Mushroomhead, another up-and-coming US band, a theatrical-metal eight-piece in the Slipknot mould, also namecheck Manson in 'Bwomp', a track from their debut album *XX*: 'There's no sympathetic posturing/There's no more true humanity/The old ways aren't working anymore/Let's separate the users from the whores/Creepy crawl… Twist the four-five cap and understand/That if it was up to me, I'd free Charles Manson/Throw it all away/Let's separate the users from the whores/What do we have to hope for?/Why do we even try?/Laughed at religion long ago/I doubt I'll be an angel when I die'.

Like many people I have come across, Mushroomhead singer Jay and drummer Skinny from the band are adamant that Manson was denied a fair trial and seem angry at this fact. There's not exactly a cop-out, but they stop short of saying that they admire him. 'If they released Manson, there would just be a 60-year-old guy walking around,' Jay told me when I met them both in early 2002. 'Instead, by keeping him in jail, they make him a martyr.'

Off the record, a number of established and up-and-coming bands have talked to me about Manson and all of them trot out the same stuff, like a party line. Manson is an environmental martyr. He was set up. He is innocent. Society was to blame.

These are not obscure dark-wave bands or punks playing to audiences of six and using cartoons of Manson in their handbills. Manson's new school of fans sell out stadiums and have gold records. They appear on MTV and on the cover of *Rolling Stone*.

There's an undeniable attraction to Manson because he is a figure who inspires fear in others in straight society. To many of these bands, whose members were actually born some years after the Manson murders, there is no real sense of connection to the victims, to the times or to the motives. Manson is only as real as Hannibal Lecter (the suave serial killer from the films *Manhunter* and *Silence Of The Lambs*), Freddy Kruger (from the *Nightmare On Elm Street* series), Michael Myers, Jason (from *Friday The 13th* parts 1 through 17!) or the anti-heroes of countless straight-to-video teen slasher flicks. He's part of a pantheon of sick heroes that includes 1950s serial killer Ed Gein, killer clown John Wayne Gacy and creepy cannibal Jeffrey Dahmer.

There are complex reasons why these kids will identify with such characters, but mostly it comes down to the position of weakness in which most young people feel themselves to be. They are physically weak and often the prey of bullies, they are financially weak and unable to stand on their own two feet and they are emotionally weak and unable to deal with the world around them with confidence. Wearing a Charles Manson T-shirt, an icon that will shock or revolt adults, is a sort of defence. It's like a tribal totem or a war face – by carrying the image of something terrifying, you take some of that on yourself. You become bad.

But there's also something about America and outlaws. Within a remarkably short space of time, murderers, thieves, bandits and rustlers are canonised – they become American heroes. Villains of the Old West such as the James Gang, the Hole in the Wall Gang, Doc Holliday and Billy the Kid have been retooled and rehabilitated as heroes – usually posthumously, though not always – by colourful pulp magazines, popular songs and Hollywood movies. Similarly, Depression-era gangsters like Pretty Boy Floyd, Bonnie and Clyde, Al Capone, the Barker Gang and John Dillinger have become, at worst, victims of society and, at best, freedom fighters, latter-day Robin Hoods (a man whose story was no doubt a cleaned-up biography of some real-life Norman warlord or robber baron).

That process – for better or worse, and like it or not – is taking place with Manson. Regardless of the truth, there is a perception that Manson is a true modern-day outlaw, persecuted and set up by the government. Well, if they can make heroes out of bloodthirsty killers like Butch Cassidy and the Sundance Kid, why not Manson?

In an interview with *Disinformation*, a webzine dedicated to fringe subjects, unpopular music and dissident viewpoints, George Stinson – who maintained *Access Manson*, Manson's website (currently closed because, allegedly, Manson felt it made him seem too respectable) – said of the response, 'Reaction has been overwhelmingly positive, like 90 per cent. And little of the negative mail has showed much mind beyond just saying we're crazy. Positive responses have ranged from many-paged messages expressing empathy and a willingness to help, to messages that simply say "thank you"... We've heard from students, lawyers, blue-collar people, people who are still affected by the counter-culture, all kinds. And yes, we hear from a lot of young people, many who are not familiar with Manson and his case from their own memory of the time. Kids are fine. The people who were with Manson in 1969 were mostly kids.'

The children may once again come at you with knives.

Appendix 1: A Manson Discography

CHARLES MANSON

Lie: The Love And Terror Cult
Awareness 1970; re-released ESP-DISK 1974; re-released Grey Matter 1987
Contains recordings made by Manson prior to the Tate/LaBianca murders for Terry Melcher, produced by Gregg Jakobson with Dennis Wilson, recorded 1968

Track listing:
'Look At Your Game Girl'
'Ego'
'Mechanical Man'
'People Say I'm No Good'
'Home Is Where You're Happy'
'Arkansas'
'I'll Never Say Never To Always'
'Garbage Dump'
'Don't Do Anything Illegal'
'Sick City'
'Cease To Exist'
'Big Iron Door'
'I Once Knew A Man'
'Eyes Of A Dreamer'

Live At San Quentin
Grey Matter 1983
Recorded in Manson's jail cell

Track listing:
'Boxcar Willie And Big Bad Joe'
'Television Mind'
'Marilyn Monroe Was My Childhood Shame'
'Instrumental'
'And As I Told You On This Chord Once Before'
'So As The Hour Goes On That I Will Spend With You'
'I Got A Tough Bastard Child Wants To Become A Samurai'
'So Today Has Been A Good Day'
'My Name Is Sam McGee'
'Take Me To The Summer Road'
'My Feelings Begin To Grow'
'And I'd Like To Say Hello To Some Of My Friends'
'So The Mood Was Broken'

The Way Of The Wolf
Pale Horse

Track listing:
'Universal Law'
'Blind Sky'
'All In The Motions'
'In The Infinite Mind'
'Red Snake'
'Eternal Wind'
'Dead Grass Growing In The Garden'
'Major'
'Prison Conversion'
'I'm Your Music Mind'
'I'm Doin' Fine'
'Stars'

'Friends'
'Dream Train/My Oklahoma Angel Love'
'Atwa/Computer Perfection'

Commemoration
White Devil
Recorded at the Vacaville Medical Facility, 1982–85

'Introduction'
'The Hallways Of The Always'
'A Peace In Your Heart'
'Give Your Love To Be Free'
'Atwa'
'Searchlight Dreams'
'Down In The Nuremberg'
'Father In The Universal Sky'
'Down In Dixieland'
'Monologue'
'Walking Through Forever'
'Reflections'
'A Tribute To Hank Williams'
'Be Free'
'Shakespeare's Clown'
'Hobo's Lament'
'Yellow Blues'
'The Spaceman'
'I'm Free Now'

Manson Speaks
White Devil
A collection of spoken-word material by Charles Manson containing a
reading from the Bible as well as impromptu performances of his poetry
and his thoughts on the OJ Simpson case and prisoners' rights, the
Rodney King beating, his feelings about ecology, world peace, racism
and the lies that have been told about him

Charles Manson Unplugged 9/11/67
Archer CAT Productions Inc
The 'lost' demo tapes recorded for Universal in 1967, the first in a
planned series of three

Track listing:
'Sick City'
'Run For Fun'
'Clang Bang Clang'
'Your Home'
'Monkey/Lock And Loll'
'Ego Is A Too Much Thing'
'Now Is The Time'
'The House Of Tomorrow'
'Close To Me'
'She Done Turned Me In'/'Twilight Blues'/'Your Daddy's Home'

Fire/The Hallways Of The Always
White Devil
7" vinyl 45rpm single, tracks taken from *Live At San Quentin* and
Commemoration respectively

RELATED

Manson Family Sings The Songs Of Charles Manson
ESP-DISK
Music written by Charles Manson, lead vocals by Steve 'Clem' Grogan;
back-up vocals were provided by 'Gypsy', 'Capistrano', 'Brenda',
'Ouisch', and 'Red' and 'Blue'

Track listing:
'Ride Away'
'Love's Death'
'Never Ask Why (Love Never Dies)'
'No Wrong'

'Get On Home'
'Is There No One In Your World But You?'
'I'm Scratching Peace Symbols On Your Tombstone'
'Give Your Love To Be Free'
'I'll Never Say Never To Always'
'Look At Your Love'
'What Would You Have Me Do?'
'Goin' To The Churchyard'

The Family Jams

Grey Matter 1997 re-release
Double CD accompanied by 20-page book, which contains liner notes
by Manson, Lynette Fromme and Sandra Good; CD1 listed as 'Manson
Family Sing The Songs Of Charles Manson', albeit remastered for
better sound; CD2 contains new/previously unreleased material

Track listing:
'A Gamblin' Man Come From Natchez'
'Ride Away'
'Die To Be One'
'The Fires Are Burning'
'Give Your Love (To Be Free)'
'The Young Will Overcome'
'Goin' To The Church House'
'The Fires Are Burning'
'I'll Never Say Never To Always'
'Die To Be One'
'Look At Your Love'
'I Can't Remember When'
'Give Your Love (To Be Free)'/'London Bridge Is Falling Down'

There are assorted cassette tape bootlegs and repackaging of this
material, such as Grey Matter's 'White Album' – basically a reissue of
Lie and *Manson Family Sing The Songs Of Charles Manson* in a white
sleeve that parodied the eponymous 1968 Beatles album.

CHANGES

Fire Of Life
Storm Productions
Whether this is 'related' depends on whether you subscribe to conspiracy theories involving Manson with the Process; compiled from vintage analogue open-reel recordings made between 1969 and 1974 by Changes (the Process Church's house band); like Manson, it's folky, but Changes tap right into contemporary goth, dark-wave and apocalyptic folk such as Current 93 and Sol Invictus; put together by author Michael Moynihan and Willi Stasch of German label Cthulhu

Track listing:
'Fire Of Life'
'Sweet Eve'
'Bleeding Out Your Feelings Evermore'
'The Saddest Thing'
'Early Morning Hours Of The Night'
'Memorabilia'
'Horizons That I See'
'Satanic Hymn #2'
'RIP Van Winkles Pipe Dream'
'The Stranger In The Mirror (Part 3)'
'Twilight Of The West'

Appendix 2: Manson Lyrics

The following lyrics by Charles Manson are taken from the 1970 Awareness album *Lie*.

'Look At Your Game Girl'

There's a time for livin'
The time keeps on flyin'
Think you're lovin' baby
And all you do is cryin'

Can you feel are those feelings real
Look at your game girl
Look at your game girl

What a mad delusion
Livin' in that confusion
Frustration and doubt
Can you ever live without the game?
The sad sad game
Mad game

Just to say your love's not enough
If'n you can't be true
You can tell those lies baby
But you're only foolin' you

Can you feel are those feelings real
Look at your game girl
Go on look at your game girl

If'n you can't feel
And the feelings ain't real
Then you better stop tryin'
Or you're gonna play cryin'
Stop tryin' or you're gonna play cryin'
That's the game
Sad sad game
Mad game
Sad game

'Ego' (aka 'Old Ego Is A Too Much Thing')

It's in, side
It's in the back
The front
No it's in the back
No it's in the front
No it's in the back
They shoved it in the back
They put it in the back
All the love in the back in the back
All the love in the back
Get in the back boy

And they call it your subconscious
Remember Freud
In the front is your computer
And I call him
Old ego is a too much thing
Old ego is a too much thing
He'll make you fool yourself

You'll think you're somebody else
They got the whole subway train
Makes you want to jump on up there and fight
And you can't stand left to your right

He'll make you lie
Make you cheat
Jus' so you won't be beat
He'll make you get on outta sight
You get afraid you gonna, act like a clown
And you get mad when somebody puts you down

Your heart's a-pumpin' and you pan-heart's a-jumpin'
Look out ego is a too much thing
When everything seems goin' so fine
Old ego puts itself on a bind
Your certainty turns to doubt
Then you start flippin' out
Then you ease on out of your mind

'Mechanical Man' (aka 'I Am A Mechanical Man')

I am a mechanical man
A mechanical man
And I do the best I can
Because I have my family
I am a mechanical boy
I am my mother's toy
And I play in the backyard sometime
I am a mechanical boy

The past is an illusion
Postulated mocked up through confusion
The future, will be confusion
In your, in your illusion

I had a little monkey
And I sent him to the country
And I fed him on gingerbread
Long come a choo-choo
And knocked my monkey cuckoo
And now my monkey's dead

Ban won't wear off
'Cause my monkey's dead
I'm so mechanical I–
Ban won't wear off
'Cause my monkey's dead
In your head go in and lay down
I wonder how, a brown cow
Could say moo
Down the road come my junco partner
London Bridge is falling down
Hey you're goin' the wrong way
I am?
I see you out there Joe
And you think your name is Joe
I see you out there Sam
And you think your name is Sam
You ain't Joe, you ain't Sam
You just am

'People Say I'm No Good'

People say I'm no good
But they never never do they say
Why their world is so mixed up
Or how it got that way

They all look at me and they frown
Do I really look so strange

If they really dug themselves
I know they'd want to change

Everybody says you're no good
'Cause you don't do like they think you should
Do you expect them
And do you expect you to act like them
Look at them man
Look at the fix they're in

I don't care I don't care what they say
Just let 'em sit there and burn
The young might not be so dumb after all
And from the young you might even learn

Everybody says you're no good
'Cause Charles you don't do
You don't do like they think you should
Do you expect them to act like you
Do you expect them
To expect you to act like them
Do you expect to see
Do you expect the fool to see what a fix he's in
Do you expect the fool to see what a fix he's in

In your cardboard houses
And your tin-can cars
You sit there and you wonder
You wonder where you are

Those diamond rings they're obscene
You sit there and you wonder
And you say who's to blame
Take a look at yourself
Take yourself off the shelf

You can't belong to nobody

With your Can't-Cough medicine
And your wonder drug
You got, more sickness
Than you got cures of
Cancer of the mind

'Home Is Where You're Happy' (aka 'Your Home Is Where You're Happy')

Your home is where you're happy
It's not where you're not free
Your home is where you can be what you are
'Cause you were just born free

Now they'll show you their castles
And diamonds for all to see
But they'll never show you that peace of mind
'Cause they don't know how to be free

So burn all your bridges
Leave your whole life behind
You can do what you want to do
'Cause you're strong in your mind

And anywhere you might wander
You could make that your home
And as long as you got love in your heart
You'll never be alone

Just as long as you got love in your heart
You'll never be alone, no no no
You'll never be alone, no no no no

'Arkansas'

Far, far down Arkansas
There lived a squatter with a stubborn jaw
His nose was droopy red and his whiskers grey
He could fiddle all the night and all the day (far far away)

Came a traveler down a road
Ask if he could find an inn
Can I find an inn?
C'mon, can I find an inn?

Far, far down Arkansas
Here come a government man talkin' to my pa
He told him, I jots to go to school
I got learn to be a gosh-darn fool (far, far away)
(Far, far away, far, far away)

Far, far down Arkansas
I was a squatter with a stubborn jaw (far far away)
My nose is droopy red and my whiskers grey
'Cause the magical mystery tour has taken me away
(Taken me away) taken me away

Far, far down Arkansas
I was my mother I was my pa (raised a squatter)
A government man and a-whiskey still too
And everywhere I'm a-lookin' at you

Far, far down Arkansas
Are you stubborn? Look at your droopin' jaw

'I'll Never Say Never To Always' (aka 'Always Is Always Forever')

Always is always forever

As long as one is one
Inside yourself for your father
All is none all is none all is one

It's time we put our love behind you
The illusion has been just a dream
The valley of death and I'll find you
Now is when on a sunshine beam
So bring all the young perfection
For there us shall surely be
No clothing, tears, or hunger
You can see you can see you can be

'Garbage Dump'

Oh, garbage dump, oh, garbage dump
Why are you called a garbage dump?
Oh, garbage dump, oh, garbage dump
Why are you called a garbage dump?

You could feed the world with my garbage dump
You could feed the world with my garbage dump
You could feed the world with my garbage dump
That sums it up in one big lump

When you're livin' on the road
And you think sometimes you're starvin'
Get on off that trip my friend
Just get in them cans and start cravin'

Oh, garbage dump, oh, garbage dump
Why are you called my garbage dump?
Oh, garbage dump, oh, garbage dump
Why are you called my garbage dump?

There's a market basket and a A&P
I don't care if the box boys are starin' at me
I don't even care who wins the war

I'll be in them cans behind my favorite store

Garbage dump, oh, garbage dump
Why are you called my garbage dump?
Garbage dump, oh, garbage dump
Why are you called my garbage dump?

I claim all these garbage dumps
In the name of
The garbage pickers of America
Oh but it smells
Oh pew…yeow

'Don't Do Anything Illegal'

Don't do anything illegal
Beware of the eagle
That's right in the middle of your back
Don't be the eagle
Got you in the back
They got you in a sack
And they keep you lookin' back

Don't do anything illegal
Beware of the eagle
It's got you by the neck
Don't do anything you shouldn't
And you never can say, 'Aw, heck,
I don't wanna do that'

I gotta see your ID, my friend

I gotta see your ID, my friend
I got to see where you begin
I gotta see your ID, my friend

Every time I go to the store
I gotta have an ID with me
I got to have an ID with me
I refuse, so they can see
What they wanna be
Free, I'm free

I gotta see your ID, my friend
When you come out of the hole
And you're up and down the highway
You got to have an ID
If you don't, you can't go sideways

'Sick City'

Let's see
What was we talkin' about?
Sick City, OK

Restless people, from the sick city
But they're home, now to make the sky look pretty
What can I do? I'm just a person
Just a line that we always seem to hear
You just sit
Things get worse and

Watch TV and drink your beer

Walkin' all alone, not goin' anywhere
Walkin' all alone, nobody seem to care

Restless as the wind
This town is killin' me
Got to put an end
To this restless misery

I'm just one of those restless people
Who can never seem to be satisfied with livin'
'Cause sick old sick, sick, sick old sick city
It may be too late for me to say goodbye
And it may be too late
To watch the sick old city die
Goin' on the road
Yeah, I'm gonna try to say
Sick city, so long, goodbye and die

'Cease To Exist'

Pretty girl, pretty, pretty girl
Cease to exist
Just, come and say you love me
Give up, your world
Come on, you can be

I'm your kind, oh, your kind, and I can see
You walk on walk on
I love you, pretty girl
My life is yours
Ah, you can have my world

Never had a lesson, I ever learned
But I know, we all get our turn
And I love you
Never learn not to love you
Submission is a gift
Go on, give it to your brother

Love and understandin'
Is for one another

I'm your kind, I'm your kind
I'm your brother

I never had a lesson I ever learned
But I know we all get our turn
And I love you
Never learn not to love you
Never learn not to love you
Never learn not to love you

'Big Iron Door' (aka 'Clang Bang Clang')

Clang bang clang
Went the big iron door
They put me in a cell
With a concrete floor
Nine other men in that cell with me
Moaning their date with destiny

Clang bang clang
Clang bang clang clang
Early in the mornin'
At the crack of dawn
They wake us to the tune of a bong bong bong
Line up for chow
Munchin' on bread
Drinkin' black coffee with that noise in my head

Clang bang clang
Clang bang clang bang clang
The judge said to me, 'Now, boy
You've had it'

I Once Knew A Man

I once knew a man
So love he was to be
I once knew a man
Whose heart open you could see

Sadder than a dream
Is that he should pass us by
Sadder than the scheme
Is in the dreams within the sky

Lonelier than I
Could I ever dream of a place to go
Much further than before?
Time as it seems would be passive
If it were knocking at your door

Why wonder why dream in a night
Why argue hate and fight
The love that grows in the hearts of the men that I see
Is happenin', is comin' home forever

In the path, I should wander alone
And a dream would not be mine to say
And a dream, no, the dream
Never do more than it seems should I obey

The love in my heart says
Give yourself away
The love in my heart says
You're loose today

Now is forever lasting constant in the mind
Illusions with memories scheming at my end of the mind

All the time

One and one are one if you find
A man who's got to find
Of the man who lives behind the gun
Of the man that lives behind the gun

Where has his love gone and come from?
He is your brother
He is your loved one

'Eyes Of A Dreamer' (aka 'Eyes Of The Dreamer')

It's all in the eyes of a dreamer
It's all in the eyes of a man
All the things that we've done in life
And all the things that we've planned

Can the world be sad as it seems?
Where are man's hopes?
Where are man's dreams?
Aw, the eyes of a dreamer
In the eyes o' the man

All the songs have been sung
And all the saints have been hung
The wars and cries have been wailed
And all the people have been jailed

The world, it's yours, my friend
It's yours to begin or to end
Oh, the eyes of a dreamer
In the eyes of the man

Take nothing from nothing, brother

And it's all just the same
For the loser is the winner
And there ain't no blame
Except the end of the game

The moment is ever constant in the mind
Everywhere I look, the blind lead the blind
Here's your chance to step out of time
There ain't no reason and there ain't no rhyme

For the trouble you bring is the trouble you bring
And a thing is a thing just a thing is a thing
In the eyes of a dreamer
It's in the eyes of a man

It's all in the eyes of a dreamer
It's all in the eyes o' the man
All the things that you've done in life
And all the things that you plan

Is the world, as sad as it seems?
Where are your hopes?
Where are your dreams?
In the eyes of a dreamer
All in the eyes of the man
And you are the man

The following lyrics by Charles Manson were found at Spahn ranch.

The pass where the Devil you can see
Flying along in sight for all to see
On the edge of infinity
Santa Suzana is the pass where you look to be
Santa Suzana is the pass where you look for me
12 in the night, love or fight

Any way is right
If you come out in the night
It's so out of sight in Devil's Canyon

Index